Translation Tools and Technologies

To trainee translators and established professionals alike, the range of tools and technologies now available, and the speed with which they change, can seem bewildering. This state-of-the-art, copiously illustrated textbook offers a straightforward and practical guide to translation tools and technologies.

Demystifying the workings of computer-assisted translation (CAT) and machine translation (MT) technologies, *Translation Tools and Technologies* offers clear step-by-step guidance on how to choose suitable tools (free or commercial) for the task in hand and quickly get up to speed with them, using examples from a wide range of languages. Translator trainers will also find it invaluable when constructing or updating their courses. This unique book covers many topics in addition to text translation. These include the history of the technologies, project management, terminology research and corpora, audiovisual translation, website, software and games localisation, and quality assurance. Professional workflows are at the heart of the narrative, and due consideration is also given to the legal and ethical questions arising from the reuse of translation data.

With targeted suggestions for further reading at the end of each chapter to guide users in deepening their knowledge, this is the essential textbook for all courses in translation and technology within translation studies and translator training.

Andrew Rothwell is Professor Emeritus of French and Translation Studies at Swansea University, UK, where he trained translators and taught translation tools and technologies for over 20 years.

Joss Moorkens is Associate Professor at the School of Applied Language and Intercultural Studies at Dublin City University, Ireland. He is General Co-Editor of the journal *Translation Spaces* and sits on the board of the European Masters in Translation network.

María Fernández-Parra is Senior Lecturer in Translation and Interpreting at Swansea University, UK, where she teaches and researches translation and technology topics and where she currently directs the MA Translation and Interpreting and MA Professional Translation programmes.

Joanna Drugan is Professor of Translation and the Head of the Department of Languages and Intercultural Studies at Heriot-Watt University, UK. Her research focuses on translation quality and ethics.

Frank Austermuehl is Professor of Languages and Intercultural Communication at Nottingham Trent University, UK, with specialisations in Translation Studies and Political Discourse Analysis.

T0386439

Routledge Introductions to Translation and Interpreting

Series Editor

Sergey Tyulenev is the Director of the MA in Translation and Russian Studies at the School of Modern Languages and Cultures, Durham University, UK.

Advisory Board
Luise von Flotow, University of Ottawa, Canada
Ricardo Muñoz Martin, University of Bologna, Italy
Kobus Marais, University of the Free State, South Africa
Nike K. Pokorn, University of Ljubljana, Slovenia
James St André, Chinese University of Hong Kong, China
Michaela Wolf, University of Graz, Austria

Routledge Introductions to Translation and Interpreting is a series of textbooks, designed to meet the need for teaching materials for translator/interpreter training. Accessible and aimed at beginning students but also useful for instructors designing and teaching courses, the series covers a broad range of topics, many of which are already core courses while others cover new directions of translator/interpreter teaching.

The series reflects the standards of the translator/interpreter training and professional practice set out by national and international competence frameworks and codes of translation/language service provision and are aimed at a global readership.

All topics combine both practical and theoretical aspects so as to ensure a bridging of the gap between the academic and professional world and all titles include a range of pedagogical support: activities, case studies etc.

Most recent titles in the series:

Translation Project Management
Callum Walker

Translation Ethics
Joseph Lambert

Translation Tools and Technologies
Andrew Rothwell, Joss Moorkens, Maria Fernández Parra, Joanna Drugan, and Frank Austermuehl

For more information on any of these and other titles, or to order, please go to https://www.routledge.com/Routledge-Introductions-to-Translation-and-Interpreting/book-series/RITI

Additional resources for Translation and Interpreting Studies are available on the Routledge Translation Studies Portal: http://cw.routledge.com/textbooks/translationstudies

Translation Tools and Technologies

Andrew Rothwell, Joss Moorkens, María Fernández-Parra, Joanna Drugan, and Frank Austermuehl

Routledge
Taylor & Francis Group

LONDON AND NEW YORK

Designed cover image: Getty Images | Blue Planet Studio

First published 2023
by Routledge
4 Park Square, Milton Park, Abingdon, Oxon OX14 4RN

and by Routledge
605 Third Avenue, New York, NY 10158

Routledge is an imprint of the Taylor & Francis Group, an informa business

© 2023 Andrew Rothwell, Joss Moorkens, María Fernández-Parra, Joanna Drugan and Frank Austermuehl

British Library Cataloguing-in-Publication Data
A catalogue record for this book is available from the British Library

Library of Congress Cataloging-in-Publication Data
Names: Drugan, Joanna, author. | Moorkens, Joss, author. |
Fernández Parra, Maria, author. | Rothwell, Andrew, author. |
Austermuehl, Frank, author.
Title: Translation tools and technologies/Joanna Drugan, Joss Moorkens, Maria Fernández Parra, Andrew Rothwell, Frank Austermuehl.
Description: First edition. | Abingdon, Oxon; New York: Routledge, 2023. |
Series: Routledge introductions to translation and interpreting |
Includes bibliographical references and index.
Identifiers: LCCN 2022047707 | ISBN 9780367750336 (hardback) |
ISBN 9780367750329 (paperback) | ISBN 9781003160793 (ebook)
Subjects: LCSH: Translating and interpreting–Technological innovations. |
Machine translating.
Classification: LCC P306.97.T73 D78 2023 |
DDC 418/.02028–dc23/eng/20230120
LC record available at https://lccn.loc.gov/2022047707

ISBN: 978-0-367-75033-6 (hbk)
ISBN: 978-0-367-75032-9 (pbk)
ISBN: 978-1-003-16079-3 (ebk)

DOI: 10.4324/9781003160793

Typeset in Sabon
by Deanta Global Publishing Services, Chennai, India

Access the Support Material: http://routledgetranslationstudiesportal.com

Contents

Series Editor's Foreword   *vi*
Abbreviations and Acronyms   *viii*
Glossary   *x*

1   Introducing Translation Tools and Technologies   1

2   Principles of Computer-Assisted Translation (CAT)   11

3   Translation Memory, Matching, Alignment, and Data Exchange   33

4   Managing Terminology in CAT Tools   55

5   Electronic Corpora   75

6   Current Machine Translation Technologies   97

7   Advanced Leveraging in CAT Tools   114

8   Translation Project Management   130

9   Subtitle Editing Tools   152

10   Software, Web, and Game Localisation   174

11   Translation Quality Assurance   190

12   Human Factors in Translation Tools and Technologies   202

Afterword   *213*
Bibliography   *219*
Index   *235*

Series Editor's Foreword

Translator and interpreter training programmes have become an integral feature of the present-day professional educational landscape all over the world. There are at least two good reasons for that. On the one hand, it has been realised that to work as a translator or interpreter, one needs more than to speak a couple of languages; a special training in translation and interpreting is a must. On the other hand, translator/interpreter training programmes are seen as a practical way to start a career in the language-service provision industry or to earn a degree as a Translation/Interpreting Studies scholar. These programmes may be part of the university curriculum or stand-alone courses in various formats of continuing studies or qualification upgrading.

Yet there is still a dearth of teaching materials geared at novices in translation or interpreting. In every class, students are either given sheaves of handouts which, by the end of the course, build up into a pile of paper or referred to a small library of publications for a chapter here and a chapter there. As a result, the student struggles to imagine the subject area as a coherent whole and there is no helpful textbook for references while in the course or after.

The lack of coursebooks makes life little easier for translator/interpreter trainers. Even if they find a suitable book or monograph, a great deal of adaptation must be done. The instructor has to adjust the book to the length of the course and individual teaching sessions, to add exercises and assignments, questions and topics for presentations to facilitate students' engagement with the materials, and to help them go beyond the 'read-only' mode of working with the recommended book(s).

The purport of the series *Routledge Introductions to Translation and Interpreting* is to put into the hands of the translator/interpreter trainee and trainer ready-made textbooks. Each textbook is written by an expert or a team of experts in the subject area under discussion; moreover, each author has vast experience in teaching the subject of their textbook. The series reflects what have already become staple courses and modules in translator/interpreter training – but it also introduces new areas of teaching and research. The series is meant as a kind of library of textbooks – all books present various aspects of a translation and interpreting training programme viewed as a whole. They can be taken as a basis for developing new programmes and courses or reinforcing the existing ones.

The present textbook is one amongst several in the series which introduce the technological side of translation. Technology plays an ever-growing and vital role in the present-day translation industry. Translators cannot afford to be ignorant about this aspect of their profession. This book is intended as a convenient primer which presents the fundamental concepts of technological tools used by translators. Every effort is made to enable the reader to work not only with the tools available today or the tools s/he works with at present but to prepare him or her for other possibilities both existing and those that will be developed in the future.

The textbook is useful for introductory courses of translation technology and tools in translator training programmes and for self-directed learning. The book is written in such a way as to be helpful for translation trainees and trainers alike. The number of chapters fits an average term/semester length. There are plenty of practical exercises and assignments for hands-on application of the discussed topics. The book will lay a sound foundation for further, more specialised explorations of translation technologies. A thorough glossary of terminology and a comprehensive list of abbreviations and acronyms will equip the reader with the keys to understanding (and potentially contributing to) sophisticated discussions of translation technological software and tools. An especially valuable feature is that the reader is pointed to accessible resources which are available either free of charge online or in trial versions.

The team of authors are experts in translation technology. They are not only seasoned users of the tools they discuss, but also world-leading researchers and experienced teachers. This textbook is an opportunity for the global translation community to benefit from their collective expertise.

Sergey Tyulenev

2022

Abbreviations and Acronyms

API	application programming interface
ARIA	accessible rich internet applications
AI	artificial intelligence
AEM	automatic evaluation metrics
ALPAC	Automatic Language Processing Advisory Committee
ASR	automatic speech recognition
ATE	automatic term extraction
AVT	audiovisual translation
BLEU	Bilingual Evaluation Understudy
BPE	byte pair encoding
CPL	characters per line
CPS	characters per second
CSS	Cascading Style Sheets
CAT	computer-assisted (or aided) translation
CMS	content management system
DDL	data driven learning
EBMT	example-based machine translation
GILT	globalisation, internationalisation, localisation, and translation
HTER	Human-Targeted Translation Edit Rate
HTML	Hypertext Markup Language
IAA	inter-annotator agreement
ISO	International Organization for Standardization
KWIC	keyword in context
LISA	Localization Industry Standards Association
LSP	language service provider
MT	machine translation
MLV	multi-language vendor
NMT	neural machine translation
OS	operating system
PM	project manager/management
PO	purchase order
PoS	part of speech

PBSMT	phrase-based statistical machine translation
QA	quality assurance
QC	quality control
QE	quality evaluation
REGEX	regular expressions
RTF	Rich Text Format
RBMT	rule-based machine translation
SEO	search engine optimisation
SLV	single language vendor
SaaS	software as a service
SL	source language
ST	source text
SMT	statistical machine translation
SRT	SubRip Text
TL	target language
TT	target text
TBX	TermBase eXchange
TB	termbase
TMS	terminology management system
TMX	Translation Memory eXchange
TMS	translation management system
TM	translation memory
TQA	translation quality assurance
TU	translation unit
UTF-8	Unicode
UI	user interface
WYSIWYG	what you see is what you get
XLIFF	XML Localisation Interface File Format
XML	EXtensible Markup Language

Glossary

100% match   See **exact match**.

101% match   See **context match**.

102% match   See **perfect match**.

active segment   The selected segment on which the translator is currently working.

active terminology lookup   A process that can be activated in **CAT tools** to automatically extract and display potential term matches in a separate window as you translate with the CAT tool. Also referred to as **automatic term lookup**.

adaptive MT   An MT engine which is customised on the fly in response to corrections made by a human post-editor, not just by batch retraining (compare **interactive MT**).

affordances   The possibilities for action that a user perceives when interacting with a tool or interface (from the fields of human-computer interaction and interaction design).

agile workflow   Applies to translation jobs (especially common in the software domain) where translation starts before the ST has been finalised and new and/or revised text needs to be incorporated and translated on the fly.

align   Connect an ST and a TT electronically in such a way that each sentence (sometimes paragraph) is linked to its corresponding translation.

analysis   Process by which a CAT tool compares each segment in an ST with those held in an associated TM/fuzzy index, to establish the number and quality of matches that can be leveraged for the translation task.

Application Programming Interface (API) key   A special code that validates a connection between two programs to allow data to be exchanged between them.

ARIA (Accessible Rich Internet Applications) label   An internet software attribute intended specifically for accessibility.

artificial intelligence (AI)   The term used for software intended to behave in a human-like or rational way. At the time of writing this usually involves the use of **machine learning**.

assistive technology A technology tool to assist and facilitate people with disabilities.

attention Within a transformer neural network, the attention mechanism can prioritise one item from the source data over another.

augmented translation Translation activity supported (rather than supplanted) by and interacting with technology.

automatic evaluation metrics (AEMs) Software to automatically measure translation quality in the form of a numerical score, usually by comparison with a reference translation.

automatic speech recognition (ASR) Software that enables the recognition of spoken language and its conversion into text.

automatic term extraction (ATE) The process of using computer programs in order to identify strings of text that are potential terms. The extracted strings are referred to as **term candidates** (compare **term extraction**).

automatic terminology lookup See **active terminology lookup**.

back-translation The use of monolingual target language data that has been machine translated to the source language in order to increase the amount of training data for MT.

base form See **canonical form**.

batch checks A range of QA checks run at the same time by the system, usually on multiple files.

bitext A pair of documents which are translations of each other.

BLEU (Bilingual Evaluation Understudy) An **AEM** that compares **n-grams** (usually up to four) between a reference and MT segment, with modifications for repeated words and averaging results over a corpus.

byte pair encoding (BPE) A process whereby words are analysed and broken down to their most commonly-occurring chunks. Used for **ASR** and **NMT**.

canonical form The most basic form of a word or expression, without plurals or tense endings and in lowercase (except for proper nouns). Also referred to as **dictionary form**, **citation form** or **base form**.

character encoding Mappings between computer bytes and characters in a text to ensure that the correct characters are displayed.

characters per line (CPL) A measure of the space taken up on screen by a subtitle, with implications for reading speed and viewer distraction from the visual content (compare **characters per second**).

characters per second (CPS) A measure of the reading speed of a subtitle, calculated by dividing the total number of characters (including spaces) by the number of seconds it is displayed on screen (compare **characters per line**).

circular definition Definition where two concepts are defined in terms of each other – for instance, the definition of *textile industry* as *Branch of industry that produces textiles* would be circular. The problem with circular definitions is that they assume knowledge which the reader may not have. Circular definitions should be avoided in terminology (compare **tautological definition**).

citation form See **canonical form**.

cleaning and maintenance (of a TM database) Editing operations such as removal of duplicate TUs, alternative translations etc. designed to ensure the TM works efficiently.

client A piece of computer hardware or software that accesses a service made available by a server as part of the client–server model of computer networks. (Not to be confused with the same word for a translator's customer!).

closed captions See **closed subtitles**.

cloud/cloud-based Software accessed remotely via internet, hosted in a data centre rather than on a local computer.

closed subtitles Subtitles that are not displayed on screen by default but need to be switched on by the viewer (compare **open subtitles**).

code Proprietary binary (non-printing) markers used by different text-editing and other programs to control formatting (compare **tag**).

cognitive effort Amount of mental capacity required to perform a given task or tasks.

cognitive friction Cognitive irritation when faced with a mismatch between expected and actual behaviour, usually of a software or device.

cognitive overload An overload of working memory, caused perhaps by a complex task or its presentation, or by too many simultaneous tasks.

computer-assisted (or aided) translation (CAT) Software, typically including **translation memory** and **termbase** facilities, that helps translators during the translation process (compare **machine translation**).

concept-oriented termbase A termbase that is organised around concepts, not words. Each concept is recorded once, and all the associated information will be included in that entry.

concordance A list of *all* words and phrases from a text, often showing their frequency of occurrence in the text. Concordances can be analysed with **concordancers** (see also **Keyword in context** or **KWIC**) (compare **term extraction**).

concordance search Search allowing any user-selected SL or TL string to be looked up in an active TM or fuzzy index, from which any TUs containing the string will be retrieved and displayed. Useful to find out how a phrase, etc. was previously translated.

concordancer A tool to access and exploit the texts available in a corpus (compare **Keyword in context** or **KWIC** and **concordance**).

content management system (CMS) Software that allows non-technical users to create, manage, and modify content on a website.

content word Word that possesses semantic content and contributes to the meaning of the sentence in which it occurs. Nouns, adjectives, adverbs and verbs are examples of content words.

context match (101%) A TU match from a TM/fuzzy index where the SL segment is identical (characters and formatting) to the active segment of the document being translated, and the previous and/or following segment(s) are also identical (compare **exact match, repetition match, fuzzy match, perfect match**).

controlled language Pre-editing to constrain a source text using rules so as to avoid MT errors. Used most commonly and effectively for **SMT**.

corpus (pl.: corpora) A principled collection of naturally occurring texts which are stored on a computer to permit investigation using special software (Evans, n.d.).

cross-platform software Applications that can be run on different operating systems (e.g. Windows, Mac OS, Linux).

culturalisation Examination and adaptation of cultural elements, assumptions, and choices within a game to a target locale.

data curation Creating, organising, and maintaining data for reuse. The ability to understand the uses and value of data falls into the larger concept of data literacy.

data sparsity A term often used in relation to databases, referring here to an insufficiency of data for NMT to produce high-quality translations of unseen source text.

dictionary form See **canonical form**.

domain A specialised, often technical area of knowledge and corresponding lexis (see **terminology**) which is qualitatively distinct from 'general' or 'everyday' knowledge and language.

edit distance The minimum number of single-character edits (insertions, deletions or substitutions) required to change one character string into another.

encyclopaedic information In a termbase, the additional background or contextual details and information about a concept which do not form part of the definition.

ergonomics/human factors Analysis of the interaction of people and their environment to maximise well-being and efficiency of performance.

evaluation metric A measure used to assess quality, usually of a data-driven model.

exact match (100%) A TU match from a TM/fuzzy index where the SL segment is identical (characters and formatting) to the active segment of the document being translated (compare **repetition match, fuzzy match, context match, perfect match**). Also referred to as a **full match**.

example-based MT (EBMT) Automatic translation paradigm that attempts to find and recombine equivalent phrases or words from bilingual corpora.

export Convert a file back from the standard format used in a CAT tool to its original format (compare **import**).

extensible markup language See **XML**.

familiarisation A period of playing and reading documentation before beginning to localise a game.

fansubber Amateur translator of subtitles who wants to make a foreign language video production available to other fans in their own language.

feedback loop Part of a system in which some or all of the system's output is used as input for future operations (e.g. MT training).

filter (n. & v.) Routine by which a CAT tool separates translatable text from the formatting **codes** or **tags** in a file for translation. Filters are specific to each originating program.

full match See **exact match**.

fully localised website One in which all elements have been translated and adapted to the target locale.

function word Word that has little lexical meaning and expresses grammatical relationships among other words. Determiners, prepositions and articles are examples of function words.

fuzzy index An alternative to a TM database used notably by Star Transit, in which matches are calculated between, and extracted, from reference documents, and are held temporarily in the form of an index updated on the fly with new translated segments, rather than permanently in a database.

fuzzy lookup The process of finding partial matches, either in the **translation memory** or in the **termbase**, rather than **exact matches**.

fuzzy match (< 100%) A TU match from a TM/fuzzy index where the SL segment is different (in characters and/or formatting) from the active segment of the document being translated. The degree of similarity is represented as a percentage (compare **exact match, repetition match, context match, perfect match**).

fuzzy match repair The process of modifying the TL segment of a fuzzy match proposal to make it into an accurate translation of the active ST segment.

fuzzy match threshold User-configurable value that sets the minimum degree of similarity (fuzzy match percentage) below which translation proposals from the TM/fuzzy index will not be displayed (typically, 70% or 75%).

game localisation **Localisation** of video games and associated material.

game situations Parts of a video game with different levels of interaction.

GILT (globalisation, internationalisation, localisation, and translation) The steps or processes required in software localisation to produce a global product.

global gateway The place in a website or application where users may choose the version for their locale.

globalisation Organisation-wide consideration of the needs and consequences of making a product globally available

glossary A basic list of lexical equivalents between two or more languages, with minimal additional information (compare **termbase**).

hard coded **Open subtitles** are hard coded, or 'burnt' (from the old days of celluloid film), into the video file, and cannot be turned off.

hotkey A key or key combination that triggers a function in an operating system or application.

HTER (Human-Targeted Translation Edit Rate) A metric used to measure the number of edits needed to edit MT output to produce a reference (or post-edited) translation.

HTML Hypertext Markup Language. A standardised system for tagging text files to achieve font, colour, graphic, and hyperlink effects on World Wide Web pages. (Compare **XML**).

import Convert a file from an original format (e.g. PowerPoint) to the standard format used internally by a CAT tool (compare **export**).

in and out times The start and end times for a subtitle to be displayed on screen.

inline (tag, code) Format information (e.g. for boldface or to indicate a hyperlink) that occurs inside a translatable segment.

interactive MT An MT system that can adjust its proposed translation on the fly to take account of user input (compare **adaptive MT**).

interlingual subtitles Translated subtitles, in a different language from the video (compare **intralingual subtitles**).

internationalisation The act of making a product (and related documentation) translatable and culturally adaptable from the very outset of its development.

intralingual subtitles Subtitles in the same language as the video, mainly for accessibility purposes (compare **interlingual subtitles**).

ISO 3166-1 Part 1-alpha 2 of the *International Organization for Standardization's standard 3166* provides a 2-letter (upper-case) code for the countries of the world (www.iso.org/iso-3166-country-codes .html).

ISO 639-1 Part 1-alpha 2 of the *International Organization for Standardization's standard 639*:2002 provides a 2-letter code (lower-case) for most of the major languages of the world (www.iso.org/iso -639-language-codes.html).

keyword in context (KWIC) A central tool in computerised text analysis in which text lines are sorted by the searched word or phrase (i.e. the 'keyword in context'). In this way, users can see what words or phrases come immediately before or after the KWIC. It is widely used by **concordancers**.

language model A representation of the target language in SMT based on monolingual training data. It assigns output from the translation model a probability to indicate how likely it is to occur in the target language. The language model should maximise the fluency of SMT output (compare **translation model**).

language pair A source language and a target language (note that en>zh and zh>en are two different pairs).

legacy translation Any previously completed translation project.

leverage (n. & v.) When performing a new translation, existing data from a legacy translation can be re-used (leveraged) to save time and enhance consistency.

lexicon   A special type of electronic dictionary, mono-, bi- or multi-lingual, used in some MT systems, especially rules-based systems. Entries typically contain grammatical as well as lexical information. Used in a different sense by Déjà Vu X3 (see Chapter 7).

'lights-out' project management   Automated, or partially automated, project management.

lip-synchronous   Synchronicity with lip movement in dubbing.

locale   a region in which a particular language or dialect is spoken.

localisable (n.)   A type of numerical **placeables** which may need to be adjusted to match different target **locale** conventions.

localisation (L10n), localise   The linguistic, cultural, and technical adaptation of technology for a user group within a defined **locale**.

localisation kit   A set of the tools, documentation, translatable files, and resources required to localise a software product.

long-tail language   The long tail is the portion of a distribution graph that slowly tails off. Long-tail languages may be minoritised languages or languages-of-lesser-diffusion, for which there are few speakers or few linguistic resources, or perhaps those deprioritised due to a low return of investment for localisation.

low-resource language   Language for which there is little training data or with few natural language processing tools.

LSP (language service provider)   More general term for 'translation company' (LSPs may provide many other language-related services than just translation).

machine learning   Software that identifies patterns in data, either with or without an explicit instruction.

machine translation (MT)   Automatic translation of text or speech performed by computer software, with or without human intervention.

macros   Programmed sequences of activities or commands, usually triggered by a hotkey.

mandatory field   In a termbase, a field that you must populate with data before the software allows you to close and save the entry. Compare to **multiple field**.

match (n. & v.)   A source segment in a translation memory or termbase that is found by a CAT tool to be identical (exact match) or similar (fuzzy match) to the active source segment currently being translated. (See **exact match, fuzzy match, context match, perfect match**).

match penalty   Difference between a **fuzzy match** and an **exact match** (100%): e.g. a 95% fuzzy match has a 5% penalty.

metadata   Data that provides information about other data (e.g. in a TM, ID of the linguist who created the TU, date when the TU was created, modified, last used, SL and TL identifiers, etc.).

MT for assimilation   MT that will be used without editing or review.

MT for dissemination   MT used as part of a translation process. This will usually involve **post-editing**.

multi-language vendor (MLV) A company that offers translation into multiple languages.

multiple field In a termbase, a field that can appear more than once in one entry. For instance, a field such as 'Example of usage' may appear more than once in an entry to show various examples of that term in context. Compare to **mandatory field**.

neural AEM An AEM that produces a quality score based on a pre-trained neural model.

neural MT (NMT) Software that uses artificial neural networks to automatically predict the most likely translation of a source text based on many previous translations.

n-gram A string of text made up of a certain number of words. The *n* represents the number of words, so that a 2-gram is a 2-word string of text, a 3-gram a 3-word string of text and so on. N-grams are often used in **machine translation** and **corpus** analysis.

on the fly While working, without opening a different program.

open subtitles Subtitles that are permanently displayed and are encoded in the video stream (compare **closed subtitles**).

open-source software Software code designed to be publicly accessible – anyone can see, modify, and distribute it as they wish.

operating system (OS) Low-level software that supports a computer's basic functions, such as scheduling tasks and controlling peripherals. Examples include MS Windows, Mac OS and Linux.

paradigmatic relation In a termbase, a relation between terms that belong to the same **part of speech**. Examples of this type of relation include (but are not limited to) hyperonymy/hyponymy, holonymy/meronymy, synonymy/antonymy. For instance, the terms *petal* (meronym) and *flower* (holonym) are in a paradigmatic relation because they are both nouns (compare: **syntagmatic relation**).

paradigms of MT Models for training MT systems.

parallel corpus (plural: parallel corpora) A **corpus** and its translation.

parsing (v. *parse*) The analysis of a text carried out by a computer program.

part of speech (PoS) Grammatical category of a word.

partially localised website One in which portions of the site are made available in multiple languages.

perfect match (102%) A **TU** match from aligned reference documents where the SL segment is identical (characters and formatting) to the active segment of the document being translated, and the previous and/or following segment(s) are also identical (compare **exact match, repetition match, fuzzy match, context match**).

phrase-based statistical machine translation (PBSMT) SMT using sequences of words in the form of **n-grams**.

phraseology The study of word combinations and of the preferences of word combinations. (Compare **terminology**)

picklist   In a termbase, lists of finite values used for fields which have a limited number of options available, e.g. part of speech (noun, verb, adjective, adverb), register (formal, informal, jargon), etc.

pivot language   Where direct translation (human or machine) between language A and language B is not available, it may be achieved in two steps, via a third (pivot) language P (A → P → B). English is commonly used as a pivot language.

placeable   A non-translatable element in a source segment that simply needs to be copied across to the target side (compare **localisable**).

plain text file   A file consisting entirely of printable characters, with no binary **codes** and any formatting information contained in text-only **tags**.

platform   As of the late 2010s, this term is used to describe a digital infrastructure that can facilitate functionality and user interaction.

populated   Not empty: e.g. a TM containing TUs, a TB containing term entries.

post-edit (v.)   Correct the raw output of an MT system to a defined quality level (e.g. light post-editing, full post-editing).

pretranslation   Process by which a **CAT tool** automatically replaces ST segments with a **100% match** or better in the TM/**fuzzy index** with its TT equivalent, before the translator starts to translate the document.

process quality   A measurement of whether the process is likely to produce a quality product, usually by adhering to recommended workflow steps.

product quality   Human or automatic measurement of whether (or not) a target text has been produced to a defined quality level that fits the translation brief and conforms to stylistic guidelines.

quality assurance (QA)   Quality management activities that have the objective of auditing processes and procedures to provide confidence that stakeholder requirements can be fulfilled (source: theMQM.org).

quality control (QC)   Quality management activities for monitoring and assessing real-time performance in order to verify that stakeholder requirements are being fulfilled within prescribed limits (source: theMQM.org).

quality evaluation (QE)   Quality management activities for determining whether stakeholder requirements have been fulfilled through inspection and measurement of product properties (source: theMQM.org).

read-only   A file attribute meaning that a program can read data from the file (e.g. a TM), but not modify it, e.g. by adding new TUs (compare **read-write**).

read-write   A file attribute meaning that a program can both read data from the file (e.g. a TM), and modify it, e.g. by adding new TUs (compare **read-only**).

regular expressions (RegEx)   Text strings that run specific searches.

repetition match   A segment that occurs more than once in the ST, whose translation can be used as a 100% match for all occurrences.

respeaking A method of producing almost immediate subtitles by repeating what is heard into speech recognition software trained on an individual's voice and pronunciation.

rule-based MT (RBMT) Automatic translation paradigm based on bilingual dictionaries and (usually hand-coded and language-specific) rules.

screen reader Software that allows a blind or partially sighted user to access text on-screen, using either braille or text-to-speech.

search engine optimisation (SEO) Methods for optimising a website's ranking in search engine results.

segment (n. & v.) Minimal significant units of translatable text (sentence, title, heading, spreadsheet cell, etc.) into which a CAT tool divides (**segments**) a text before translation.

shortcut A key or key combination that triggers a function from a menu in an operating system or application.

simship Simultaneous publication or shipment across **locales**.

single language vendor (SLV) A company (or freelancer) that offers translation in a single language pair.

social quality Who does what, and under what conditions? Coined by Kristiina Abdallah, who identified social quality as an undermeasured aspect of translation quality that is indivisible from product and process quality.

software as a service (SaaS) Software access paid for by recurrent (generally monthly), volume-related subscription rather than by outright purchase.

software localisation **Localisation** of computer software

source language (SL) Original language of a text that is to be translated (see **target language (TL)**).

source text (ST) Text in the original language, for translation into another language or languages (compare **target text (TT)**).

spotting Setting the **in and out times** when a subtitle will be displayed on screen (also known as cueing or timecoding).

statistical MT (SMT) Automatic translation paradigm that uses a translation model (based on parallel corpora) to produce the most probable translation and a language model (based on monolingual target text corpora) to ascertain whether the translation is likely to appear in the target language.

stoplist In term extraction and corpus analysis software, a list of all words and phrases (i.e. **stopwords**) that you do not want showing up in particular search. This often includes **function words** such as *the, on, at,* etc.

stopword Words and phrases that you do not want showing up in a particular search when using term extraction and corpus analysis applications. A list of stopwords is referred to as a **stoplist**.

string Sequence of characters.

sub-segment match A match between SL and TL strings (words or phrases) contained within longer segments.

synonyms   Two or more words or expressions with the same meaning.

syntagmatic relation   In a termbase, a relation between terms that co-occur in the same sentence or text. For example, the term *greenhouse gas* is in a syntagmatic relation to *climate change* because they can appear in the same sentence or text (compare **paradigmatic relation**).

tag (n.)   Printable, non-binary markers used to control formatting, often distinguished from text by enclosure in <angled brackets> (compare **code**). Tagged text formats include RTF, HTML and XML.

tag (v.)   To specify how a piece of text (in a markup language) should be displayed or interpreted.

target language (TL)   Language into which a text is to be translated (see **source language (SL)**).

target text (TT)   Text translated into a second language (compare **source text (ST)**).

tautological definition   Definition in which the component words of the terms are used to define the concept (see de Bessé 1997), for example defining *roll-call vote* as *A vote carried out by roll-call*. The problem of tautological definitions is that they are repetitive, redundant and do not provide any clarity or new information. Tautological definitions should be avoided in terminology (compare **circular definition**).

TBX   From TermBase eXchange, an XML-based standard for moving terminological data between **CAT tools**. Historically, though, it has not been widely adopted.

template   In a termbase, a pre-established list of fields which allows for a consistent display of those fields in the same pre-established order in every entry of the termbase.

TEnT (Translation Environment Tool)   A term preferred by some to refer to a **CAT tool**.

term   A word or multiword expression used to convey specialized knowledge.

term candidate   The words, phrases or strings of text extracted from a text or corpus that are likely to be terms (compare **term extraction**). Term candidates are not considered **terms** yet – they would need to go through **validation** before they are confirmed as terms.

term extraction   A list of *selected* words and phrases from a text that are likely to be terms. The extracted words and phrases are referred to as **term candidates** (compare **concordance** and **automatic term extraction**).

termbase   A database containing rich linguistic and optionally encyclopedic information about terminology in one, two or more languages (compare **glossary**).

terminology   The set of practices and methods used for the collection, description and presentation of terms (see Kageura 2015: 45) (compare **concordance** and **automatic term extraction**).

terminology management system (TMS)   A computer program or software that helps translators manage terminology efficiently (e.g. by extracting, storing and retrieving terms, among other tasks). Not to be confused with a **termbase**, which is a terminological database in **CAT tools**. Not to be confused with **translation management system**, which has the same acronym.

test set When translation data is used for training and tuning an MT system, a **test set** is set aside and used to test the system and evaluate output quality.

TMX Translation Memory eXchange. The near-universal standard for exchanging TM data between users and different CAT tools.

transcreation A term combining 'translation' and 'creation', referring to the process of adapting a message from one locale (language and culture) to another so that it evokes the same emotions and carries the same implications in the TL as in the SL.

translatable assets The elements of a game to be localised.

translation alignment The process of connecting an ST to its TT, usually at segment level, to create **translation units** (**TUs**) such that a search for the SL segment will allow its translation to be retrieved.

translation data Similar to corpora, a collection of previous translations, either bilingual or multilingual, to be reused for training of MT or another machine learning application.

translation environment tool See **TEnT**.

translation extract A subset of TUs extracted following analysis by a CAT tool from a TM or reference **fuzzy index** (e.g. in Star Transit) which give good matches (e.g. 75% or better) with segments of an ST analysed against the TM/fuzzy index.

translation management system (**TMS**) A centralised platform that allows translators to create and manage translation projects. Translation management systems may include a **CAT tool** but also more advanced project management, invoicing and client management tools than typically offered in CAT tools. Not to be confused with **terminology management system**, which has the same acronym.

translation memory (**TM**) A database of bilingual (source and target) segments or **translation units** typically at sentence level, i.e. sentences, captions, headings, etc, although it can also include paragraphs. The TM allows translators to reuse previously translated content and helps them maintain cross-document consistency.

translation model A representation of the relationship between two languages in SMT at the word or phrase level, based on bilingual training data. The translation model should maximise the accuracy of SMT output (compare **language model**).

translation quality assurance (**TQA**) Widely used to describe all processes performed to check, measure or improve translation quality. In translation quality specialist discussions, the MQM definition is useful: Quality management activities that have the objective of auditing translation processes and procedures to provide confidence that stakeholder requirements can be fulfilled (source: theMQM.org).

translation unit (TU)   Pair of source and target segments that are translations of each other and are linked together (**aligned**) and usually stored in a TM database.

Unicode (UTF-8)   A universal character encoding system that allows many different scripts (e.g. Chinese ideograms) to be represented and manipulated by software.

user interface (UI)   The visual/display part of an application where users can view and interact with it.

validation   The process of confirming that a **term candidate** is an actual term.

variable   A data value that can change depending on the condition.

voiceover   Voice recording over a film or moving image.

web localisation   **Localisation** of websites and **platforms**.

wildcard   A character, such as an asterisk (*), that can be used to represent any other character or string of characters. For instance, a wildcard search using the search string translat* could be used to retrieve the term record for translator or the term record for translation, etc. More sophisticated TMSs [Terminology Management Systems] also employ fuzzy matching techniques. A fuzzy match will retrieve those term records that are similar to the requested search pattern, but which do not match it exactly (Bowker 2003).

word embeddings   Numerical representations of words (machine-)learned from a corpus based on sequence and distribution, placing words that are often collocated in proximity within a vector space.

workplace research   The term for research that takes place in a place of work, rather than a controlled or laboratory environment.

WYSIWYG   'What-You-See-Is-What-You-Get' – an editing environment in which the text looks as it will appear, once finalised, in the originating program.

XLIFF   XML Localisation Interface File Format. The standard text-only bilingual workfile format into which most CAT tools silently convert the numerous different input file types that they support, for translation in their internal editor.

XML   EXtensible Markup Language. A text-based markup language that allows you to define your own **tags** (as opposed to **HTML** which comes with predefined tags) and which can be used to share or transmit across systems or platforms, either locally or over the internet.

1 Introducing Translation Tools and Technologies

> **Key Questions**
>
> - Why is translation challenging, for humans and for machines?
> - What are the main types of computerised tools available to help translators?
> - What are the main differences between machine translation (MT) and computer-assisted translation (CAT)?
> - What is translation memory (TM)?
> - What is the history of these tools?
> - Who uses translation technology?
> - How does this textbook work?

Introduction

Anyone who has learnt a new language after the closure of their 'critical period' (Birdsong, 2014) in which a child spontaneously picks up any language they are immersed in, knows what a difficult task it is, and how many years of thinking, remembering, and practice are required to get anywhere near the competence acquired so naturally by children. Languages differ systematically from each other in many fundamental ways, the two most familiar categories being grammar and syntax on the one hand, and vocabulary structure and distribution (lexis) on the other. By whatever method, the second-language learner needs to develop as detailed a mental map as they can of these interlinked, multidimensional differences, many thousands of items in the case of a competent user. When it comes to reading a text (any piece of coherent, purposeful writing) in the second language, grammar and lexis are rarely enough: our learner will also need knowledge of the cultural background from which the text originates, and an accurate appreciation of related features of socio-linguistic usage to judge issues such as politeness and level of formality, rhetoric, or irony. If the text is from a technical domain, the second-language reader will have to acquire a large

DOI: 10.4324/9781003160793-1

set of terminological correspondences, but it is also the case that domain experts often express themselves using different phraseological conventions in different languages (scientific writing in English, for instance, uses many passive constructions where in French active verbs in the second person plural might be expected). All these challenges for the language learner present themselves most acutely to the translator, a learner turned professional mediator between texts, cultures, and experts, the depth and accuracy of whose foreign language acquisition are put critically to the test with every new job. If learning a language is hard, reaching professional competence as a translator is much harder.

Which makes it surprising that, almost at the dawn of the computer age, some scientists (linguists weren't invited to comment) should have thought that translation could be done automatically, by a computer. It is true that, in the period following the Second World War, the discipline of Translation Studies barely existed and there was still little understanding of the cognitive and cultural variables in play during translation; also that the ideological and military imperatives of the Cold War made the utopian project of automatic translation of documents from Russian to English look both desirable and fundable to the US government. As outlined below, that dream and much of the funding soon evaporated, but the genie was out of the bottle and the question of how the growing power of computers could best be brought to bear on translation would spur research and development in the field, both government-funded and commercial, for many decades up to the present. We now have a much better understanding of the nature of both translation and the relevant capabilities of computer systems, as a result of which the modern translator has available to them an arsenal of sophisticated technologies designed to make their work more accurate, efficient, and cost-effective. The downside of this situation is the potentially bewildering range and complexity of the tools on offer: how do they work, what might their benefits be, how should a translator choose which to use, and learn to use them effectively? These questions, of crucial relevance to students of translation and early-career professionals alike, are at the heart of this book, which is intended to introduce you to contemporary translation tools and technologies, the principles on which they work, their place in current and likely future translation workflows, and the motivations and ethical considerations behind each technology.

Mastery of translation technologies is now a key professional requirement, and they are developing at an unprecedented rate. The vast and growing amounts of digital content being created, much of it time-sensitive, means that there is far more material to be translated than there are human translators available to do the work. There is now very little translation that could not be considered a form of human-computer interaction, as noted by O'Brien (2012), from working within a text-editing interface with automatic spelling and grammar checking, to making use of online **machine translation (MT)**, based on huge repositories of previous translations, with many tools and options for assistance and automation in between. As a key and highly visible example of **artificial intelligence** (**AI**) in action, MT is the most widely used translation technology today, but there are many other tools that translators work with when producing a high-quality translation. The development of many of these tools grew from the earliest efforts to digitise and automate translation. Automation is when computers carry out repetitive functions such as word counting or spell checking that were previously carried out by humans, but that 'humans do not wish to perform, or cannot perform as accurately or reliably as machines' (Parasuraman et al., 2000: 286). In the next section, we follow the timeline of development that led to current translation tools and technologies.

A Brief History of Translation Technology

Before the appearance of the digital computer, translation by human translators was the only available option for overcoming language barriers. Philosophers and intellectuals suggested creating shared universal codes, languages in which there would be a one-to-one mapping between concepts and words, but this proved an impossible ideal: human language seems inherently riven with polysemy (words having multiple meanings) and ambiguity. In the early 20th century, prior to the computer era, patents for mechanical translation machines were issued that either used bilingual dictionaries or proposed translation via a **pivot language**. The spur for automatic translation as we now know it, utilising derivatives of the proto-computers devised for codebreaking during the Second World War, came from American scientist and mathematician Warren Weaver, then vice-president of the Rockefeller Foundation. His famous 1949 Memorandum on translation starts by noting 'the obvious fact that a multiplicity of language impedes cultural interchange between the peoples of the earth, and is a serious deterrent to international understanding' (Weaver, 1975: 15). Weaver proposed automatic translation by computer as the scientific solution to this problem, using context, logic, cryptography, and a belief in language universals – that there is a common basis underlying all languages, however different their surface forms may be.

Work began on MT using early computers, and the first full-time MT researcher, the philosopher and mathematician Yehoshua Bar-Hillel, was employed by MIT in the USA in 1951. The 1950s was a period of great optimism in MT research, peaking with a high-profile public demonstration in 1954. The 'Georgetown-IBM experiment' brought the media to see a **rule-based MT** (**RBMT**) system translate from Russian into English with the help of six linguistic rules and a dictionary of 250 lexical items. The theory underlying RBMT was that since any language should be describable in terms of its vocabulary items and a set of grammatical rules for combining them, translating between languages should just be a matter of converting one computerised representation into another. The rudimentary MT system demonstrated at Georgetown and the researchers' optimism about rapid improvement were reported throughout the USA and beyond. Over the following years, researchers in the USA, USSR, and Europe all developed improved RBMT systems, focusing either on adding to the system **lexicons** or making rules and adjusting syntax.

By the end of the 1950s the optimism had dissipated, and Bar-Hillel (1960) opined that fully automatic high-quality MT was unattainable. The US government assembled the Automatic Language Processing Advisory Committee (ALPAC) in 1964 to evaluate the progress in MT research and its report, delivered two years later, was damning and dissuaded funders for MT projects in the USA and Europe. The report did, however, suggest that 'machine-aided translation may be an important avenue toward better, quicker, and cheaper translation' in the future (ALPAC, 1966: 32). Despite the reduced interest in MT research, some work continued, particularly in the USSR and Canada. A 'sublanguage' approach to MT development had been proposed as early as the 1950s, essentially meaning that MT would be developed for a particular subject area or **domain**. This was the approach taken by researchers at the University of Montreal in building an RBMT system for translating weather forecasts from English into French, funded by Environment Canada. This system, called MÉTÉO, was deployed in 1981 and remained in use until 2001, the MT output lightly **post-edited** by translators (the output was already estimated to be 97% accurate), with great success.

Using Technology to Repurpose Previous Translations: Translation Memory

At roughly the same time, some translators and researchers such as Arthern (1979), Kay (1980/1997), and Melby (1982) proposed a translation edit-ing interface that would make use of previous translations. Rather than 'solving' the problem of translation, these proposed automation tools were intended to assist translators, building on the ALPAC (1966) proposal of 'machine-aided translation'. Automation is not necessarily all or nothing, and discussions of technology augmenting human work had been around for some time. The keynote, Kay (1997: 11) wrote, was modesty: 'At each stage, we will do only what we know we can do reliably'.

Efforts to develop such a tool began shortly afterwards, but the first com-mercial **computer-assisted** (or **aided**) **translation** (**CAT**) tools that incorpo-rated **translation memory** (**TM**) and **terminology** databases did not appear until the early 1990s, helped by the increasing standardisation of hardware platforms. TM allowed users to recycle or **leverage** previously translated sentences or headings, as described in Chapter 3. While these tools were ini-tially not well received by many translators, over time they became widely accepted. The tools gradually became more stable, usable, and feature-rich, leading to the range of CAT tools and interfaces we present in Chapter 2.

Whereas TMs were initially envisaged as a way for individual translators to leverage their own previous work, many contemporary tools are networked, facilitating access to huge repositories of previous translations and the sharing of translation resources by teams of translators. Contemporary CAT tools also incorporate MT (see Chapter 7), the development of which continued in parallel.

Using Technology to Repurpose Previous Translations: MT

RBMT remained the dominant paradigm until Nagao (1984) proposed that MT should make use of the growing repositories of **parallel corpora**, previous translations that are stored digitally alongside their source texts as in a TM, automatically searching for phrases and sections of text from **legacy translations** to reassemble. The MT research community began exploring this new paradigm of **example-based MT** (**EBMT**) until Brown and colleagues from IBM (1988) proposed a new method of utilising legacy translations: allowing the MT system to choose the most statistically likely translation. The idea was considered shocking, to the extent that one reviewer of a Brown et al. paper wrote that the 'crude force of computers is not science' (Way, 2010: 181), and led to a split in the MT community for a time. However, the statistical approach won out and **statistical MT** (**SMT**) became the dominant paradigm. This had two repercussions: first, MT engineers were no longer required to have detailed linguistic knowledge alongside programming skills, and second, previous translations were now seen as data for training and testing MT. As MT providers gathered more data for their systems, output quality improved, and after free online MT systems became available in the late 1990s, MT became ubiquitous, with almost a dozen providers offering free online MT services by the turn of the millennium (Gaspari & Hutchins, 2007) (Figure 1.1).

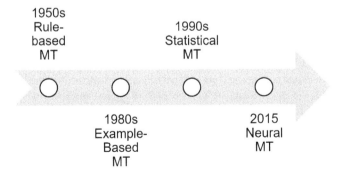

Figure 1.1 Timeline of MT paradigms.

By the 2010s the quality of SMT output in well-supported language pairs (those for which sufficient data was available to create workable systems) had plateaued. Many system builders added language-specific pre- and post-processing steps that were essentially rule-based to boost their output quality. Then, in 2014 and 2015, the first research publications on **Neural MT** (**NMT**) appeared, and by 2016 NMT systems were shown by academic and industrial research teams to outperform previous approaches. Neural systems had been proposed as early as the 1940s but required sufficient computing power to be put into practice. By 2016 that time had arrived, and free online providers such as Google and Microsoft gradually moved to NMT for many of their **language pairs**. NMT became, and continues to be at the time of writing, the dominant MT paradigm.

The early researchers working on MT considered multilingualism and translation as problems to be solved, but, as Hutchins (1986: 15) wrote, they were also 'motivated by idealism: the promotion of international cooperation and peace, the removal of language barriers, the transmission of technical, agricultural and medical information to the poor and developing countries of the world'. The extent to which these goals have been achieved is debatable and there are other impacts of MT that were not foreseen. However, MT can now produce surprisingly good output in many language pairs, especially between languages that are closely related, making it useful for both translators and end users. You can read more about MT paradigms, some impacts and uses of MT, and in particular about NMT, in Chapter 6.

CAT Today

CAT software has grown from relatively simple tools that often worked alongside a text editor such as Microsoft Word, to become feature-rich (and often expensive), networked environments within which translation jobs can be managed, carried out utilising a range of different inputs, and checked, as described in Chapters 2, 7, 8 and 11. García (2014) charts the progress of these tools, from initially favouring enterprise users to becoming an invaluable aid to the vast majority of freelance and in-house translators, according to translator surveys. Contemporary tools either facilitate networked production via shared servers or are browser-based, with the usage billed via the cloud in a **software-as-a-service** (**SaaS**) model. While historically the gap between TM and MT widened due to their parallel development as described previously, this gap has recently become fuzzier, with MT output being offered for post-editing (or as a predictive typing suggestion) in the absence of a **match** from the TM (Chapter 7).

According to a study by Pielmeier and O'Mara (2020) of CSA Research, 88% of almost 7,000 translators surveyed use TM or CAT tools (66% for most projects, with another 22% using it if requested by their client), 81% use terminology management, and 55% use MT. Most respondents say that the quality of TMs received is good. The main selling point for TM is that it should make work more efficient and promote consistency, but the downside is that the use of TM can also propagate errors. Only 23% of survey respondents were paid for the **cleaning and maintenance** of TMs. The ideal scenario for the use of CAT tools is that they are under the control of the translator with various kinds of resources at their fingertips, to augment their work. As evidenced by the lack of payment for maintenance, the focus is often on maximising short-term efficiency rather than on the maintenance of linguistic resources for longer-term reuse by translators with a good deal of autonomy. As many agencies move translation work to their own purpose-built online platforms, this element of translator control becomes more variable. In general, however, these platforms operate on the basis of leveraging previous translations and terminology as CAT tools have done since the 1990s.

How This Book Works

The widespread use of CAT tools in the industry means that knowledge of translation technologies is now a required competence for both translation graduates and professional translators. This textbook introduces readers to key concepts and principles in translation technology, the contexts behind the development of translation tools, and some critical points to consider in their use. The authors combine decades of experience of using, teaching, and researching a broad range of translation technologies, with specialist interests that are reflected in the writing of individual chapters. They have all played senior roles in Master's-level translator training programmes at universities in Europe which are current or former members of the European Commission's European Master's in Translation (EMT) Network, whose widely adopted EMT Competence Framework (EMT Board, 2022) three of them helped devise. The explanatory framework used in this book is designed to be compatible with, and help readers to achieve, the EMT's 'Technology' competence, but it also opens the topic of technology up to the other four main competence domains, especially 'Personal and Interpersonal' (focusing on teamwork and soft skills), and 'Service Provision' (use of the tools in a professional context to deliver a translation product to a client).

Some aspects of a textbook such as this will inevitably become dated due to the rapid pace of technological change in the field. The recent trend towards consolidation in the translation tools industry through company mergers and acquisitions also seems likely to continue. In November 2020, for instance, British language technology firm SDL, which had owned the well-known Trados suite of CAT tool products since 2005, was taken over by its even larger British competitor RWS, creating the world's biggest technology and language services provider. As this book was going to press (in September 2022), the long-established Memsource Cloud tool was rebadged as Phrase TMS, one component of a newly constituted Phrase Localization Suite, following the acquisition of Phrase by Memsource in January 2021.

Such industry consolidations look likely to continue. Software versions will also undoubtedly evolve and introduce new functionalities, features, and interfaces, while completely new tools may well also come along in the next few years. We have therefore not attempted to offer comprehensive coverage of the many tools on the market today (an impossible task anyway in the scope of a single book), or step-by-step guidance in how to master all the capabilities of any given tool – such training is probably best left to the manufacturers, whose online materials are generally accessible and of high quality (we give some pointers to such materials in the companion websites linked to each of the book's chapters).

We have chosen instead to focus on the key *concepts* underlying modern translation tools and technologies, and to illustrate how they are implemented in the design and use of individual tools selected as representative of specific features and approaches. We have tried to make our explanations generalisable, so that what the reader learns about one tool is transferrable to others that they may want to use or be required to pick up later in their professional life. In this sense, the book takes it as axiomatic that learning in this area means learning how to learn, how to ask the right questions, and to drill down from a general understanding of the principles on which a technology works, to their practical implementation in a specific tool. We therefore intend it as a contribution to helping readers achieve the 26th (Personal and Interpersonal) competence of the EMT Framework, to 'Continuously self-evaluate, update and develop competences and skills through personal strategies and collaborative learning and acknowledge the importance of lifelong learning' (EMT Board, 2022). Since the book progresses chapter by chapter from fundamental, generic considerations to more specialised aspects of the topic, it is designed to be used by individual readers in the manner of a self-directed continuing professional development (CPD) course. But we hope it will also be helpful to trainers, both academic and commercial, tasked with devising learning materials to provide a practical introduction to translation tools and technologies, and will offer them ideas, strategies, and examples on which to base their courses, supplemented by the companion website. The 'Follow-up tasks and reflection' sections at the end of each of the following chapters are designed to provide the first steps towards this objective.

We know from experience that it is important not just to talk about translation tools, but to show how they work and encourage students to gain confidence by experimenting for themselves. That is why, despite the risks that some of them might become outdated, we have used extensive practical examples illustrated by screenshots to support the discussion in many of our chapters. We have tried to illustrate representative features from a wide range of software tools being used in projects in different languages (always in combination with English, the language of this book). In addition to their representativeness, our choice of tools to discuss and illustrate has also been motivated by the criterion of accessibility: we give priority to those that are available either completely free of charge, or in fully functional trial versions for a useful length of time, and/or to tools that offer free academic licences to universities. Our choice of tools in no way implies that we endorse any provider's product in preference to any other, or that we are making any claims about one or other tool being particularly 'advanced' or 'state-of-the-art'. We are simply concerned to draw interesting features and capabilities to the reader's attention, in tools to which they will have easy access to experiment for themselves. However, we are also aware that the licence charges imposed by certain manufacturers put their tools essentially beyond the reach of many academic institutions and trainers around the world, so we regard it as important to show that fully industry-standard learning materials can be devised using inexpensive software that performs well and implements the same key concepts as more costly applications.

Following on from the brief overview of the history of translation technology above, Chapter 2 introduces the design objectives and essential features of today's CAT tools. Chapter 3 then covers the fundamental principle of **translation alignment** on which all modern translation technologies, key among them TM, are based. The following two chapters discuss ways of extracting fine-grained linguistic equivalences from bilingual data: Chapter 4 focuses on specialist terminology and how it can be managed in CAT tools, while Chapter 5 looks more widely at constructing and searching comparable and parallel corpora to extract domain knowledge and the corresponding terminology. The focus shifts in Chapter 6 from computer-assisted to automatic translation tools, with an examination of the principles on which current MT technologies work. Chapter 7 brings together CAT and MT, showing the different ways in which the two types of technology are being combined in today's advanced tools to provide the translator with ever-greater support. Chapter 8 moves away from the individual translator to examine how tools can support larger translation projects, potentially involving many languages and collaboration between teams of linguists. The following two chapters then examine specialised types of translation tools, those used to produce subtitles for audiovisual productions in Chapter 9, and to **localise** websites, games, and software more generally in Chapter 10. The final two substantive chapters discuss important general issues affecting translation technology: the complex question of **translation quality assurance** (**TQA**) when so many different technologies are being applied to the translation task (Chapter 11), and the cognitive demands made on translators by the use of tools (Chapter 12). The book closes with an Afterword that considers likely future developments, and some ongoing controversies, in this fast-moving field.

Key concepts discussed throughout the book are explained in a succinct Glossary (pp. x-xxii) and are highlighted in **boldface** the first time they occur in each chapter. Translation technology is a field characterised by the use of many abbreviations, some confusingly similar (e.g. TM = 'translation memory', MT = 'machine translation'), others potentially ambiguous (e.g. TMS may stand for 'translation memory system', 'terminology management system', or 'translation management system', the sense in which we use it here). A full list of abbreviations and their meanings in this book can be found on pp. viii-ix. Readers can supplement the learning from this textbook with links to tool developer guidelines and other online materials on our web portal at http://routledgetranslationstudiesportal.com/resources/9780367750329.php, as well as publications listed in the 'Further Reading' section that closes each chapter, with full details in the Bibliography.

Further Reading

There are many interesting overviews of the history of translation technologies since the Second World War, among the most accessible of which is Chan Sin-Wai's 'The development of translation technology: 1967–2013' (Chan, 2015b), Chapter 1 of the *Routledge encyclopedia of translation technology*, which he also edited. John Hutchins' book *Machine translation: past, present, future* (Hutchins, 1986) gives an authoritative account of the history of RBMT. Another helpful perspective is offered by the opening pages of Ruslan Mitkov's chapter on 'Translation memory systems' in the *Routledge encyclopedia of translation and memory* (Mitkov, 2022).

2 Principles of Computer-Assisted Translation (CAT)

Key Questions

- What are CAT tools and how do they work?
- How are they different from office-style text editors?
- How do you get a translation job into a CAT tool?
- What are a CAT tool's main components?
- What special features do they offer a translator and how are these features used?
- How do CAT tools help organise translation projects and workflows?
- What different CAT architectures are currently available?
- What advantages and disadvantages do these architectures present?
- What are some major current issues to be aware of when you use CAT tools?

Introduction

As outlined in Chapter 1, the development of **computer-assisted** (or **aided**) **translation** (**CAT**) tools was driven by the commercial imperative to make translation quicker and more accurate, by turning the general-purpose computer into what the late Martin Kay, in a research paper written in 1980 for Xerox Labs, called a 'translator's amanuensis', or assistant (Kay, 1997). Rather than trying to perform translation automatically, as **machine translation** (**MT**) does (see Chapter 6), CAT leaves all the linguistic and cultural decisions in the hands of the translator, but exploits (**leverages**) key strengths of the computer to prompt them with useful information and relieve them of some of the routine and repetitive aspects of the job. Computers are better than people at storing, comparing, searching for, and accurately recalling items from potentially huge volumes of data, and it is above all these qualities, applied to linguistic resources created during previous translation assignments, that CAT was developed to exploit. Assuming suitable **legacy translation** data is available, a CAT tool will typically present you with sentences of the **source text** (**ST**) for translation one at a time (**segments**), automatically looking up

DOI: 10.4324/9781003160793-2

each word in a customised **glossary** or **termbase** and simultaneously checking a different data resource, usually a **translation memory** (**TM**), to see if the sentence, or sentences similar to it, has been translated before. Any **matches** found by the system are displayed for the translator to reuse, editing as necessary to make the closest proposal fit the new context: the CAT mantra is never to waste effort translating the same sentence a second time. With a suitable combination of ST and translation data, this approach can significantly reduce the **cognitive effort**, time needed, and therefore, it is argued, the cost of the translation. At the same time, it also increases consistency: the same words and phrases are translated the same way every time. This can be a critical requirement in a whole range of administrative, and technical text types, as well as reducing ambiguity in cases where, for instance, users of the **target text** (**TT**) might be reading it in a language in which they have limited competence.

The release of the first IBM Personal Computer in August 1981 raised for the first time the prospect of ordinary individuals having a business-capable machine on their desks. Unlike Apple's Macintosh, launched in January 1984, the IBM PC had an open design specification and **operating system** (**OS**), which allowed other manufacturers to develop cheaper and more powerful compatible hardware, and encouraged programmers to apply their inventiveness to practical problems in myriad domains. The backing of the giant IBM corporation made the PC the *de facto* standard in many fields, including translation. At the time of writing, with the exception of Wordfast Classic, the only stand-alone CAT programs that will run natively on a Mac or a Linux machine are ones built on the Java cross-platform programming language. Those currently available include the open-source, freeware OmegaT, and paid tools Fluency Now, Swordfish, Wordfast Pro, and CafeTran Espresso. The advent of Microsoft Windows in November 1985, along with IBM's philosophy of ensuring that both its hardware and OS are backward-compatible with legacy equipment, made the PC dominant in CAT and gave it the lion's share of the market; however, IBM's own CAT tool Translation Manager, originally released for the firm's short-lived OS/2 operating system, was not widely adopted (though it is still available for free as OpenTM2). The situation became more flexible with the development of internet-based CAT tools accessible from a web browser on any platform, including tablets and mobile phones (see below), but the world market for Windows-based CAT tools remains buoyant and updated versions continue to be developed.

CAT Core Functionality

File Import and Export

A key attribute of CAT tools is that they are designed to handle many different types of electronic documents, or files. A translator may be commissioned to translate a Word document or a PowerPoint presentation, a magazine article laid out in InDesign, a spreadsheet, a set of web pages, a PDF leaflet, online Help files, an iPhone app, or text held in any one of dozens of other file formats. A single assignment may well involve files in multiple formats, between which the translations need to be kept consistent (for instance, a software application may come with online user documentation and a marketing website, or a new pharmaceutical product may require translation of online information, a patient information leaflet, and packaging). The applications used to create these diverse types of files are monolingual and not designed to aid translation, and even if they were, it would be unrealistic to expect a translator to own licences for the different programs and know how to use them all. What is needed is a single editing environment that can extract the translatable text from a source file in any format, display it in a standard way for translation using relevant linguistic resources, and then rebuild the target file in the original format afterwards, so that it looks and functions just like the original, only in a different language. That way, the translator can translate text from many different formats, but only needs to learn one new program, a CAT tool – an exception being software localisation, the specific requirements of which are more easily met with a specialised tool such as Passolo or Lokalise (see Chapter 10).

An early approach to creating such a translation tool was to turn the familiar monolingual environment of Microsoft Word itself into a bilingual CAT editor. In addition to its native document format, Word already had the built-in ability to handle various other file types (plain text, Rich Text, HTML from web pages, PowerPoint). Word could open and edit these different formats, and it also possessed (and still does) several features which made it possible to create a Word add-on (template) that turned it into a CAT tool able to work with a limited range of common document formats. These features included both a powerful macro programming language, which allowed sequences of commands to be automated and the editing environment to be customised, and the capability of exchanging data with other applications (especially databases). The idea was to allow the translator to work in the familiar environment of their office text editor, while using macros, accessed by buttons on a special toolbar or (from Word 2007 onwards) ribbon, to add the functionality of looking up previous translations in databases, and customising the editor so that as each SL sentence was activated for translation, a colour-coded space in which to insert the translation opened up below it. The first and most successful implementation of this idea was the Windows version of Trados Translator's Workbench, launched in 1994 (a version for Mac came later), which was quickly adopted by the European Commission and remained a popular CAT tool until it was discontinued in 2009 (Figure 2.1).

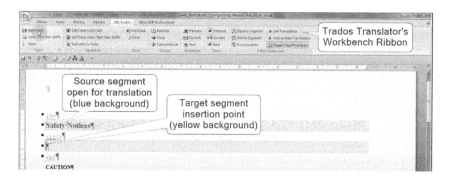

Figure 2.1 Trados Translator's Workbench interface with Word 2007.

A similar macro-based implementation is still available today in the form of Wordfast Classic (see e.g. Díaz and Zetzsche, 2022: 168–9).

While this approach allowed a few common document types to be translated 'natively', a wider (and potentially extensible) range of formats could only be handled by a dedicated program, written for the specific purpose of aiding translation. Many tools of this type have been developed since the 1990s, the first on the market being Déjà Vu in 1993, and they all have in common that the translator is no longer working natively, in the familiar environment of an originating program such as a text processor. Instead, source files need to be processed for **import** into the CAT environment before they can be translated, then processed again for **export** back into their original format once the translation is complete. Despite their many differences, such program-independent CAT tools all need to perform three crucial processing functions (Box 2.1).

Box 2.1: Key CAT Tool Functions

- Whatever the original format of the ST, the CAT tool must be able to extract (**filter**) the translatable text from the file and present it for translation in a standard editing environment.
- It must also break up the text in a logical way into manageable chunks, usually called segments, for the translator to work on and for the system to look up in its resources of previous translations.
- When the translation process is complete, the CAT tool must be able to rebuild the original file format around the translated text, so that the TT looks and functions exactly as the ST did.

Anything other than a **plain text file** for translation consists of translatable text embedded among **binary codes** (or, for text-based formats such as HTML, **tags** typically comprising understandable text enclosed between <angled brackets>) which determine things like the format and structure of the document, the position of graphics or links, the name and size of fonts, etc. These codes and tags are usually specific to each originating application, so for the CAT tool to identify them accurately it needs to run a program-specific filter on the source file (a typical CAT tool will have dozens of such filters, and most will be able to work out automatically which one to apply). When a CAT tool has a filter for a file format, that format is said to be *supported by* the tool. In this first import process, therefore, codes and tags are separated from translatable text, their locations in the source file are marked, and they are stored away separately, ready to be reinserted at the end of the translation task, when the TT is exported for delivery to the client. It is this system of filtering that allows the text from files of different types to be translated together in a single CAT environment, using the same resources.

The second key import process is *segmentation*, in which the CAT tool uses language-specific cues to divide the text into meaningful units (segments) for translation. Segments are often full sentences, bounded by primary punctuation such as a full stop, question mark, or exclamation mark, but they may also be coded or tagged structural units in a document (e.g. the title, different levels of heading, etc.), or, in the case of a spreadsheet, the contents of individual cells. Users can often *configure* (adjust) the segmentation rules for a given language, for instance, to specify whether they want the colon or semicolon to mark a segment boundary. Each segment of the source text (ST) is treated as a **string** of characters, including spaces (remember, CAT tools have no linguistic knowledge), which can subsequently be looked up in relevant translation resources (see below). Once the import process is complete, the text(s) for translation are displayed as a series of discrete segments in the CAT tool's editor, where they have the same basic appearance, in whichever application they were originally created.

Essential Environment Components

However sophisticated they have become, CAT tools in the specific sense in which the term is used here basically comprise a bilingual editing environment with linked resources and information-retrieval capabilities optimised in various ways for translation. The CAT environment window typically comprises three main panes that can often be arranged in different ways to suit the user (Box 2.2 and Figure 2.2).

Box 2.2: Key CAT Tool Environment Panes

- *Bilingual translation editor*, usually in the form of a spreadsheet-like grid or table in which each SL segment occupies a cell, with a corresponding empty cell alongside (or sometimes below) it to receive the translation as the translator types or pastes it in. Segments of the ST are generally displayed in this workfile in the order in which they occur in the text, but in some instances alphabetical order may be selectable, allowing related items (e.g. when translating the menu system of a piece of software, 'File', 'File > New', 'File > Open') to be presented for translation together.

- *Segment lookup* pane, in which identical or similar SL segments retrieved from the resources (generally a TM) are displayed along with their translation. Proposals are ranked by percentage in descending order of similarity (see Chapter 3), which means the most similar (useful) ones appear at the top of the list. Differences between the **active source segment** and any retrieved source segments are marked up to highlight the points where editing would be needed.

- *Terminology lookup* pane, in which any matches between words in the active source segment and entries in the glossary or termbase are displayed. If a new term is found in the active segment, it can often be added to the glossary or termbase **'on the fly'**, along with its translation and other relevant information such as its **part of speech (PoS)**, definition, or an example of usage (see Chapter 4).

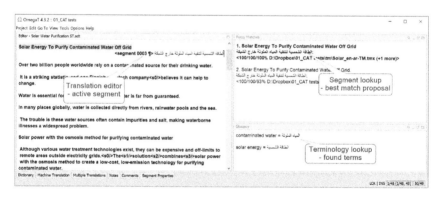

Figure 2.2 Basic translation environment (OmegaT 4.3.2).

As you work on a new segment in the translation editor, you can use the mouse or a quick-key combination to paste in any relevant segment or term proposal(s) from the lookup panes, then edit the draft target segment to correct lexis, word-order, inflection, etc. as necessary, rather than having to invent the translation from scratch. Once you are happy with the translation, you *confirm* the **translation unit (TU)**, typically using the key combination

CTRL+Enter (or sometimes Ctrl+↓). Confirming a segment normally results in three actions:

1. The completed segment is sent (*appended*) to the TM database (or reference document fuzzy index – see Chapter 3), where it is *saved automatically* and immediately becomes available for reuse.
2. The edit-point (cursor) moves down to the next untranslated segment, which becomes active.
3. Automatic segment and term lookup is immediately performed on the new active segment, and relevant proposals are again displayed.

A side benefit of this interaction between the translation editor and the TM is that if anything happens to disrupt the software (e.g. a power cut), the latest state of the translation is still available in the saved resource file, so that the ST can be automatically retranslated up to the point where the incident occurred, and no work is lost.

Additional Features

To optimise the assistance provided to translators, many CAT tools offer one or more of the following additional features:

1. *Interface configuration*: the translator may have the freedom to choose which panes are displayed, and/or resize them, and drag them to different parts of the program window. It is sometimes also possible to configure a tool to display the ST segment and TT editing space either side by side, or one above the other. These **ergonomic** options help you adjust the tool to your preferred way of working.
2. *Tabbed interface*: the main CAT window may be tabbed to allow the translator to switch quickly between different documents, a termbase, a translation memory, etc., each of which can be opened in a separate tab inside the same environment (see e.g. Déjà Vu X3).
3. *Preview* function: this shows how the ST and/or the in-progress TT will look in the originating program (e.g. Word, Excel, InDesign, etc.). It gives the translator quick access to the document *context* in which the active TT segment will need to work. The Preview pane may be permanently displayed as part of the interface (e.g. in memoQ, Déjà Vu X3) or expand on demand by clicking an icon or tab (e.g. in Trados Studio). Some tools generate the preview using the original program (which must be installed on the PC), others convert the TT to a generic format such as HTML or PDF. Déjà Vu's and memoQ's preview panes display a hybrid view of the text, with the TT shown up to the end of the active segment, and the ST thereafter. Previews may be static or updated in real time – so the translator can see exactly how the TT will look up to the point they have reached in the translation job.

4. *Inline formats* display: many CAT editors offer a partially **WYSIWYG** ('What-You-See-Is-What-You-Get') display of ST segments, where **inline** character formats (occurring inside the segment) such as bold, italics, larger or smaller fonts, etc. are displayed. This helps the translator quickly to apply the same formatting to the correct parts of the TT segment, often using familiar Office icons or key combinations (e.g. CTRL+B for bold). Before the advent of WYSIWYG in the editor, ST segments were displayed in a single font with the location of inline formats indicated by special place-marker codes or tags, which could often (but not always, e.g. in Déjà Vu) be expanded to provide a description of their function. More complex tags (e.g. those designating inline URLs or footnote anchors) are typically still displayed in this way, to avoid visual clutter.

5. *Placeables*: these are elements from the ST segment that the program identifies as non-translatable, such as numbers, proper names, URLs, email addresses, and the inline format tags referred to in 4 (above). Typically, for a given segment the tool will present the translator with a list of placeables from which the correct one can be selected and inserted. This avoids retyping, which saves time but also avoids the risk of error. Some CAT tools (e.g. Matecat – see Chapter 7) will 'guess' the correct placement of inline format tags in the TL segment, usually saving the translator even the trouble of selecting them from the list.

6. *Localisables*: a type of numerical placeable which may need to be adjusted (in some cases, automatically by the CAT tool) to match different target **locale** conventions. These include dates (for instance, French DD.MM.YYYY becomes MM.DD.YYYY in US English, but DD/MM/YYYY in UK English) and decimal separators (e.g. English 1,999.75 is written 1 999,75 in French and 1.999,75 in German).

7. *Concordance search*: allows the user to search the source side of the current TM(s) for a particular word or phrase, to find out how it was translated before, displaying all occurrences. This helps remind the translator of previous solutions and aids consistency. Some tools can perform this lookup automatically (see Chapter 7).

8. *Autotext*: as in many office applications, some CAT tools allow the translator to set up a table of frequently occurring strings (e.g. 'President of the United States') that would be complex and time-consuming to type out each time, along with an abbreviated code (e.g. 'potus') for each. To insert the full string, the translator types the short code and hits a particular key (e.g. F3 in MS Word) to expand it.

9. *Autotype*: some CAT tools can use a termbase, a TM, and other available data to 'guess' the next word or words that the translator wants to type, much like predictive text on a smartphone (see Chapter 7). The translator sees a pop-up list of candidate words which changes as you type more letters until the correct word or phrase is identified, at which

point you can just hit Enter to insert it. This potentially saves time but also aids accuracy and consistency.

10. *Propagation*: once a Translation Unit (TU) has been confirmed, the system may search for identical SL segments throughout the text and optionally insert the same translation automatically in each case it finds.

11. *Reference documents*: in addition to (or, in the case of Star Transit NXT, instead of) translation memory, some CAT tools allow segment-level proposals to be extracted from pairs of previously translated documents (also known as **bitexts**) that have been **aligned**, either manually or automatically. For more on this topic, see Chapter 3.

12. *Machine translation (MT) integration* (see Chapter 7): many CAT tools now have a facility to link, usually via a paid-for **API** (**application programming interface**) **key**, to one or more automatic translation systems to provide draft translation suggestions for ST segments for which no (good) match is found in the translation memory or reference documents. The translator can edit, correct, and insert such MT-derived proposals in much the same way as proposals coming from the TM, except that the points for correction are not indicated by the system.

13. *Quality assurance (QA)*: most CAT tools can exploit the rigorous search accuracy of the computer to run a series of quality checks on the TT before it is finalised. These may be run on the fly during the translation process, or at the end as a separate QA step. The translator's attention is drawn directly to any anomalous segments, rather than relying on fallible proofreading alone, and you may be required to resolve any identified issues (sometimes including the option of explicitly ignoring them) before moving on. QA routines include spelling and (often) grammar checking, sometimes using external resources such as those built into an installed office suite. CAT-specific QA routines, which may be user-selectable, include checking for:
    - TUs with empty target side (no translation).
    - TUs with identical SL and TL segments.
    - TUs where the SL and TL segments are of significantly different lengths (this may indicate omitted material).
    - Identical SL segments that have different translations (inconsistent translation).
    - Unedited fuzzy matches or MT proposals (errors may remain uncorrected).
    - Inconsistent use of terminology from the termbase.
    - Different numbers, dates, etc. in SL and TL segments.
    - Different (numbers of) inline tags in the SL and TL segments.
    - Extra or missing spaces around punctuation marks.

      It is common for the tool to prevent finalisation (export) of the TT until QA checks have been completed, as a means of ensuring the formal accuracy and consistency of the TT (of course, such mechanical checks cannot ensure the linguistic or cultural suitability of the translation). For a more detailed look at QA in CAT tools, see Chapter 11, and Díaz & Zetzsche (2022: 252–5).

The multiple sources of translation assistance can be very useful to a translator, but learning to use them effectively takes time, and the amount and variety of information on offer from some of the most fully featured CAT tools can initially seem daunting. You need to develop an instinct for scanning the different proposal sources and quickly selecting those that are most relevant. However, learning to do this efficiently adds a new cognitive challenge (effective information management) to the already complex task of translating. CAT tool developers have tried to use colours, fonts, layouts, icons, and menu systems to guide the user around their interfaces in a clear manner (see, for example, Figure 2.3), but translators still sometimes complain of visual clutter and information overload.

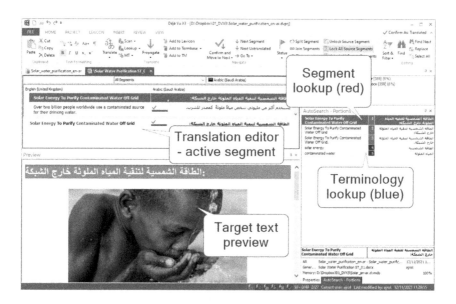

Figure 2.3 Fully featured CAT environment (Déjà Vu X3).

The newest generation of online CAT tools has reacted against this tendency by creating pared-down browser environments displaying a minimum of vital information, with many processes happening behind the scenes, out of the translator's view (see, for example, Figure 2.4).

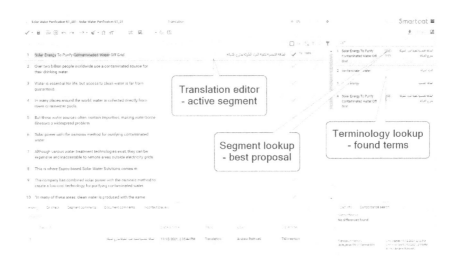

Figure 2.4 Online CAT interface (Smartcat).

However useful the facilities of CAT tools may be, it is worth stressing once more that they are only programs that prompt the translator with relevant proposals for the piece of text on which you are working and guide you on how best to make use of it. *CAT tools do not themselves perform translation*, they are just data matching and retrieval systems that have no knowledge of any of the languages with which they are used (this is what makes them *language independent*). The decision about which CAT proposals (if any) to use in crafting the final translation rests with the translator, without whose linguistic and cultural skills the tools on their own would be all but useless. As an assistant, however, a CAT tool can make the translator's work quicker and more consistent, and it can also sometimes suggest solutions that you might not have thought of. It is in this sense that CAT can be said to *augment* the powers of the human translator (Lommel, 2018a), rather than replacing them.

CAT Data Organisation and Workflow

Translation Projects

For a quick and simple job, a CAT tool can be used to translate a single SL file, with confirmed segments being sent to a new (empty) TM and use of a glossary or termbase optional. This allows you to start work straight away and build up your translation resources interactively, as you go. With more complex assignments, particularly those involving multiple documents, more than one TL, and/or reuse of existing translation resources, it is usually advisable to set up a translation project to keep the different materials, and the links between them, organised. In addition to STs, potentially of different file types, a project can contain multiple, indeed multilingual, translation resources (TMs, termbases, glossaries, reference bitexts, connections to MT systems, etc.). For the moment, we will look at projects from the perspective of a freelance translator using their own workstation-based CAT tool. However, it is worth noting already that in a server- or cloud-based collaborative environment (see below), the translation resources may be built and allocated by a project manager as just one stage of setting up a more complex and sophisticated type of centrally controlled project, allowing various modes of access to potentially many participants with different roles (for more on project management, see Chapter 8).

Setting up a basic CAT translation project on a workstation normally includes the following steps:

1. Decide what to call and where to store the project. Informative names and logical drive and folder hierarchies are essential, as you may well need to find the data quickly and reliably for use in a future project, and over time, file numbers will grow to unmanageable levels if you don't keep them under careful control: 'effective personal file management is the precursor to successful CAT tool operations' (Mitchell-Schuitevoerder, 2020: 1). Among other options, texts and resources may be organised by **language pair**, project, client, domain, or any combination of these (see also Chapter 3).
2. Select the source and target languages, and optionally their complete locale (e.g. en-GB for British English; see Wright, 2015). Using the full locale can be helpful (you should get the correct spell-checker suggestions, for one thing), but it can complicate data import – for example, some CAT tools will regard British and American English as different languages and will not import material marked as one into a database designated as the other. Many CAT tools also use their own variant combinations of the standard 2-letter **ISO 639-1** language and **ISO 3166-1** country codes, which can also lead to data exchange problems if the receiving tool fails to recognise the language code of the material you want it to import.
3. At this point, you are often invited to give the project a 'friendly' (more informative) name, and/or enter a description of it – again, helpful in keeping track of the data in the future.
4. Select and import the ST(s) that you want to translate, which may be files in different formats.
5. Add the *translation resources* you want to use. These may be existing TMs, termbases (TBs), or reference bitexts, perhaps from previous projects you have completed in the same domain, or legacy material supplied by the client to aid translation consistency. Alternatively, they may be newly created for the project. Often, it will be appropriate to use existing TMs and TBs for lookup but leave them unchanged by

marking them as **read-only**, while the TUs and any new terminology from the active translation are sent to a new, empty TM and TB, created for the project and marked as **read-write** or for update (for more on these decisions, see Chapter 3).

6. At this point many CAT tools will let you perform an *Analysis* of the new ST(s), to establish what proportion (if any) of the material for translation is already present in a useful form in the TM(s) and/or reference bitexts selected for the project. In this process, each ST segment is systematically looked up in the reference data and any matches found are scored for their degree of similarity (see Chapter 3). This can give a helpful indication of how much work the resources are likely to save you, and therefore potentially allow you to quote a lower, more competitive price for the job. However, analysis is also routinely used by translation companies to reduce the price they pay to freelancers (see below).

7. Optionally, the tool may also perform a **pretranslation** of the project ST(s), during which the translations of any new SL segments with exact matches in the reference resources (see Chapter 3) may be inserted automatically into the TL side of the bilingual grid. This may give you the impression that the CAT tool has 'translated' part of the text for you, but in fact all the system has done is match strings of characters, and even exact matches will need to be checked. For segments without an exact match, some tools will allow automatic insertion of highly similar matches, down to a match percentage specified by the user (e.g. 98% similarity, which might indicate just a minor difference of spacing, punctuation, or formatting). Alternatively, any matches from the termbase may be inserted at this point.

Now that the project has been set up and (optionally) pretranslated, you can begin work in earnest, making use of the proposals supplied by all the features described above as you perform the translation. As you work, you can normally add new terms to the termbase or glossary, and every completed segment, once it is confirmed, is saved as a new TU for potential reuse. Once you have finished, you will normally run QA checks on the translation (see above) and carefully review each issue highlighted by the CAT tool, fixing any errors. At this stage, the editor display will normally change to show only TUs that have QA alerts, along with an explanation of the potential problem; sometimes the translator can even filter the alerts to deal with one type at a time. After QA, the Translation phase of the project is complete and all TUs have typically been marked with the status of 'Translated'.

Revision, Review, Sign-Off

Translation of the ST(s) is only the first, if the most important, phase of the professional project workflow. Once the draft translation has been completed, it normally needs to be revised, by either the same or a different translator. The definition of revision given by the International Organization for Standardization (ISO) is: '*bilingual* examination of target language content against source language content for its suitability for the agreed purpose' (ISO 17100:2015(en)). Some CAT tools, including Trados Studio, confusingly refer to this workflow step as Review, which is really a separate operation, the ISO definition of which is: '*monolingual* examination of target language content for its suitability for the agreed purpose' (ibid.) – on this important distinction, see also Declercq (2015: 483–5). Revision involves a careful rereading of each TL segment to ensure that it is an accurate translation of the ST, and to check for readability, ambiguity, and any other defects that may affect the usability of the TT, as well as for the overall coherence and cohesion of the text (i.e. ensuring that the linguistic and logical links between one segment and those around it are correct). Many CAT tools have a Revision mode in which the command ribbon or menu bar of the editor changes to provide easy access to the specific functions needed for revision (compare Figure 2.5 with Figure 2.6).

Figure 2.5 Trados Studio 2022 Translation ribbon.

Figure 2.6 Trados Studio 2022 Review ribbon.

If the original translator also does the revision, any corrections and other modifications can be made directly, confirmed, and saved into the active TM or index, normally *overwriting* the original entry, so that only the revised (corrected) translation is preserved for future use. If the translation is revised by a different reviser, who is normally paid a lower rate for the job because it should take less time, the reviser may also make changes directly to the TL segments and resources. However, in some CAT tools, including Trados Studio and Phrase TMS (formerly Memsource Cloud), the reviser can instead use a system of *tracked changes* like that available in Microsoft Word or the Suggesting mode in Google Docs, to recommend changes without making them directly. There is often also a Comment facility which allows the reviser to ask a question or explain the reasons for a proposed change, and sometimes a system of drop-down menus allowing the type and severity of an error to be indicated by simple selection (this also potentially gives a project manager or **LSP** (**language service provider**) a crude way of quantifying the translator's accuracy, or lack of it). Once the reviser has finished working through the project in this way, it may be returned to the original translator or forwarded to a third linguist who will read the comments and decide whether to accept or reject any proposed changes, before confirming each revised TU as before. In revision mode, each time the reviser confirms a TU, it is marked in the editor with the new status of 'Revised'.

A single stage of revision is usually sufficient (and cheaper) for most projects, but for some safety-critical translation assignments (e.g. in domains like pharmacology or aerospace), an extra step of monolingual Review of the TT may be required to ensure that it makes accurate sense to a domain expert. This may be done outside the CAT environment, but some CAT tools have a third editing mode, sometimes referred to as *Sign-off*, which may be used for expert review. Alternatively, sign-off may be performed by a project manager, who will check the formal aspects of the job to ensure that they correspond to the client's brief, often across multiple target languages. It may not be necessary to sign off TUs one at a time: once the PM is happy with it, the whole project can usually be signed off in one go, updating all TUs to the status 'Signed Off'. The importance of this status is that it certifies that all stages of the translation task have been completed to a satisfactory standard and in accordance with the workflow procedures agreed between the client and the LSP or translator. At this point, the final TT is ready to be generated by *export* and sent to the client, along with the invoice for the job.

CAT Tool Architectures

Stand-Alone, or Networked?

The potential involvement of multiple participants in the translation project workflow raises the question of how the data can be exchanged and controlled in appropriate ways between them, for instance, to avoid a proliferation of 'out of step' versions, each containing different edits. The answer depends on the overall *architecture* of the CAT tool – a metaphor for the structure of a piece of software, resulting from the most fundamental decisions about its organisation.

In the case of CAT tools, differences in architecture relate mainly to where the program resides and runs, and where the translation resources are stored. These design options, which have evolved from the early 1990s to the present in line with the general huge increase in network connectivity, have an important effect on the capabilities of the tools and the complexity of the workflows they can support. There are three main categories, all of which are currently represented in the professional marketplace, where they aim to appeal to different types of users (Box 3.2).

Box 2.3: CAT Tool Architectures

- *Workstation* tools, sometimes known as *workbenches*, traditionally appealed to freelance translators (and still do). This is the original architecture, in which the program is installed on a stand-alone computer (PC), along with all the major resources needed to perform a translation. Translators will of course use email and other tools for communicating with clients and collaborators, and will certainly browse the web for information, but the CAT tool and its associated translation projects all reside on a local machine – which makes it essential to have an effective backup regime. OmegaT is a free, open-source workstation CAT tool; commercial tools, which can be expensive, include long-established 'big names' such as Across, Déjà Vu X3, Star Transit NXT, Trados Studio, or Wordfast Pro, all of which require the one-off purchase of a software licence, generally with support included. Some paid tools (e.g. Trados Studio, CafeTran Espresso and Déjà Vu X3) offer time-limited or reduced functionality evaluation versions that can be downloaded and installed for free: these are a good way of getting a feel for a tool before committing to purchasing it.
- *Client-server* tools were the first extension of the workstation architecture in the direction of connectivity and collaboration, often labelled as 'team' versions. Taking advantage of the rise first of the local area network (LAN), then of the internet, they allow the workstations (PC **clients**) of potentially numerous translators, revisers, terminologists, project managers, and other participants, many of whom may work remotely, to be linked together and managed via a server, typically installed on the premises of a translation company (LSP). A big advantage of this architecture is that translation resources can be held on the server, rather than on individual workstations, and shared in real time between teams of translator-revisers, optionally under the overall supervision of a project manager, allowing the company to take on larger, often multilingual projects. Once a segment has been translated by one translator and the TU committed to the TM, it can be made instantly available to other translators in the team for reuse. Disadvantages of client-server tools include the generally high cost of team licences, and the complexity of installing and maintaining the server infrastructure, which typically requires significant in-house IT expertise.
- *Cloud-based* tools move the server out of the LSP, into a secure location in the cloud, where the system is managed (maintained

and updated) by the tool vendor, with whom the client (in the sense of customer, e.g. an LSP, individual translator, or even end user) has an account allowing a defined level and volume of access. CAT tools of this type (e.g. Phrase TMS, XTM Cloud, Wordbee, Matecat, Smartcat, Lilt), sometimes badged as **translation management systems** (**TMS**) (see Chapter 8), are becoming increasingly popular with both companies and freelancers because they offer all the project management sophistication of a client-server architecture without the overhead of running a server, and allow translators and clients access from any browser, sometimes even from a dedicated smartphone app (e.g. Phrase). One cloud-based tool designed primarily for translators, but which has recently acquired significant company-oriented project management features, is Wordfast Anywhere (discussed in detail in Chapter 8).

The fact that each of these architectures has specific strengths is demonstrated by the development of different varieties of *hybrid* systems. On the one hand, the heavyweight workstation tools now offer different degrees of network connectivity: for instance, memoQ Project Manager edition and Trados Team 2022 are complete TMSs with comparable project management capabilities to a cloud-based tool such as Phrase (see Chapter 8), while the Freelancer version of Trados Studio, which has now seamlessly incorporated the cloud-based Trados Live features introduced in the previous version, allows individual linguists to work either online or locally, but without the resource-sharing ability of the Team version. On the other hand, cloud-based tools such as Lionbridge Translation Workspace and Phrase offer for download and local installation a workstation-based editor which closely mimics the functionality of their online editor, allowing linguists to continue working when away from the internet and resynchronise their work with the cloud-based project once they are back online. Wordfast Anywhere's online TMs and Glossaries can now also be shared with users of the workstation-based Wordfast Classic and Wordfast Pro, as long as users have an internet connection. The effect of these developments is to blur the distinction between the three basic architecture types, and it is fair to say that whether they began life on the workstation or in the cloud, many of the most popular CAT tools are converging on a model combining local and online access to projects with variously sophisticated resource-sharing and project management capabilities. Ultimately, Trados Studio has become more like Phrase, and vice versa – to the extent that both now also offer a mobile app, so you don't even need a laptop to carry on translating.

Architecture-Related Issues

Feature Sets

Workstation and client-server CAT tools tend to be more fully featured, both because they have evolved over a longer time, during which developers have continually added more 'bells and whistles' in the attempt to gain market share, and because the Windows programming environment is inherently more flexible than the web (though the gap is rapidly closing). On the other hand, some users dislike the complexity that this can cause, complaining of 'information overload' and preferring the more streamlined environments typically offered by cloud-based tools (see Chapter 12), which explains why 'hybrid' systems aim to get the best of both worlds.

CAT Tool Ownership and Licensing

Workstation tools generally appeal to individual translators who work on their own or with a small number of collaborators. They can offer a reassuring sense of software ownership, a familiar editing environment, and professional expertise, often supported by communities of fellow users on translators' forums such as ProZ (www.proz.com) and TranslatorsCafé (www.translatorscafe.com/cafe). The translator may also control and manage their own translation projects and associated resources, which enhances a sense of independence, though increasingly LSPs and end clients are claiming ownership of the resources and will supply only relevant extracts from them when a job is commissioned (see below, and Chapter 8). Users must feel confident to choose, install, maintain, and update their own workstation software, and will need to budget for periodic upgrades. Many freelancers find that they need to use more than one CAT tool because different clients specify different tools, though major tools can increasingly open and save to each other's data formats.

Networked tools, whether client-server or cloud-based, appeal particularly to LSPs for their project management capabilities. Cloud tools increasingly offer business features as well, acting as vendor platforms through which clients can directly commission translations. An example is Smartcat, launched in 2015, which Wikipedia describes as 'a cloud-based translation and localization platform that connects businesses, translators, and translation agencies in a single "Connected Translation" delivery loop' (Wikipedia, 2021). In such an integrated model, the individual translator may feel like rather a small, disempowered cog in a big machine (see also Chapter 8), responding to email alerts of online jobs where resources have been prepared by someone else and they will not be able to retain their own work after it is submitted. On the plus side, if they work for an LSP in this way, they do not need to pay for the CAT software, to which the LSP will subscribe on a scalable **software-as-a-service (SaaS)** model, depending on the number of languages, users, and/or the wordage they generate. Díaz &

Zetzsche (2022: 263–4) offer some useful tips about choosing among the different CAT tool types.

Collaboration

Shared access to data is a key strength of both networked architectures because the language data (bilingual workfile, TMs, termbases, etc.) does not need to be sent anywhere: it stays in one place, on the server, in a single copy, and different project participants (translator, reviser, project manager) are given appropriate access privileges to it so that they can complete their specific tasks in the appropriate sequence. The case of a freelancer working with a workstation-based CAT tool is more problematic: how can they send work to a reviser, and receive it back again, in a way that retains all the advantages of the CAT environment? Recent versions of some of the bigger workstation tools (e.g. Trados Studio, Déjà Vu X3) solve this problem with a system of *project packages* that can be emailed between participants. Packages are basically zip archives (compressed folders) that contain user-selectable parts of a translation project (minimally, the bilingual workfile but optionally also relevant translation resources). When a reviser receives a package, they open the translation in their local version of the CAT tool, perform the revision, then zip it up into another package for return to the translator, who then opens the return package in their own workstation project, checks and signs off the revisions, updates the TM, and generates the TT. In cases where the reviser does not have the same CAT tool, it may be possible to export a bilingual Word file and send it to the reviser, who marks corrections in Word using tracked changes and comments. When the translator receives the Word file back, it can be imported into the project for checking, sign-off, and updating in the usual way (see also Chapter 3).

Confidentiality and Data Security

In many translation commissions, confidentiality (commercial, legal, medical, political, etc.) can be essential: the translator is working on material that must not be passed on to anyone else, or allowed to 'leak out' in other ways, such as through malicious hacking, malware, etc. Not just the ST, but also any TM, TB, and reference resources used to translate it, may be highly sensitive, so the question arises as to which CAT architecture can be considered more secure. Is it safer for a client to send a confidential ST, along with a TM containing previously translated sensitive documents of a similar type, to a known freelancer to translate on their workstation, or upload them to a cloud-based platform for use by an unknown translator commissioned by an LSP? The answer is not straightforward, because either option has its risks. The freelancer may well have signed a Non-Disclosure Agreement, or NDA with the client or the LSP, but how can they be sure that the person will not keep the TT and resources, especially the TM, for their own future use, rather than deleting them at the end of the job? Moreover, while it is on a PC, the data could be vulnerable to hacking, particularly if the system security is not up to date, laptop loss, etc. On the other hand, the cloud has a deserved reputation for vulnerability to data theft, leading cloud-based CAT developers to offer their clients, in a lengthy online 'Privacy Notice' or similar document, reassurances about the precautions they take to ensure the security of their systems. LSPs who use such services also stress the benefits of centralised *project management*: each individual in the supply chain only sees the minimum of confidential information necessary to allow them to do their job, and typically they will have no further access to that data once they submit their work. On balance, the central control offered by the cloud, which is business-critical for both developers and their LSP clients, may outweigh the advantages of local storage offered by the workstation solution. It is worth noting, however, that many CAT tools also help mitigate risks to confidentially by allowing just relevant *extracts* from translation resources to be accessed by the translator, rather than whole TMs or reference documents: this is another benefit of the Analysis process described above, which can enable only those TUs that closely match segments in the new ST to be extracted from a confidential TM or set of reference bitexts (see also Chapter 3).

Conclusion: Some Unresolved CAT Issues

The advent of CAT tools and their rapid development have had a huge impact on both the language services industry and the working practices of translators, most of whom have had little option but to become as expert and efficient as they can in using CAT if they want to keep their customers. In addition to imposing on translators a steep learning curve and the continuous requirement to update their skills, CAT has also introduced into the whole business of translation several new issues which have yet to be fully resolved, including those in Box 2.4.

Box 2.4: Some Current CAT Issues

- When applied to suitable material, CAT has been shown to accelerate translation, but who benefits from the increase in speed? In the early days, freelancers could both save time and gain a pricing advantage over competitors who were not CAT-equipped, but LSPs quickly seized the advantages for themselves, using TM analysis statistics to pay lower rates to translators for material already present in the database in different degrees of similarity (see Chapters 3 and 8).
- Who owns a translation memory? This is a complex and much-discussed topic. Translators often feel that, since a TT embodies

their own linguistic skill and translation expertise, they have a claim to the intellectual property in the TM (and therefore should be allowed to reuse it in their own later projects). For an LSP, possession of a regular client's TM gives a commercial advantage, so contracts will often require a freelancer to submit the project TM to the LSP along with the TT. But the client also has a legitimate claim: it is after all their ST and they are paying for it to be translated. The question has recently become more urgent with the development of a market in TM data, particularly for rarer language pairs or domains, for use in training machine translation systems (see Chapter 6 and Afterword).

- What additional cognitive demands does using CAT technology make on translators, and how can the tools be further improved to make them more intuitive to use? It is clear from translation process research that the savings in time and gains in efficiency that they enable come at the cost of additional mental effort on the part of the translator (Ehrensberger-Dow & Hunziker Heeb, 2016).

A further question, among the most important, relates to training: how can translators, both beginners and experienced professionals, many of whom come from non-technical backgrounds, best acquire, then update, the skills they need to become confident choosers and users of CAT tools? LSPs rarely provide any training for freelancers, whom they generally expect to already own and use a relevant tool (or, in the case of cloud-based platform companies such as Translated.com, the owners of Matecat, adapt to using the company's tool). Many universities offer relevant degree courses, professional organisations provide opportunities for CPD (continuing professional development) and networking, online forums and user-communities offer advice and help with troubleshooting, and some tools vendors (e.g. Trados, Phrase or memoQ) provide their own online training and certification materials. Most of these options, however, carry a significant cost in both money and time, which needs to be factored into a translator's business planning.

Follow-Up Tasks and Reflection

1. Select a fairly short electronic text (300–1,000 words will be plenty) in your L2 that contains some character formatting (e.g. bold, italics, different font sizes, etc.), and maybe a picture or a table as well. It should be in a domain that interests you, as this 'Practice ST' will be the basis of the follow-up exercises for several further chapters, so you won't want it to be too boring! Read it carefully and make

a note of the linguistic challenges you expect to encounter when translating it into your L1.

2. Choose a workstation CAT tool to work with – it might be free to use (like OmegaT), a trial version of a paid-for tool such as memoQ, CafeTran Espresso, Déjà Vu X3 or Wordfast Pro, or a full version to which you have access personally or through your university, etc. On the basis of what you have read in this chapter, work out how to install your chosen tool and use it in a basic way, taking advantage of any learning materials (sample data, Help files etc.) provided by the developers.

3. Once you are familiar with its interface and core functionality, use your chosen workstation tool to create an empty TM called Practice TM1, import your Practice ST into the tool and translate approximately the first half of the text, sending confirmed TUs to the TM. Then export the half-translated TT (make sure you know where it will be saved!) and open it to check the formatting: is everything present and correct?

4. Now select a free-to-use online CAT tool (e.g. Matecat, Smartcat, Phrase TMS Team trial), make an account for yourself as necessary, and repeat the learning process outlined in Step 2 above for the second tool.

5. Create an empty TM in your cloud-based tool called Practice TM2 (make sure you know whether it will be private to you or shared with other users), upload your Practice ST, and translate the second half of it. (If MT proposals appear automatically, make sure to turn MT off for the moment.) When you have finished, export the TT and check the formatting.

6. You now have some basic experience of using two CAT tools with different architectures. Which did you prefer, and why? What were the main differences between them? (Make sure you know where the files from these exercises are stored because you will need them again after the next chapter.)

Further Reading

Authoritative discussions of the history and functioning of CAT tools can be found in various chapters of the *Routledge encyclopedia of translation technology* (Chan, 2015a), the most comprehensive reference resource to date on translation technology. For helpful overviews of specific tools and practical tips on how to use them effectively, the latest (15th) version of *The translator's toolbox* (Díaz & Zetzsche, 2022) is invaluable, while 'Investigating the cognitive ergonomic aspects of translation tools in a workplace setting' (Teixeira & O'Brien, 2017) gives a clear overview of ergonomic issues associated with translation tools. The websites of all the major tools developers have downloadable guides, user manuals, and other training resources, and there is a wealth of material on YouTube showing how to use different tools to complete specific tasks (a good place to start is the support page for this chapter on our online portal).

3   Translation Memory, Matching, Alignment, and Data Exchange

<hr>

Key Questions

- How can **legacy translations** be reused within a CAT tool?
- How are **bitexts** used as reference documents?
- Which is better, **translation memory (TM)** or bitexts? Or both together?
- How does translation matching work?
- What are **match penalties** and how are they useful?
- What do the main types of **matches** mean? (**exact, fuzzy, context, perfect**)
- How do you 'repair' a fuzzy match?
- How is **analysis** used to set rates and to create a **translation extract**?
- What is **alignment** and how is it done?
- How do you use a graphical alignment editor?
- What are **TMX, XLIFF**, and Word bilingual files, and how are they used?

<hr>

Introduction

As we saw in Chapter 2, a primary function of CAT tools is to enable effective reuse (**leveraging**) of existing (**legacy**) translations, and efficient storage of new translation data for future searching and reuse The key technology making this possible is the translation memory (TM), a database of **translation units (TUs)** made up of source language **segments** and their target language translations. Each time the user opens a segment of the new ST, the CAT tool searches for **matches** in any previously translated texts stored in the database. In addition to TMs, the present chapter will describe an alternative approach to leveraging legacy translations using sets of source texts and their translations, often referred to as **bitexts** (as in 'bilingual'). The advantages and disadvantages of the two approaches will be discussed, as well as the reasons why some major CAT tools offer both, treating them as complementary.

DOI: 10.4324/9781003160793-3

The principles by which the two types of resources are searched for relevant information, and the different types of **matches** they can identify, will then be described before a practical explanation is given of **aligning** translations for reuse. The final section will describe three different file formats for exchanging segment-aligned translation data, and illustrate their use.

The theoretical principle underlying all CAT leveraging is **equivalence** between source and target segments – a principle whose adequacy has, of course, been questioned by translation scholars at least since the 1970s (Koller, 1995), which on the face of it brings CAT into conflict with translation theory. However, the objections to equivalence mainly relate to expressive text types (Reiss, 1981) such as literature, marketing materials etc., where different types of cultural adaptation are often required and for which TM has traditionally been seen as less suitable, though technological advances are increasingly challenging these earlier views. In the almost limitless range of informative text types and domains where CAT is designed to be useful, the pragmatic guiding principle is usually that the target text needs to be *equivalent in meaning* to the original source text if the end-user is to rely on it for information.

The extension of this principle to equivalence *between* documents cannot, however, be taken for granted. We might assume that if a source sentence has a specific, equivalent translation in one document, the same sentence in a second document should logically be translated the same way. But there is an important objection which goes to the heart of the distinction between the TM and bitext approaches: the same sentence in a second document may occur in a completely different *context*, where it may have a different meaning and therefore require a different translation. Suppose, for example, you are translating a text about wind turbine technology from English into French that contains the sentence: 'Turbine blade fatigue is no longer a significant cause of failure'. Your translation memory suggests an exact French equivalent, which you accept without realising that the proposal actually comes from a document about water turbines, which is the wrong **domain**. As a result, to translate *blade*, which in English is the correct term in both domains, your translation uses the incorrect French term *aube* instead of the required term *pale*, wrecking its in-context meaning. This is a potential trap to which all users of TM tools need to remain alert: the translator may have to intervene to adjust a translation proposal to fit its new context, even if the **string** being translated is identical to one that has been translated before. This is just another example of the constant requirement for human linguistic skill and sensitivity to context in overseeing even the most apparently automatable parts of the translation workflow.

Translation Memory or Bitext?

Almost all CAT tools store legacy translations in TM databases (the major exception being Star Transit NXT, which leverages only reference bitexts by creating a **fuzzy index** from them), while some of the most popular tools (memoQ, Trados Studio) offer retrieval from both TM and bitexts (which memoQ calls LiveDocs). This raises the question of the differences between the two approaches, and their relative benefits and disadvantages. Both a **populated** TM database and a pair of indexed translation bitexts can yield relevant proposals based on previous high-quality translations done by expert linguists, but the quality guarantee they offer operates at different levels. Using TM, a CAT tool accurately computes whether the database contains an identical or similar source string but cannot make any document-level assessment of whether it comes from the correct context or domain, even if the originating filenames are displayed, because TMs do not store TUs in document order and so do not normally allow the originating ST and TT to be reconstructed (but see context matches, below). On the other hand, reference bitexts are selected (whether by the project manager or the freelance translator) explicitly for their relevance to the job in hand, so the context/domain problem should not arise, but precisely because they are so 'on topic', they may provide narrower coverage of segments using non-specialised language, and so offer weaker leverage. So which approach is more useful? A practical example may help to assess the issues.

Suppose an LSP has already worked for several years with two clients in the same sector: Client A is a mass-market vendor, while Client B sells into the lower-volume premium sector. The LSP is commissioned by both A and B to keep their marketing website and online catalogue updated and has available their legacy translation assets in the form of both TMs and bitexts (incidentally, the commercial advantage of this situation to the LSP is obvious: a competitor who wanted to bid for one of the accounts would be at a disadvantage without access to the time- and money-saving legacy materials). Imagine you are the project manager (PM) in charge of both accounts, aiming to make the most efficient use of each LSP's translation assets. Assuming there were no contractual obstacles, would you keep all the legacy data for both clients in a single large TM and have it updated by the freelancers who work on their commissions? This could give an advantage in coverage (more of a new translation assignment might be matched in the TM), but at the risk of blurring the commercial identity (brand image) of the two clients – they not only sell different products, but they need to appeal to different types of customer, using different language. On the other hand, if your translators are just supplied with the legacy bitexts, they may well miss out on a significant amount of general-language leverage that the big TM might have offered, making the job slower, more expensive, and probably linguistically less consistent (because segments that might have been extracted from the TM and used consistently end up being retranslated differently, perhaps by different translators).

This illustrates how the two approaches can in fact be complementary, explaining why some CAT tools offer both options (indeed, Melby et al. note that 'the distinction between translation memory and bitext systems is blurring' (2015: 412)). However, for those tools (the majority) that do not use bitexts, it is possible to achieve many of the same benefits by careful structuring and management of the TM data. The most obvious first step is not to store all the data from both clients in the same big TM! Assume now that you have one TM per client, TM_A and TM_B. When a new commission comes in from Client A, you can set up the project to use TM_A as the primary reference TM, and have your translators update it if you choose (alternatively, new translations could be sent to a third, initially empty, project TM), but you could additionally associate TM_B with the project in **read-only** mode (so that it doesn't get updated with the wrong client's data). Most CAT tools allow you to specify the search order of two or more TMs, so that the translator would see proposals from TM_A first, and you can even add an automatic **match penalty** (see below) to all proposals from TM_B to make them appear lower down the list of translation candidates. That way, the translator can benefit from seeing proposals from the other client's dataset without being prompted by the system to use them uncritically.

Matching

Whether your translation project is set up to use one or more TM(s), reference bitexts, or both, the CAT tool searches this previous translation material in the same way: by comparing each active segment in the ST you are translating with the legacy ST material, to look for identical or similar TUs. If one or more useful **matches** is found, each legacy ST segment will be presented along with its corresponding TT segment as a translation *proposal*, with an indication of the differences (if any) between the new and the old ST segment, to show the translator where the legacy translation needs to be adapted to the new context. The details of how this *lookup* is performed vary from tool to tool and can only be inferred from *black box* testing, because the search algorithms are commercially confidential. However, the basic mechanism is a calculation of the similarity between two **strings** of characters (corresponding to each active ST segment on the one hand, and the set of legacy ST segments on the other), which allows extraction of those TUs with the highest (most useful) level of similarity to the new ST segment. The calculation is based on the principle of **edit distance**, the best-known variant of which is Levenshtein distance, named after the Soviet mathematician Vladimir Levenshtein who proposed it in 1965 (Wikipedia, 2022). In simple terms, the edit distance between two strings is the minimum number of single-character edits (insertions, deletions, or substitutions) required to change one string into the other (spell checkers use this same principle to propose corrections). The more numerous the edits needed to transform the legacy ST string into the new ST string, the higher the **match penalty** that will be applied in the CAT tool's calculation of the relevance (usefulness) of the translation proposal, expressed as a similarity percentage with the penalty figure deducted from 100 (so a 95% match, with a 5% penalty, will be more similar, and useful, than an 83% match with a 17% penalty, and will be ranked above it in the CAT tool interface).

Box 3.1: Match Categories

- A **100% match**, or **exact match** is a TU whose SL segment string corresponds exactly (in characters, spaces, punctuation, as well as formatting) to the active segment;
- A **repetition match**, conceptually similar to an exact match, indicates that the same segment recurs more than once in the project – so you only need to translate the first occurrence and the translation can be propagated automatically to the others, as if they were all 100% matches;
- A **fuzzy match** is any match of less than 100% similarity (named after *fuzzy logic*, which goes beyond the absolute distinction between True and False to accommodate degrees of partial truth).

There are two additional cases, used by some CAT tools only, where match scores are *higher than 100%*, meaning that the system is even more confident that the proposal is likely to be correct:

- In a **context match**, usually abbreviated as 'CM' and scored at **101%**, not only does the ST segment of the TM proposal correspond exactly to the active segment, the *preceding* segment in the TM is also identical (and for some tools, the *following* segment as well), which indicates strongly that the proposal is coming from the correct context (typically, a previous version of the same document);
- A **perfect match**, usually abbreviated as 'PM' and scored at **102%**, is even more likely to be correct in context because it comes not from a TM, but from the reference corpus of bitext documents explicitly selected for their relevance to the project.

When **pretranslating** a new ST, a CAT tool that offers both TM and bitext retrieval will give preference to a 102% match from a bitext (if available) over a 101% or 100% match from a TM. At the opposite end of the scale, to avoid information overload and wastage of time from too many poor-quality matches, CAT tools also have a user-configurable **fuzzy match threshold** (usually set by default at around 70%), below which proposals are considered not to be useful; they will therefore not be displayed. If no match above the threshold is found, some CAT tools will attempt to construct a proposal from fragmentary equivalences extracted from different reference sources (Déjà Vu was the first to attempt this with its *Assemble* feature).

A useful attribute of CAT tools is that whenever a usable fuzzy match is found, they typically show the translator the differences between the active segment and the TM proposal using a comparison system of *tracked changes*, as in Figure 3.1.

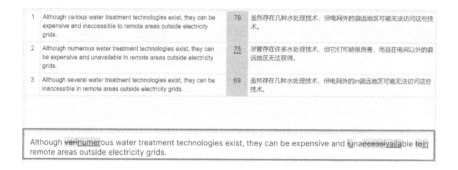

Figure 3.1 Fuzzy match differences in Phrase TMS

Here, Phrase has searched the project TM and found two fuzzy matches, scored at 78% and 69%, for the active English segment: 'Although numerous water treatment technologies exist, they can be expensive and unavailable in remote areas outside electricity grids'. (In between them, scored at 75% with a dotted underline, is an MT proposal – for more on this, see Chapter 7). The best (78%) match is selected (light orange background) and beneath the proposal window, the tracked changes panel (outlined) identifies the edit distance between the best match and the active segment, using strikethrough with pink shading to indicate deletions, and underlining with green shading to indicate additions (this shows that 'various' in the TM segment has changed to 'numerous' in the new ST segment, 'inaccessible' has become 'unavailable', and 'of' has been changed to 'in'). These are the equivalent changes that need to be made in the editor *on the target (Chinese) side* to repair the fuzzy match and turn it into an exact translation of the active English segment. Tracked changes thus allow the translator to home in on the parts of the TL proposal that need to be modified.

At the start of a project, when the project manager or translator runs an **analysis** of the new ST(s) against the legacy resources (TM and/or bitexts) allocated to it, the result is a report structured according to different *match bands*, the percentage boundaries of which are adjustable in some tools.

Figure 3.2 is an extract from a Trados Studio report, exported to Excel, on an English to Spanish project containing three SL files totalling 253 segments and 2,474 words.

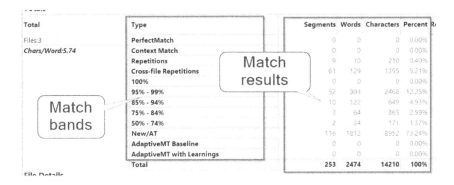

Total		Type	Segments	Words	Characters	Percent	R
Files:3		PerfectMatch	0	0	0	0.00%	
Chars/Word:5.74		Context Match	0	0	0	0.00%	
		Repetitions	9	10	210	0.40%	
		Cross-file Repetitions	61	129	1395	5.21%	
		100%	0	0	0	0.00%	
		95% - 99%	52	303	2468	12.25%	
		85% - 94%	10	122	649	4.93%	
Match bands		75% - 84%	3	64	365	2.59%	
		50% - 74%	2	34	171	1.37%	
		New/AT	116	1812	8952	73.24%	
		AdaptiveMT Baseline	0	0	0	0.00%	
		AdaptiveMT with Learnings	0	0	0	0.00%	
		Total	253	2474	14210	100%	
File Details							

Figure 3.2 Extract from Trados Studio analysis report

It shows there are no Perfect, Context, or 100% matches, but 52 segments fall in the highest fuzzy band (95%–99%) and another 70 are repetitions. Altogether, 135 segments (628 words, or 25.38% of the project) are matched in the resources at a useful level of 75% or above, and since it should be quicker to edit a high-value fuzzy match than translate the segment from scratch, this suggests a significant potential time saving, which in turn allows the freelancer or project manager to quote a lower price for the translation job. Some CAT tools allow analysis reports to be linked directly to a configurable *net rate scheme* specifying what discounted percentage of the full *rate per word* will be paid for different types of matches (so a translator might be paid 80% of the full rate for correcting a 75%–84% fuzzy match, but only 10% for checking an exact match, etc.), which means the job's financial quote can be generated automatically. Another benefit of the analysis process is that it potentially allows a project manager to extract from the project resources only relevant TUs (e.g. those with a match score of 75% or higher) and supply just that translation extract to the translator, usually in the form of a new TM. This offers significant benefits for confidentiality, as outlined in Chapter 2.

CAT tools are often said to be *language-independent*, i.e. they work in the same way and equally well with whichever languages they are used. Matching and analysis, which are concerned solely with strings of characters (to the computer, numbers), with no involvement of linguistic analysis (syntax, morphology, etc.), might appear to support this view, and indeed they work well for many quite different languages. The case of Arabic, however, exposes the limits of this language independence. Three features of written Arabic are problematic for algorithms designed to extract strings of similar meaning to the SL segment solely on the basis of string matching (Ben Milad,

2021: 5–12): flexible word order, complex morphology, and orthography (spelling). Unlike in many languages including English, a sentence in Arabic can be written with the words in several different orders without changing the meaning, so to a string-matching CAT tool, two sentences with the same meaning can look so different that their match score falls below the fuzzy match threshold, and the TU is therefore not displayed. Arabic also has a high incidence of inflectional morphology, with many grammatical relations conveyed by the addition of affixes and clitics to base word forms, and again, a relatively minor grammatical change (e.g. from singular to plural, or present tense to past) can lead to a significant number of character differences, resulting in a higher edit distance and therefore match penalty than the change in meaning alone would deserve. Finally, Arabic spelling is characterised by a complex system of diacritics which can distinguish between very different meanings of the same word form, but in practice are often omitted when the meaning is clear from the context, again creating edit distance and leading match penalties to be applied inappropriately to strings with identical meaning. To overcome these limitations, which taken together mean the translator working from Arabic is likely to miss a considerable number of potentially useful match proposals, researchers have suggested adding routines for handling the movement of blocks of identical characters, morphological preprocessing, and orthographical normalisation to the matching routines of CAT tools, among other techniques (ibid: 40–45). The absence of such customisations in current tools may go some way to explaining their slow adoption in Arabic-speaking countries, and in other countries/locales where complex features make adopting the tools less straightforward.

Alignment

The equivalence principle that underlines all leveraging of legacy translations is implemented in CAT tools through the mechanism of statistical (probabilistic) *alignment*, first formulated by Gale and Church (1993) as an algorithmic method for constructing parallel (translation) corpora for use in NLP (Natural Language Processing) applications. Alignment binds together a given source segment and its equivalent translation in one or more target languages as a translation unit (TU), along with relevant **metadata**, much of it added automatically by the system (e.g. date and time of the TU's creation and/or revision, ID of the translator or reviser, name and location of source and target files), but some of which (e.g. project name, client ID, domain, etc.) may be user-customisable. The resulting TU may be stored in a TM database or, in the case of bitexts, simply indexed for subsequent retrieval direct from the documents. In addition to NLP applications, alignment is now at the heart of all CAT tools, whether they use TM, bitexts, or both, but it is also fundamental to the creation of training corpora for machine translation (see Chapter 6 and Afterword).

As described in Chapter 2, alignment occurs automatically on the fly during translation in a CAT tool editor. Typically, whenever the translator *confirms* a segment, the TU is compiled and sent to a translation memory or (in the case of Star Transit) a fuzzy index for storage, subsequent search, and reuse. *Searching* a TM or fuzzy index, either automatically or through a manual **concordance search**, will retrieve relevant chunks of translated text, but *filtering* (a task often performed by a Project Manager) additionally allows a set of TUs to be retrieved that meet specific selection criteria based on either text or metadata (e.g. TUs created by a particular translator, or between a specific date range, or for a specific client, etc.). When you first acquire and open a typical CAT tool, you won't find any TM databases built in: you must start by creating an empty one in which to store the TUs generated by your new translation activity. As with project creation (see Chapter 2), this means deciding on a name and storage location for the TM, selecting source and target languages, and (optionally) adding metadata about the client, project, etc.

You are now all set to store and reuse any new TUs you create, but suppose you already have some existing (legacy) translations that you would like to reuse? If you or someone else made them in a CAT tool, that's no problem: the TUs can be exported from the originating program (it doesn't need to be the one you are planning to use) in the industry-standard TMX format (see below) and quickly imported into your new TM, which then is no longer empty. But what if you only have the legacy ST and TT in Word or PowerPoint format, or, worse, on paper? In the last case (and also with certain types of encrypted PDF files), you'd need to start by digitising the texts with a scanner (or your phone) to make an image of each page, then use an OCR (optical character recognition) tool – the free Online OCR program (https://www.onlineocr.net) is a good place to start – to convert the images to text. Once your legacy ST and TT are in electronic format, you can then bring them into the CAT environment, either leaving them as bitexts (if your tool supports that mode of retrieval) or, more commonly, by turning them into a TM. If TM import is intended, each pair of files (ST and TT) needs to be aligned, normally at *segment level* (some CAT tools also give you the option of aligning at paragraph level) to convert them into a series of independent TUs which can be imported into your TM. Bitexts may appear to be aligned only at *document level*, but for retrieval purposes the CAT tool actually needs to align and index them at segment level as well, usually automatically and in the background, so in fact both TM and bitexts rely on a comparable alignment mechanism. Before you commit time and effort into aligning legacy translations, however, it is important to consider how useful the results will be, i.e. how many high-quality matches you are likely to find for future translation jobs, which depends on how closely related to them the new and legacy materials are likely to be:

Alignment can be a very powerful tool if you have specific sets of already translated documents that correspond closely to new documents that now have to be translated. The amount of time you can save and the level of consistency and quality you can achieve by aligning the existing documents and using that as the basis for your translation can be immense.

(Díaz & Zetzsche, 2022: 223)

There is much less point in aligning lots of less relevant material which is unlikely to repay the cost in terms of useful leverage. If you do have a large volume of less relevant translations that you want to bulk align anyway, Díaz and Zetzsche recommend using the speedy, relatively accurate, and entirely automatic AlignFactory by Terminotix, which has a free online version called YouAlign (https://youalign.com).

Most CAT tools (a notable exception being Wordbee) include a component that performs segment-level alignment, and there are other stand-alone programs such as the very useful freeware LF Aligner that are not part of a CAT package and give you close control over the alignment process. They vary in the number of file formats they can handle: LF Aligner for instance is limited to TXT, DOC, DOCX, RTF and HTML, whereas the aligners of major CAT tools can handle any format for which they have an available **filter** to separate text from tags and codes (see Chapter 2). Just like the early steps that happen when a new ST is imported into a CAT tool, the aligner first identifies the filetype it is working with and filters the files: because the alignment products (TUs or indexes) are for reference use rather than for producing a finished target document, the inline tags and codes may be discarded by default (this behaviour is user-configurable in some tools), which can improve match scores by removing formatting penalties. Once the files have been filtered, they are segmented, typically using the same language-specific segmentation rules a CAT tool would apply to a new ST in the same language.

Next, the aligner carries out a first pass attempt to align the source and target segments automatically, before (usually) offering the user the opportunity to review the alignment and manually correct any errors. To achieve this, it works with the structural features of the two documents, trying to identify as many points of correspondence as possible (so the default assumption of equivalence between ST and TT holds on the level of structure as well as meaning). When evaluating whether an ST and a TT segment are equivalent and so should be aligned, the aligner typically considers text features such as those listed in Box 3.2.

Box 3.2: Text Features Used for Alignment

Document structure, including:

- Relative position of the segments in the two documents (i.e. segment number);
- Position relative to other TUs that have already been aligned, especially when they have been manually confirmed (see below);
- Segment length (do the segments contain a similar number of words, or characters?).

Aligners may also use certain features of segment content to refine their confidence judgements, but this typically makes the alignment slower (for this reason Across, for example, makes their use optional):

- Presence of numerals, dates, abbreviations, measurements, named entities and other **placeables** and **localisables** (see Chapter 2) in both SL and TL segments;
- Inline formatting (e.g. do both segments contain words in italics?);
- Styles and other structural information (e.g. are both segments formatted as Heading 1?).

Of course, contrary to the simplistic assumption of structural equivalence between documents, there may be cases where one ST segment is translated by two or more in the TT, or vice-versa: an efficient aligner should also be able to make a good attempt at handling these so-called *one-to-many* and *many-to-one* cases (as well as the less common *many-to-many* instances where more than one SL segments need to be aligned with more than one TL segments in different relative positions). Partly for this reason, LF Aligner supplements structural information with dictionaries (for 32 languages including most European ones and Arabic, Chinese, Hebrew, Japanese, Korean, Russian, Swahili, and Turkish) to establish some word-level equivalences between segments, thus increasing alignment accuracy (Díaz & Zetzsche, 2022: 225). Similarly, the XTM Advanced Text Aligner uses Big Data 'lexicons' for 50 languages and claims to be able to repair structural misalignments between the two documents, as well as offering the option to extract bilingual terminology (see Chapter 4) during alignment (comparable capabilities in 46 languages, 2,070 language pairs, are also offered by the Chinese tool TMXmallaligner). Note, however, that even tools that use dictionaries or lexicons are still just matching strings of characters in the same way as TM systems do: they do not perform linguistic analysis. Having assessed the various parameters for each candidate segment alignment, the aligner assigns a confidence score to each possibility and retains across the project the candidates with the highest scores, which it may subsequently display to the user (e.g. in XTM).

Once the first automatic alignment has been completed by the system, the user is generally given the opportunity to review it in a dedicated alignment editor and correct any misalignments. Significant exceptions here are Phrase and XTM, which export their automatic alignments to Excel, where they can be manually corrected before import into a TM (this is also an option in LF Aligner). Smartcat exports its alignment directly in TMX format (see below), which can be corrected in a tool such as the freeware TMXEditor (which uses LF Aligner), while in addition to outputting a Wordfast format text-based TM, the Wordfast Online Aligner also exports to Excel and TMX. Manually correcting an alignment project can be quite a lengthy process, so depending on the expected value of the legacy translations for the project in hand and/or as a resource for the future, you may quite legitimately decide not to bother and accept that some of the resultant translation proposals may be incorrectly aligned. Similar considerations apply in the case of reference bitexts: memoQ, for instance, uses its LiveDocs corpus by default in automatic alignment mode, but the user has the option of reviewing and correcting the alignment, which can also be exported, if you wish, to TMX and made into a TM. Whether your alignment is being used to create a TM or a bitext pair, if you do decide to correct it manually, you will have turned your expertly-produced legacy translations into a flexible resource of known high quality – here again, qualified human review is essential to give this assurance.

Two broad types of graphical interfaces have been developed to help visualise and facilitate alignment correction, which achieve the same goal but conceptualise the problem slightly differently:

- Segment-manipulation aligners;
- Connection-manipulation aligners.

Both approaches present the user with a familiar grid view of the source and target segments side by side, but whereas the first allows you to move individual SL and TL segments spatially in relation to those on the other side until they line up, the second leaves the segments in their original position but invites you to make and break graphical connections between them. As will be seen from the examples below, both types can handle one-to-many and many-to-one alignments, but the second has the added flexibility of allowing connections to cross, to accommodate the (quite rare) case where a segment on one side is in a different position relative to the rest of the document than its corresponding segment on the other side. The examples below illustrate how the two types of aligners handle the same ST and TT pair, a small text in English (left column) and its German translation (right column).

Segment-Manipulation Aligners

Figure 3.3 shows a typical segment-manipulation aligner, the freeware LF Aligner referred to above. The grid contains the outcome of the tool's first-

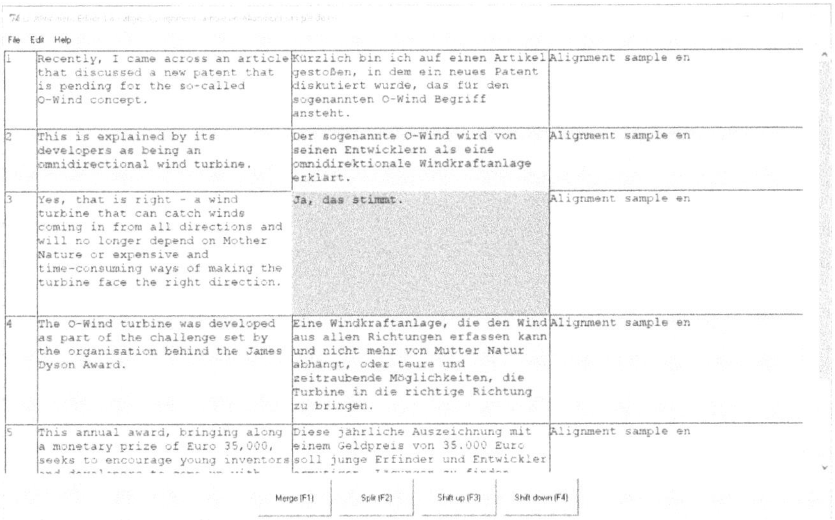

Figure 3.3 Segment manipulation alignment (LF Aligner 4.21)

pass automatic alignment (the third column gives the name of the ST file), from which it is immediately clear that Row 3 is wrong: a long SL sentence split by a dash has been aligned with a short TL sentence ending in a full stop (selected).

This misalignment can be corrected by manipulating the segments using just four commands, accessed by clicking on the buttons at the bottom of the window or through Function keys. These allow two successive segments to be *merged* or a single segment to be *split* at the cursor point, or any individual segment to be *shifted* either *up* or *down*, and in

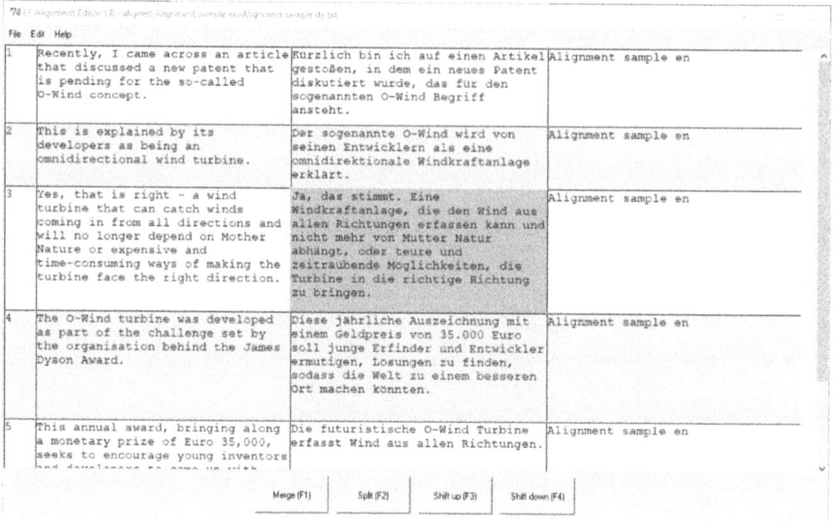

1	Recently, I came across an article that discussed a new patent that is pending for the so-called O-Wind concept.	Kürzlich bin ich auf einen Artikel gestoßen, in dem ein neues Patent diskutiert wurde, das für den sogenannten O-Wind Begriff ansteht.	Alignment sample en
2	This is explained by its developers as being an omnidirectional wind turbine.	Der sogenannte O-Wind wird von seinen Entwicklern als eine omnidirektionale Windkraftanlage erklärt.	Alignment sample en
3	Yes, that is right - a wind turbine that can catch winds coming in from all directions and will no longer depend on Mother Nature or expensive and time-consuming ways of making the turbine face the right direction.	Ja, das stimmt. Eine Windkraftanlage, die den Wind aus allen Richtungen erfassen kann und nicht mehr von Mutter Natur abhängt, oder teure und zeitraubende Möglichkeiten, die Turbine in die richtige Richtung zu bringen.	Alignment sample en
4	The O-Wind turbine was developed as part of the challenge set by the organisation behind the James Dyson Award.	Diese jährliche Auszeichnung mit einem Geldpreis von 35.000 Euro soll junge Erfinder und Entwickler ermutigen, Lösungen zu finden, sodass die Welt zu einem besseren Ort machen könnten.	Alignment sample en
5	This annual award, bringing along a monetary prize of Euro 35,000, seeks to encourage young inventors	Die futuristische O-Wind Turbine erfasst Wind aus allen Richtungen.	Alignment sample en

Merge (F1)   Split (F2)   Shift up (F3)   Shift down (F4)

Figure 3.4 First alignment error corrected.

combination they can handle any common alignment problem. In this example, the first step is to merge the short TL segment in Row 3 (highlighted as the active segment) with the segment in Row 4, to produce the result seen in Figure 3.4.

This has fixed the problem in Row 3 but introduced a new misalignment in Row 4, because the German segment that has moved up to fill the gap left

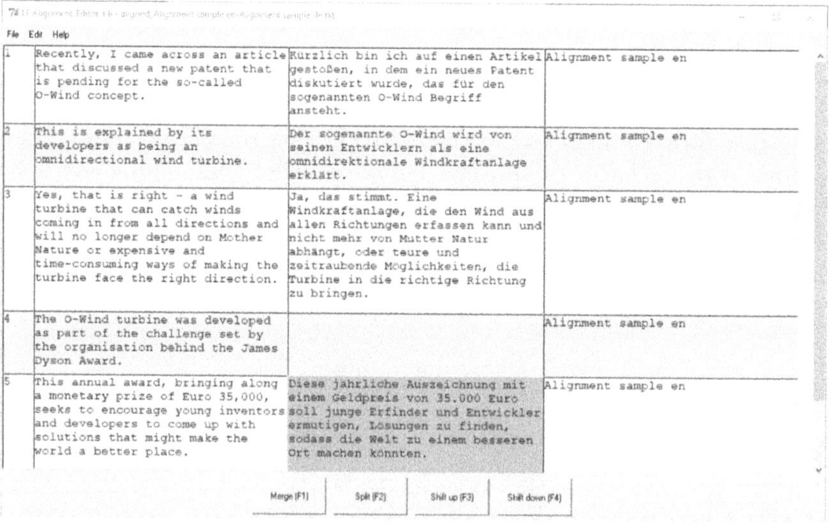

1	Recently, I came across an article that discussed a new patent that is pending for the so-called O-Wind concept.	Kürzlich bin ich auf einen Artikel gestoßen, in dem ein neues Patent diskutiert wurde, das für den sogenannten O-Wind Begriff ansteht.	Alignment sample en
2	This is explained by its developers as being an omnidirectional wind turbine.	Der sogenannte O-Wind wird von seinen Entwicklern als eine omnidirektionale Windkraftanlage erklärt.	Alignment sample en
3	Yes, that is right - a wind turbine that can catch winds coming in from all directions and will no longer depend on Mother Nature or expensive and time-consuming ways of making the turbine face the right direction.	Ja, das stimmt. Eine Windkraftanlage, die den Wind aus allen Richtungen erfassen kann und nicht mehr von Mutter Natur abhängt, oder teure und zeitraubende Möglichkeiten, die Turbine in die richtige Richtung zu bringen.	Alignment sample en
4	The O-Wind turbine was developed as part of the challenge set by the organisation behind the James Dyson Award.		Alignment sample en
5	This annual award, bringing along a monetary prize of Euro 35,000, seeks to encourage young inventors and developers to come up with solutions that might make the world a better place.	Diese jährliche Auszeichnung mit einem Geldpreis von 35.000 Euro soll junge Erfinder und Entwickler ermutigen, Lösungen zu finden, sodass die Welt zu einem besseren Ort machen könnten.	Alignment sample en

Merge (F1)   Split (F2)   Shift up (F3)   Shift down (F4)

Figure 3.5 Second alignment error corrected.

by the first shift operation is not a translation of the English. In fact, segment 4 of the ST has not been translated at all in the TT, so to restore the alignment below Row 3 you need to introduce a blank TL segment in Row 4 by shifting the German sentence down one place (see Figure 3.5).

After you have scrolled through the document and corrected any further alignment errors (as well as any spelling, translation, etc. errors you may come across in the texts), the program invites you to export the alignment in TMX format (see below) ready for import into a TM of the CAT tool of your choice. Current CAT tools with segment-manipulation aligners include CafeTran Espresso, Déjà Vu X3, OmegaT, Star Transit NXT, and Stingray, the alignment partner of the Swordfish CAT tool. The Matecat aligner is also of this type, but with the additional command option to *switch* segments to resolve the cross-linking problem referred to above.

Connection-Manipulation Aligners

Rather than manipulating the boundaries and locations of segments, when manually reviewing an alignment project in a connection-manipulation aligner you *confirm*, *disconnect*, or *reconnect* the candidate links between them. Figure 3.6 shows the outcome of a first-pass alignment of the same small sample file by Trados Studio, heir to Trados's classic WinAlign program (originally T-Align) that pioneered this approach. A key difference from LF Aligner is the central column between the seg-

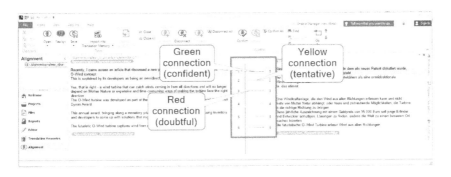

Figure 3.6 Connection-manipulation alignment (Trados Studio 2022).

ment numbers (outlined), in which the program uses dotted lines to indicate candidate connections between SL and TL segments, colour-coded (green, yellow, red) to indicate its degree of confidence in the proposed alignment.

Segments 1, 5, and 6 have their source connected to their target by dotted green lines and since those alignments are correct, you can select them individually (they become highlighted in light blue) and click the Confirm button, which turns the dotted lines solid to indicate that they are now confirmed. Our problematic third segment is, however, red, and because of that, 2 and 4 are marked appropriately as tentative (yellow), though in fact the alignment of segment 2 is correct and so it too can be confirmed. To correct the misalignment of segment 3, you need to make a new 'one-to-many' link to connect the long segment on the SL side to *both* segments 3 and 4 on the TL side. The first step is to disconnect the existing incorrect alignments of segments 3 and 4 (remember, segment 4 does not belong in a TM at all, because the target side is empty). Deleting a connection works in a similar way to confirming it: just select each pair of segments and click Disconnect, which 'breaks' the dotted line between them. Next, to create the new one-to-many link, click the number 3 (not the segment text to the left of it) on the source side, then hold down the CTRL key and click numbers 3 and 4 on the target side, so that all three segments are highlighted in light yellow; next click the Connect button and you will see the result shown in Figure 3.7,

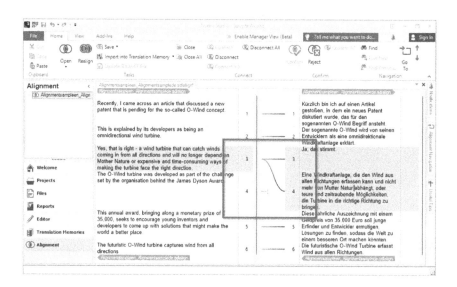

Figure 3.7 'One-to-many' alignment in Trados Studio 2022.

which effectively means that, just as in the segment-based alignment, target segments 3 and 4 have been joined together and aligned with source segment 3, while the translation of source segment 4 is left empty, so that TU will not be exported.

Now that all the alignments in this little sample have been confirmed, they can be exported (in Trados Studio) directly to a TM you nominated at the start of the project, or (in other CAT tools) to a TMX file that you can subsequently import into a TM of your choice (see below). Among other current CAT tools with connection-manipulation aligners are Across, memoQ, and Wordfast Pro.

Aligned Data Interchange Formats

There are two main interchange formats for segment-aligned bilingual data, TMX and XLIFF, which are both tagged-text formats belonging to the Open Architecture for XML Authoring and Localization (OAXAL) reference architecture (https://en.wikipedia.org/wiki/OAXAL). A third option is the tabular Microsoft Word bilingual document, supported by an increasing number of CAT tools, which is mainly designed to allow a reviser to work on a translation outside the CAT tool that originally produced it, capturing their changes for subsequent re-import into the original CAT project.

Box 3.3: Main Interchange Standards for Aligned Data

- *TMX 1.4* – Translation Memory eXchange. The near-universal standard for exchanging TM data between users and different CAT tools. It is an XML-based text-only format that encodes TUs and associated metadata in a text-only, tagged format that all CAT tools can read and convert into their own internal TM database or fuzzy index format. However, since CAT tools have different segmentation rules and encode inline formats differently, they may process (import and export) TMX files from other tools in slightly unpredictable ways (Díaz & Zetzsche, 2022: 258).

- *XLIFF 1.2* – XML Localisation Interface File Format. XLIFF is the standard text-only bilingual workfile format into which most CAT tools silently convert the numerous different input file types that they support, for translation in their internal editor. Some tools have added customisations onto the basic standard format (e.g. Phrase has MXLIFF, Trados Studio has SDLXLIFF etc.) (Díaz & Zetzsche, 2022: 259). Some (e.g. memoQ, Smartcat, XTM Cloud) allow the XLIFF workfile to be directly exported for translation in a different CAT tool, then re-imported, while others (e.g. Wordfast Anywhere) allow import and editing of external XLIFFs. XLIFF files can be used natively (without conversion) as bilingual reference corpora by some tools (e.g. memoQ). Project packages (see Chapter 2) used to exchange ongoing translation and revision assignments between linguists typically include the XLIFF workfile.

- *Word bilingual file* – Some CAT tools including memoQ, Phrase, Smartcat, and Trados Studio allow export of the XLIFF workfile into a multi-column Word table, so that linguists who do not have access to the original tool can still work on the translation. When they return the finished Word table, the tool re-imports it and updates the XLIFF workfile and connected resources with any changes.

TMX is the principal *pivot* format, allowing data conversion in all directions between aligners, translation memories, and (where they are supported) bitexts, and it is particularly useful for converting TM data from the format used in one CAT tool to that of a different tool. XLIFF allows the workfile from one tool that supports the format to be imported directly into the editing environment of a different tool, preserving as many of the CAT-specific attributes (e.g. match percentages) as possible. An example of TMX's role in alignment to TM conversion is shown in Figure 3.8, where the sample alignment created in the

Figure 3.8 TMX export from Trados Studio imported into a memoQ 9.12 TM.

previous section has first been exported from Trados Studio as a TMX file, then imported into an empty TM in memoQ 9.12, where it is open for editing.

Figure 3.9 illustrates how the structure of the third TU (outlined) is represented in a TMX file, which has been opened as a text-only file in Notepad++. The whole entry is enclosed between opening and closing XML tags (<tu> and </tu>) and the first eight lines contain metadata, recording the date and time of the TU's creation, the user who created it, etc., along with properties such as the originating program, source and target filenames, TU status (ApprovedSignOff) and translation equivalence quality

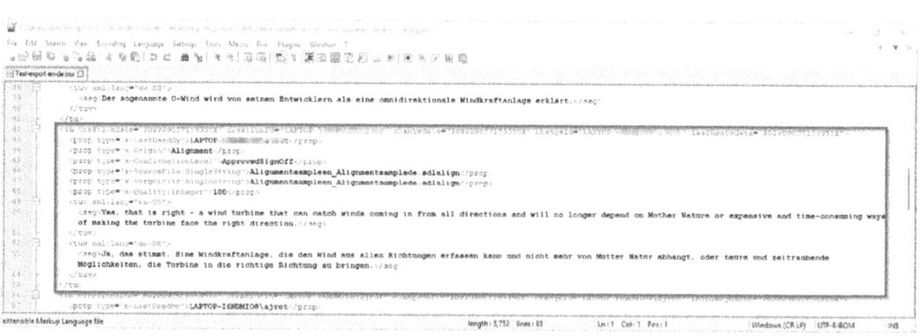

Figure 3.9 Part of a TMX 1.4 file opened as XML text in Notepad++.

(>100<) – set by default to 100% because the alignment of SL and TL segments has been signed off by the user:

Below the metadata fields come the SL and TL segments, marked by their **ISO locale codes** <tuv xml:lang="en-GB"> and <tuv xml:lang="de-DE"> respectively (if you ever need to change a locale in a TM, you can do it by editing the TMX file in a text editor to replace these values with the new ones and re-saving the file as 'Text only'). For comparison, Figure 3.10

Figure 3.10 Smartcat XLIFF export file opened in Notepad++.

shows the same file exported from Smartcat in XLIFF format and opened in Notepad++: The layout may be slightly less easy to read than the TMX export above, but the text-only file architecture, with metadata in the header and TUs in the body represented by nested structural units enclosed between angled brackets, is quite similar.

To illustrate the role of the Word bilingual export format, we can create a project to translate a revised version of the sample wind turbine text using Phrase TMS, starting by creating a new TM and importing the aligned TMX file into it. In Figure 3.11, exact and high-value fuzzy match proposals from the TM have been used, corrected, and confirmed for segments 1, 2, 3, and 5; segment 4 (missing from the alignment) has been machine translated (as indicated by the match score of 75% with a line of dashes underneath),

Figure 3.11 Aligned TMX in use in the Phrase TMS editor.

while the best match for the active segment 6 (87%) has been inserted but not yet corrected.

Like memoQ, Smartcat and Trados Studio, Phrase allows a translation job to be exported from the bilingual editor for revision by a linguist who does not have access to the CAT tool, generating a Microsoft Word table that contains most of the information in the translation grid: TU numbers, SL and TL segments, original match percentages, and an extra column for comments by the reviser. In Figure 3.12, the reviser is ready to check the

Figure 3.12 Export from Phrase TMS to a Bilingual DOCX table in Microsoft Word.

existing TUs, especially the machine-translated No. 4, and add comments in the far-right column as appropriate.

When the revised file is subsequently returned to the project manager, Phrase compares the Word document with its original MXLIFF file and updates both that file and any linked TM(s) with the changes made by the reviser.

Conclusion

It is no exaggeration to say that alignment, a materialisation of the principle of textual-linguistic equivalence, is the core concept on which all modern translation technology is built. Vast corpora of automatically aligned bitexts, many of them crawled from the web, are used to train probabilistic MT engines (see Chapter 6), while in the CAT domain, TM and reference bitexts also form types of parallel corpora constructed by alignment, automatic and/or manual, before, during, and after the translation process itself. Sophisticated searching and matching algorithms have been developed to perform the edit-distance calculations that allow the extraction of re-usable translation units from CAT corpora. Meanwhile, the standard TMX format for importing, editing, and exporting the aligned data makes TMs and bitexts usable in any CAT tool, or indeed for MT training, while XLIFF and Word bilingual export give added flexibility to data exchange and revision. So even if you as a translator do not find yourself having to make your own alignments, it is valuable to have an understanding of the underlying principles, the different file formats, and their implications for the design and use of translation tools.

Follow-Up Tasks and Reflection

(You will need access to the data you created during the tasks from Chapter 2).

1. Start by combining the two partial TTs you exported previously into a single file, so that you now have a complete translation of the Practice ST, which we will now refer to as the Practice TT.
2. Open the Practice TT file and save it with a new name (e.g. Practice TT2). Now make some changes to it: delete two short sentences, add two new ones, break one or two long sentences into two parts using a full stop or a colon, and combine two sentences into one using a comma. Save the file and close it.
3. You will now practice aligning your Practice ST and Practice TT2 files into a TM. Choose and (if necessary) install an alignment tool: LF Aligner is a good free choice, but if your chosen workstation CAT tool has an alignment component you may prefer to use that.
4. Import Practice ST and Practice TT2 into the aligner and experiment with correcting the misalignments that will have been caused by the

changes you made to the TT in Step 2. How easy is it to do this? Is it preferable to recombine the split TT sentences or break the corresponding ST sentence in the same place? How do you handle the sentences that are only present on one side of the alignment (hint: your TM is only useful if it contains complete TUs, so there is no point in including segments that have no translation).

5. When you have finished the alignment, export it as a TMX file, then practise importing that TMX file into a new TM, named Practice TM3, in each of the two CAT tools that you experimented with previously.

6. Now, in each of your CAT tools, create a new project including Practice ST and Practice TM3, and retranslate the ST using the new combined TM data. If you have done the alignment properly in Step 4, you should find exact match proposals (including Context matches if they are supported by the tool) for all segments except those with a missing translation. You could also experiment with the tool's Pretranslation function (if there is one), which should present you with an almost fully translated text from the start, requiring you only to work on the segments that don't already have a translation available in Practice TM3.

7. Finally, go back to your original TM1 and TM2 files. Export a TMX file from TM2 and import that TMX into TM1 (and, if you wish, the other way round as well). This demonstrates how easy it is to use the TMX format to move translation data between one CAT tool and another. You can repeat these procedures with as many different tools as you can get your hands on!

Further Reading

On the important Functionalist theory of text types, see Katharina Reiss's (1981) article 'Type, kind and individuality of text: decision making in translation'. For a brief overview of theories of translation equivalence, see 'Equivalence in translation theories: a critical evaluation' (Panou, 2013) and for a more detailed discussion, Werner Koller's (1995) article 'The concept of equivalence and the object of translation studies'. For more on translation memory, see Chapter 2 of this book, and the corresponding chapter of the *Routledge encyclopedia of translation technology* (Melby and Wright, 2015). The same encyclopedia contains a wide-ranging discussion of 'Bitext', including in translation tools (Melby et al., 2015). 'A program for aligning sentences in bilingual corpora' (Gale and Church, 1993) offers a useful description of the first alignment program, while for the statistically minded, Lars Ahrenberg's (2015) chapter on 'Alignment' in the *Routledge encyclopedia of translation technology* gives a technical account of different types of alignment algorithms. Wikipedia has well-informed entries for 'TMX' and 'XLIFF'.

4 Managing Terminology in CAT Tools

> **Key Questions**
>
> - Why do you need a terminology database (i.e. **termbase**) in addition to a **translation memory?**
> - What is the difference between a **glossary** and a termbase?
> - What is the difference between words and **terms** (simplified)?
> - What criteria should be used to select items for a termbase?
> - How do you create and manage termbases in a **CAT tool?**
> - How do you look up terms and information about them in a CAT tool?
> - Why is **phraseology** as important for translators as terms?

What Is a Termbase and Why Do You Need One?

As we have seen in the previous chapter, a **translation memory (TM)** is a database of bilingual sentences in the SL and TL, which allows translators to reuse those sentences, or parts of those sentences, in similar translation projects. However, despite the usefulness of translation memories to increase a translator's productivity, there is no dedicated mechanism in translation memories that helps translators to check or improve the consistency of the terminology used throughout a translation project. Ensuring consistency of terminology is one of the most important aspects of the translator's work for many reasons, and not only for quantitative ones. For example, Nkwenti-Azeh (2001: 249) found that terminology tasks can take up to 60% of the translator's time. Another reason is that terminological errors can lead to negative consequences for the users of the translation, particularly in medical and legal domains, costly delays in republishing, and substantial damage to the company's or translator's brand and reputation. While translators are already proficient users of their working languages, it does not necessarily follow that they are experts in a particular subject area (henceforth referred

DOI: 10.4324/9781003160793-4

to as **domain**) as well or that they know the specialised vocabulary of every domain in each of their languages.

Therefore, translators need to make sure that they find and use the appropriate specialised terminology of the domain, not only to avoid mistranslating terms but also to facilitate unambiguous communication among the users of the translation. To this end, translators (and interpreters) have traditionally needed to collect bilingual lists of SL terms with the corresponding equivalent terms in the TL (which are not always literal translations of the SL terms). One way of doing this, which was extensively used by translators before the CAT tool era, was to source or prepare bilingual **glossaries,** to which translators would then refer during translation to ensure they always use the same TL term for the relevant SL term. These glossaries would typically consist of lists of word equivalences, sorted alphabetically by SL term. A much-used resource for translators in this respect has been spreadsheet software such as MS Excel (Costa et al., 2018: 60; Gornostay, 2010: 25–26).

However, spreadsheet software was not designed to contain text, let alone terminological data (Bononno, 2000: 652). The strengths of spreadsheet software lie in its capabilities dealing with numbers, formulas, etc., rather than text. This makes spreadsheet software fairly deficient in dealing with the complexities of translators' terminological tasks for several reasons, including those found by Austermühl (2001: 105) and Olohan (2016: 42):

- Limited visualisation options, especially if you want to use many columns, e.g. in a multilingual termbase.
- Files can become rather large, making searches slow.
- The search results highlight the cell where the searched word is found, rather than the word itself.
- Spreadsheets typically store the SL and TL only, without potentially useful information about the terms such as domain, definition, example of term usage, etc.
- In addition, spreadsheets cannot be integrated with CAT environments, so the translator has to do all the searching manually.

Over time, it became clear that spreadsheet software hampered translators and interpreters in effectively storing and retrieving nuanced terminological information such as synonyms, collocations, term variants (e.g. geographical or spelling differences) etc., and creating cross-references between related terms in a given domain. All this along with other terminological information is vitally important for translators and interpreters to build up their knowledge of the domain but is not readily accessible to them in spreadsheets.

Furthermore, the inclusion of graphics, useful for the clarification of concepts, not to mention the inclusion of video or audio files, would render the spreadsheet unwieldy. Translators would either have to invest a great deal of extra time and effort in finding all the relevant information about a given concept scattered in various cells of the spreadsheet, or else store this information outside the spreadsheet environment.

Given the importance of ensuring the quality and consistency of translators' terminological work for all the stakeholders in the translation process, CAT tools typically provide another database alongside the translation memory: the **termbase** (from *terminological + database*). Termbases are terminological databases integrated into the CAT environment. This integration is crucial because it allows translators to benefit from the automatic, therefore faster, lookup of terms (as opposed to previous time-consuming manual searches through a spreadsheet). CAT environments typically have a window or pane where terminology matches are displayed. From here, translators can decide to insert the translation of the term directly into the translation, or, depending on the settings available in a CAT tool, the insertion of term translations can also be automatic. Translators remain in control of term selection, as they can also ignore the matches displayed in the terminology window should they not be appropriate in a given text.

A termbase also differs from the traditional two-column glossaries/ spreadsheets in the following aspects:

- Termbases are **concept oriented**. This means that each entry is organised around a concept, not around a word (see Box 4.1). Each concept will be recorded once and all the associated information about that concept will be included in that entry. Therefore, a single entry will contain the terms in the two (or more) languages, but it can also contain all the spelling variants, geographical variants, as well as definition, domain, examples of usage, sources used, etc. Concept orientation does not mean that concepts are universal across all cultures and time periods (Melby, 2012). On the contrary, you need to remain aware of the dynamic nature of terms and keep your terms and definitions updated accordingly as they change over time. For example, since its discovery, Pluto was considered a *planet* and was defined as such. However, as advancements are made in planetary and astronomical science, Pluto was finally excluded from the definition of *planet* in 2006 by the International Astronomical Union and was re-classified as a *dwarf planet*. If you are a translator that specialises in these domains, you should update the definition of *Pluto* in your termbase, and ensure that it is no longer defined as a '*planet* which ...' but as a '*dwarf planet* which ...' (see also the discussion in ten Hacken, 2015: 3–5). It would also be worth adding a definition of *dwarf planet* to your termbase, if you didn't have it already. Staying up to date with news and developments in your chosen specialism(s) is an important part of the translator's work.
- The more sophisticated termbases are organised *hierarchically*. This means that, within an entry, translators can distinguish between

information that applies to a term, a language or to the entire concept. For example, a graphic, e.g. a photo, drawing, or diagram with or without labels, would apply to the entire concept, whereas definitions apply to a particular language and synonyms would apply to a particular term. Typically, information that applies to the entire concept is entered in the so-called *Entry level*, whereas information that applies to a language is entered at *Language* or *Index level*, and information that applies to a term is generally entered at *Term level*.

Box 4.1: The Distinction between *Words* and *Terms*

It can be difficult to distinguish between words and terms, but it is an important distinction for translators, as it can help them to select the items that should be stored in a termbase (terms) from among those that should not (words).

In a specialised domain, knowledge is organised into a system of interrelated concepts, i.e. its *conceptual network*. This means that concepts must be understood in relation to each other, rather than in isolation (Bowker, 2019: 579). The way we refer to these concepts is by using **terms**, so in this sense, terms are the specialised words and expressions used to convey specialised knowledge in a specific domain. In other words, terms are the *linguistic designations* for those interrelated, specialised concepts. Terms can be made up of a single word (e.g. *lava*) or they can be a multiword expression (e.g. *pyroclastic flow*).

By contrast, *words* belong to general language and do not carry any specialisation, nor are they connected to a specific domain. However, words can become terms when they 'assume a meaning that is specific to a subject field' (Granda and Warburton, 2001: 4). For example, *window* is a general language word but, in computing, it has acquired a specialised meaning.

As explained by Granda and Warburton (2001: 4), a concept oriented termbase allows a 'vertical and horizontal network of relations between concepts and terms' and 'transforms the data from a static lexicographical record of words and definitions to a dynamic, spatial knowledge base'. Some tools, such as OmegaT or Smartcat, offer a halfway solution between a simple two-column glossary and a full, sophisticated termbase: they offer a spreadsheet facility with **active terminology lookup**, automatically extracting and displaying term matches as you translate. Figure 4.1 broadly illustrates the difference between these three types of terminological offering:

Figure 4.1 Three levels of complexity in termbase capabilities.

'A' demonstrates a basic spreadsheet outside of the CAT environment, which means that you would not benefit from automatic term lookup. 'B' demonstrates the halfway solution, where the two-column glossary is integrated into a CAT tool (Smartcat 2021 in this case), which comes with automatic term lookup (in inset). Finally, 'C' demonstrates full termbase capabilities, allowing graphics, live hyperlinks, as well as other sophisticated features and full term-recognition capabilities too (Trados MultiTerm 2021 in this case). In the next section, we identify the various considerations to take into account when creating a hierarchical, concept oriented termbase in a CAT tool.

How to Create a Termbase in a CAT Tool

A good termbase for translators should be hierarchical and concept oriented as explained above. A thorough termbase will help you produce terminologically consistent translations over time and across translation projects. However, the reality is that many professional translators have little time to invest in creating or populating thorough termbases *while working on a project*. This is why you are encouraged to develop one or two specialisms early on, so that you have a chance to build up your terminological resources prior to becoming involved in translation projects in the same domain. Once created, your termbase(s) will need maintaining or updating as you increase your knowledge of the domain. In this section, we describe the kinds of information that a very thorough termbase might contain, fully aware that not every translator will be able to include all of it all the time.

A termbase can contain a great deal of information about the terms you enter. This information is typically organised in *fields*, which are also referred to as *data categories* (Warburton, 2015: 385). It is generally good practice to enter *only one type of information in each field*. For example, it is more efficient for translators to store *random access memory* in the Term field and *RAM* in the acronym field than enter both *random access memory (RAM)* in the Term field. In this way, acronyms can be sorted and searched separately from terms when required by translators. There are four main types of fields or data categories:

- Numeric
- Free text
- Multimedia
- Picklist

Numeric fields can be used to enter dates, for example. *Free text fields* are needed for most types of information, such as definitions, context/example of usage, notes, etc. *Multimedia fields* allow you to enter graphics, video or audio files, which are worth storing in the termbase for future reference, as they can contain useful terminological information, or they can help you understand how concepts are related in a specific domain. By collecting this information in the termbase, you should not need to carry out the same research into that domain again. In this way, any domain research you carry out can double up as terminology research.

Picklists are lists of finite values (Cerrella Bauer, 2015: 336) which are typically suited to fields which have a limited number of options available, e.g. part of speech (noun, verb, adjective, adverb), register (formal, informal, jargon), etc. The advantage of picklists is that they allow you to enter, and therefore display, the information more consistently, i.e. by selecting from a list rather than typing, thereby simplifying retrieval and standardising spelling. However, deciding the picklists you want to include, the labels you want to use for each item in the list (e.g. 'noun', 'N.', 'n.', etc), and setting the entire termbase up can be time-consuming. It is normal to feel that the preparatory work can be labour-intensive at the start, but you should benefit from it with your first translation project in that domain.

The type of information to include about the terms in your termbase, the type of field, and the level to enter it at are exemplified in Table 4.1. The list of fields in this table is by no means exhaustive. You should consider your domain carefully and add or delete fields as appropriate. For example, some domains may not lend themselves well to graphics, e.g. philosophy, whereas others would welcome audio files, e.g. acoustical engineering. Similarly, you may need to consider your client's profile, needs, and preferences and this may help you decide whether you need all the information in one termbase or several.

The list of fields and information will also vary depending on your working situation: if you work freelance on a short-term project, you might 'make use of only minimal fields, while a large, corporate documentation team working on long-term projects with complex terminology may develop comprehensive, detailed termbases according to strict guidelines' (Kageura

Table 4.1 An example of types of fields and types of information in termbases

Type of information	Field	Type of field	Level	Mandatory?	Multiple?
Administrative	Unique code or ID for the entry	Numeric or free text	Entry	YES	NO
	Date it was created	Numeric or free text	Entry	YES	NO
	Author of the entry	Free text	Entry	YES	NO
Linguistic	The term itself	Free text	Term	YES	YES
	Acronym	Free text	Term	NO	NO
	Abbreviation	Free text	Term	NO	NO
	Geographical variant	Free text or picklist	Term	NO	YES
	Part of speech	Picklist	Term	YES	NO
	Gender (if applicable)	Picklist	Term	NO	NO
	Status (e.g. forbidden, standardised)	Picklist	Term	NO	NO
	Register (e.g. formal, informal)	Picklist	Term	NO	YES
Conceptual	Domain(s) and subdomain(s)	Picklist or free text	Entry	NO	YES
	Definition	Free text	Lang.	NO	YES
	Source of the definition	Free text	Lang.	NO	YES
	Example of usage/ Context	Free text	Lang.	NO	YES
	Source of example	Free text	Lang.	NO	YES
	Encyclopaedic information	Free text	Lang.	NO	NO
	Source of encycl. information	Free text	Lang.	NO	YES
	Multimedia	Multimedia	Entry	NO	YES
	Paradigmatic relations	Free text or picklist	Lang.	NO	YES
	Syntagmatic relations	Free text	Lang.	NO	YES
Notes	Notes	Free text	Any	NO	YES

& Marshman, 2020: 67). Those might be the two ends of the spectrum with many in-between variations possible.

Administrative information is important because it helps you to know how up-to-date the information is and whether changes have been made (Keller, 2010: 9). Sophisticated termbase software will allow you to distinguish between **mandatory** and **multiple** fields. Mandatory fields are those that you must populate with data before the software allows you to close the entry and save it in the termbase. The table above shows that you should at least include the administrative information, the term itself, and its part of speech (PoS) as mandatory fields. PoS is very important as it allows you to differentiate, for example, between *scan* as a noun and as a verb, and terminologists recommend it be mandatory (Warburton, 2015: 385), as the definition of the verb will not be identical to that of the noun (Warburton & Wright, 2019: 70). In this case, *scan* should be two separate entries, one for the noun and one for the verb. Making a field *multiple* means that you can use it several times, e.g. entering different examples of usage for a term, not just one.

Encyclopaedic information, or additional contextual details about a concept, should also be recorded in the entry (Fernández et al., 2011: 18), as this provides additional knowledge not only about the term but also about its conceptual network. Paradigmatic relations, in the case of terms, typically include synonymy, antonymy, hyponymy/hyperonymy (or subordinate/superordinate), meronym/holonym (or part/whole) (Ahmad & Rogers, 2001: 749). If a hyperonym has several hyponyms, these hyponyms are said to be *co-hyponyms* of each other (or *co-meronyms* under a holonym). However, in some domains it may not be easy to establish such relationships between terms. In this respect, Sager (1990: 34–35) provides an extensive list of other possible, non-hierarchical relations between terms which can be particularly useful for translators, illustrated in Table 4.2. Many of these relations can be clearly applied to terms in medical, scientific, and engineering domains.

Sager's relations are also non-exhaustive – you can create subsets of them or new ones, e.g. PLACE – OBJECT (*tunnel – boring machine*). The point

Table 4.2 Sager's non-hierarchical term relations (1990: 34–35)

Relationship	Example
CAUSE – EFFECT	*explosion – fallout*
MATERIAL – PRODUCT	*steel – girder*
MATERIAL – PROPERTY	*glass – brittle*
MATERIAL – STATE	*iron – corrosion*
PROCESS – PRODUCT	*weaving – cloth*
PROCESS – INSTRUMENT	*incision – scalpel*
PROCESS – METHOD	*storage – freeze dry*
PROCESS – PATIENT	*dying – textile*
PHENOMENON – MEASUREMENT	*light – Watt*
OBJECT – COUNTERAGENT	*poison – antidote*
OBJECT – CONTAINER	*tool – tool box*
OBJECT – MATERIAL	*bridge – iron*
OBJECT – QUALITY	*petrol – high octane*
OBJECT – OPERATION	*drill bit – drilling*
OBJECT – CHARACTERISTIC	*fuel – smokeless*
OBJECT – FORM	*book – paperback*
ACTIVITY – PLACE	*coalmining – coalmine*

about these non-hierarchical relations (which should be used *in addition to* paradigmatic and syntagmatic ones, not *instead of* them) is that they 'may be considered equally important and more revealing about the nature of concepts' (Sager, 1990: 34).

Under the label of 'syntagmatic relations', you can collect information such as collocations and any other useful **phraseological** information. For example, *greenhouse gas* may collocate often with the verb *emit* or with the noun *emissions*. This information will be crucial when producing your translation, as this includes more than just translating the terms in the ST.

Finally, it is always advisable to add a field such as Notes, which can be used to collect any information that might not have been envisaged when designing the termbase. Any information that does not fit clearly into any of your other fields can be included here. The 'Notes' field is also important because the structure of the termbase is often difficult to change once it has been created (Warburton, 2015: 379) and, therefore, it allows you to add other types of information without having to change the structure of your termbase.

Box 4.2: Entering Terms in a Termbase

- Terms can only belong to a *finite list of grammatical categories*: single-noun terms can be nouns, verbs, adjectives and adverbs (or **content words**). A multiword term can be classed as a *noun phrase* if the headword is a noun; a *verb phrase* if it is a verb, etc. In fact, most terms are nouns or noun phrases (Bowker, 2002: 83). Terms are typically not **function words**, i.e. determiners, prepositions, articles, etc.

- You should avoid the temptation of entering terms in your termbase just as you find them in a text. Terms must be entered in **canonical form** (or **dictionary form** or **citation form** or **base form**). In a nutshell, this means that nouns and adjectives must be entered in masculine (if it applies) singular and verbs in the infinitive. Terms must also be entered in *lower case* except for proper nouns and German nouns, e.g. *Nelson's syndrome*, not *Nelson's Syndrome*, because *syndrome* is not a proper noun and therefore must not be capitalised; not *nelson's syndrome* because *Nelson* is a proper noun and must be capitalised.

- *Enter multiword terms in their written order* (Schmitz, 2009). For example, do not enter a term such as *accretionary lapillus* as *lapillus, accretionary*, as it can be confusing. It is easier for retrieval purposes to list it in full as it is used, i.e. *accretionary lapillus*.

A Special Word about Definitions

Most of the time, 'it is not the terminologist's (much less the translator's) responsibility to prepare definitions' (Bononno, 2000: 655). Definitions should ideally be prepared by experts in the domain. However, definitions are a useful tool for translators to be able to establish equivalence between terms, especially if there are no experts available for consultation. Definitions are one of the most valuable parts of the entry, although they 'can easily be the most time-consuming and expensive part' (Muegge, 2007: 19).

The purpose of the definition is to identify the boundaries of the term and how that term fits in with the rest of the conceptual network, although pinning down the boundaries may not be entirely straightforward in some domains. The usual technique is to start by providing the closest broader concept (also referred to as *definiens*) to the concept being defined (also referred to as *definiendum*), and then list the 'necessary and sufficient conditions' for that concept (de Bessé, 1997; Temmerman, 2000: 94; ten Hacken, 2015: 4). The 'broader concept' tends to be a *hyperonym* or *holonym* in many domains but if this is not clear-cut in your domain, you should consider using some of Sager's additional, non-hierarchical term relations (exemplified in Table 4.2) which is becoming increasingly widespread practice (Marshman et al., 2012: 33). In order to include appropriate, terminologically oriented definitions in your termbase, the following criteria should help:

- *Terms should not appear in their own definitions.* For example, in order to define *planet*, you should start with 'A celestial body which ...', rather than start with 'A planet is a celestial body which ...'. However, sometimes the headword of the term is its closest hyperonym and therefore you should start the definition with it (de Bessé, 1997: 70). For instance, the definition of *angel shark* can start with 'Shark which ...'.
- Avoid **circular** and **tautological definitions**. A circular definition is one where 'two concepts are defined in terms of each other' (de Bessé, 1997: 71), e.g. defining *textile industry* as *The branch of industry that produces textiles*. In a tautological definition, the component words of the term are used to define the concept, e.g. defining *roll-call vote* as *A vote carried out by roll-call*.
- *Avoid vague expressions*, e.g. *usually, typically, considerable, some*, etc. These expressions point to features that do not define the concept.
- *Avoid examples in definitions.* You can add a separate field to enter examples of usage of the term. As already mentioned, you should only enter one type of information in each field, e.g. definitions in the Definition field, examples in the Examples field.
- Avoid **encyclopaedic information**. For example, a sentence such as 'sharks range from relatively harmless bottom-dwellers to large dangerous oceanic and coastal species' should not be in a definition, because it

does not define the concept of *shark*, it simply provides some additional contextual information (referred to as 'encyclopaedic information').

- *Avoid parataxis* (i.e. semi-colons). Semi-colons (;) should be avoided in terminology-oriented definitions because they do not help in clarifying the relation between the items either side of the semi-colon.
- *Make sure that the definition belongs to the right domain*. For instance, the definition of *gluten* in a termbase of baking terms may differ from that of *gluten* in a termbase of allergies.
- *The Example of usage field must show the term used with the same* **part of speech** as found in the text. The entry for '*scan*' as a verb should contain an example of the usage of that verb, rather than of the usage of '*scan*' as a noun.

Applying all of the criteria above to definitions will often make terminological definitions look quite succinct, but *conciseness* is actually a desirable feature of specialist definitions (Varantola, 1992: 124). For translators, conciseness in definitions is also acceptable because a great deal of information should already be contained in other termbase fields such as the Example, Definition, Encyclopaedic information, Paradigmatic and Syntagmatic relations fields, to name but a few.

How to Recognise Terms in Text

When trying to spot what might constitute a term in a text, there are some clues that you can use. Authors have different ways of signalling to the reader that a word or expression is technical. In other words, they tend to treat terms in a special way in a text (although unfortunately not always). The following are some examples of special treatment of terms in texts:

- *Different formatting*: terms may be highlighted in bold or italics.
- *Different punctuation*: terms may be signalled by the use of inverted commas.
- *Context*: terms may be preceded or followed by a definition, a description, an acronym or an abbreviation.
- *Visual display*: key terms may appear in graphics (e.g. a labelled diagram) and tables (although not every word in a table or graphic may be a term).
- *Translation*: In some languages, such as Japanese or Korean, English terms are 'often provided in brackets after the corresponding terms' (Kageura & Marshman, 2020: 64).

While these clues are generally language-dependent, the principles are valid across languages (Ahmad & Rogers, 2001: 750). The above clues are based on the classical criteria for *termhood* in the narrow sense, i.e. what makes a term a term. Termhood can be used by translators as a starting point and can help decide which terms to add to the termbase and which not.

Depending on your working situation, you may find yourself working on termbases from very different perspectives. For example, in some institutional translation contexts, resources are often intended to be *prescriptive* in nature. This means that the institution or organisation 'may recommend the use of preferred terms and warn against the use of terms that are deemed less acceptable in a given context' (Bowker, 2015: 308).

At the other end of the spectrum, you may find that termbases can also be more *descriptive* in nature. Although termbases were designed to contain terms and their associated information, some translators tend to add other items to them which they find useful, but which are not necessarily terms, e.g. names of people and their roles in an organisation, or even less seemingly meaningful portions of text such as *in spite of the*. The reason for doing this is that translators can still benefit from increased terminological and phraseological efficiency and consistency, especially if those items are repeated multiple times throughout the source text.

One CAT tool that envisaged a broader use of termbases as phraseological repositories in this way is Déjà Vu, which provides the *Lexicon* feature. The Lexicon is designed as a 'third' database in the CAT tool, in addition to the termbase and TM. The Lexicon is a **concordancing** tool (see also Chapter 5), not to be confused with the search feature *concordance*), i.e. it extracts every word and contiguous fragments of text and it presents them in a list, together with the frequencies of occurrence of each word or fragment in the text. Based on the frequency of a particular word of phrase, you can identify, translate and store any repeated (non-term) items from your source text that will improve your productivity and phraseological consistency *during* translation. When you translate, you get matches from the Lexicon, as well as from the termbase and TM. The Lexicon, therefore, can be a powerful tool for *analysing and preparing* your translation task (see also Chapter 7).

In addition to the classical criteria of termhood, in commercial settings companies may use other criteria for term selection as well, such as frequency of occurrence, embeddedness, visibility or translation difficulty. Embeddedness, as explained by Warburton (2015: 382–383) means that shorter terms may be included within longer ones. To use Warburton's example, the term *sustainable development* occurs in terms such as *environmentally sustainable development* or *ecologically sustainable development economics*. Since *sustainable development* is likely to be included within other longer terms, you should include this term, as well as the long ones, in your termbase.

Input of Terminological Data

As a general rule, it is always advisable to ensure that you read your ST and prepare your terminological data in the SL and TL *before* you start to translate with a CAT tool, so that you can make the most of **leveraging** terms and information from your termbase during translation. Of course, creating a full termbase before translation is not always possible, or even practical, in all situations. There are four main ways of entering data into your termbase.

- Importing data into your termbase, e.g. from Excel files and glossaries which you created yourself or which came from your use of other CAT tools, for example.
- Manual entry: entering terms and their associated information directly into the termbase before starting to translate.
- Input of data 'on the fly' (Candel Mora, 2017: 249; Steurs et al., 2015: 229), i.e. while you translate. This is a useful method if you come across new terms or information which you had not seen before or which you decide to include in your termbase. It is generally considered a 'quick fix' for entering terms and perhaps basic information such as part of speech while you translate, leaving the input of other information such as definitions for a later date.
- Input of data with a **template**. A template is a pre-established list of fields which allows for a consistent display of the same fields for all entries in the same order. Depending on the sophistication of the CAT tool, e.g. Trados MultiTerm, you may be able to edit the fields of the template in order to create your own hierarchy of fields, although not all CAT tools allow hierarchical structures to be created (Steurs et al., 2015: 233). Investing in templates can be a timesaving inputting device for translators.

Other advanced features of termbases include finding and merging duplicate term records, the use of filters, etc. (Candel Mora, 2017: 250). Increasingly, term extraction is being integrated into the terminological functionality of CAT tools. Term extraction is discussed below.

Term Extraction

Term extraction consists of identifying 'the core vocabulary of a specialized domain' (Bowker, 2019: 581). It can be carried out manually (which is a highly time-consuming process) or you can use a computer program to extract the potential terms for you. The latter is referred to as **automatic term extraction** (or **ATE**) (Heylen & de Hertog, 2015: 203). For translators, the purpose of term extraction, whether manual or automatic, is to identify specialised terms from a text before you translate it, so that you can find their relevant translations in the TL and any other background or contextual information about them *before you carry out the translation*. Therefore, a good practice in term extraction is to first create a **corpus**, which is essentially a collection of relevant texts from a specific domain. **Corpora** can be monolingual or bilingual and are discussed in more detail in Chapter 5. For now, it is worth highlighting that in a corpus of texts in the target language, for example, which you can collect as part of your domain research or terminology research, you should be able to see not only how experts from that domain use those terms and in which contexts, but also whether there are syntactic, grammatical or phraseological preferences that you need to take into account and reproduce, or find equivalents for, in the target text. This is why corpora have become essential tools for translators.

Typically, term extraction is carried out by a terminologist, who then 'consults with a domain expert to arrive at a final list of validated terms' (Heylen & De Hertog, 2015: 203). However, since term extraction is increasingly integrated into CAT tools, translators also use term extraction to create and maintain their own terminological resources. The advantage of using a term extraction program is that of speed, but at the expense of the quality of results, as all programs end up extracting 'units that are not relevant from a terminological point of view' (Drouin, 2006: 375). This means that the results of a term extraction always require the translator's **validation**. The alternative is manual extraction which can be extremely labour-intensive but usually yields good results. However, manual extraction does not guarantee that you will extract all the relevant units and will typically miss patterns that emerge only when large quantities of text are processed (Ahmad & Rogers, 2001: 740).

There are two main approaches to term extraction, i.e. *linguistic* and *statistical*. There are also *hybrid* methods that use a combination of the two, as shown in Table 4.3.

Linguistic term extractors 'attempt to identify word combinations that match particular part-of-speech patterns' (Bowker, 2002: 83). For example, if you have a **tagged** corpus, i.e. labelled for parts of speech such as noun, verb, etc, it can then be searched specifically for nouns or noun phrases, for example, as these are very common parts of speech for terms in English. By contrast, statistical systems use probabilistic algorithms to look for repeated patterns of words and often allow you to select the *minimum frequency value*, i.e. 'the number of times that a series of items must be repeated' (Bowker & Pearson, 2002: 170) in the text in order to be selected as a potential candidate.

Term extraction can be monolingual or bilingual. Monolingual term extraction has 'mainly taken two directions, either defining the patterns of

Table 4.3 Theories and methods of term extraction

Theory behind the method	Method of term extraction
Terms belong to a few part-of-speech categories only.	Linguistic
Terms are relatively more frequent in texts belonging to their domain than in general language texts.	Statistical
The part-of-speech categories of terms can be combined with their frequency in specialised texts from the relevant domain.	Hybrid

forms that complex terms, i.e. terms consisting of more than two constituent elements, can take (as most terms in most domains and in most languages are complex), or quantitatively weighting **term candidates** to distinguish terms from non-terms (Kageura & Marshman, 2020: 62), whereas bilingual term extraction works with translation or comparable corpora. Note that the expressions selected by a term extractor are referred to as term candidates. This means that the expressions cannot be considered terms until the translator (in our case) reviews and validates the results, selecting the actual terms and discarding any non-terms.

Using Terminological Data during and after Translation

Once you have read and analysed the ST and collected all the necessary terminological information in the SL and TL, you can activate several features in CAT tools in order to access this information while you translate, often without having to open the termbase directly. With the correct settings selected in your CAT tool, you should be able to see matches of SL terms to terms in your termbase in a dedicated window or pane, from which you can often insert them directly into the segment you are working on. This process is referred to as **active terminology lookup** (Bowker, 2005: 15), also referred to as **automatic terminology lookup** (e.g. De Moraes, 2007: 33). An example (from Trados Studio 2021) is shown in Figure 4.2, where the English (in this case) ST is displayed on the left and the Arabic TT on the right.

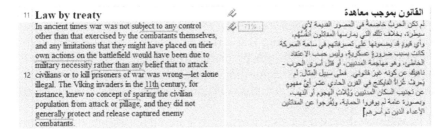

Figure 4.2 Example of active terminology lookup.

If the CAT tool finds a match between a term in the ST and a term in the termbase, it highlights it with the red brackets above words and phrases, as can be seen in Figure 4.2. Instead of brackets, other CAT tools may use other methods, e.g. highlighting the words or phrases. In any case, the red brackets or highlights alert translators to the termbase entry and, typically, the translation of the term is shown in a separate pane during translation, as the one shown in Figure 4.3.

Figure 4.3 Example of term recognition pane which translators see during translation.

Each time a **match** is shown in the term recognition pane during translation, it is up to translators to decide if they want to insert that term directly in
the current TT (typically by pressing a dedicated button, right-clicking and
choosing the relevant option, using keyboard shortcuts or automatically,
depending on the settings of the CAT tool), look up the term in the termbase
for more information, or ignore the suggestion altogether. Crucially, it is
not just seeing the matched term in the window that is important to translators, but being also able to access the term record (Bowker, 2003: 56),
which contains all the associated information about that term, including
synonyms, definitions, collocations and phraseological information to support the translation process.

In active terminology lookup, the CAT tool **parses** the strings of characters in the SL and compares them to those in your termbase. As mentioned before, CAT tools *do not have linguistic information* built in, so
they have no way of knowing if a string of letters is a noun or a verb,
for example. Instead, they work by matching strings of characters in one
language to the likely corresponding strings of characters in the other,
based on algorithms that use punctuation, formatting etc., in order to
establish the equivalences.

In addition, because terms are generally entered in canonical form into
the termbase, you may find that it is difficult for a CAT tool to match
terms that appear in a different form in the ST. For example, a CAT tool
may not be able to match the verb form *issuing* in the ST to the verb
issue in the termbase if you set the recognition settings to a high fuzzy
percentage. However, CAT tools often allow you to lower the recognition percentages and this should improve the number of correct matches.
Fuzzy lookup (De Moraes, 2007: 34) is the term used to refer to the process of finding partial matches, rather than full matches. Languages with
complex morphology, such as Arabic, and languages with a great deal
of suffixes or prefixes (see also Chapter 3), tend to achieve lower quality

matches in automatic terminology lookup than languages with simpler morphology (De Moraes, 2007: 34).

Another useful feature during translation is the **concordance search** feature. For example, if a CAT tool does not display a term as expected, you can manually look for it. Some tools allow so-called truncated searches with **wildcards** (Bowker, 2003: 55). According to Bowker:

> A wildcard is a character such as an asterisk (*) that can be used to represent any other character or string of characters. For instance, a wildcard search using the search string translat* could be used to retrieve the term record for translator or the term record for translation, etc. More sophisticated TMSs [Terminology Management Systems] also employ fuzzy matching techniques. A fuzzy match will retrieve those term records that are similar to the requested search pattern, but which do not match it exactly.
>
> (Bowker, 2003: 55)

Note that **TMS** in this quote refers to **Terminology Management Systems,** not to be confused with **Translation Management Systems,** which has the same abbreviation. You can read more about Translation Management Systems in Chapter 8.

Pretranslation (see also Chapter 3) is another feature that can help you enter the TL terms into the TT. Running a pretranslation before you start to translate will insert all the TL terms into the correct segments, *if there is no 100% match from the TM.* During pretranslation, if there were 100% matches from the TM, these would be ranked above matches from the termbase, i.e. you would not get insertions from the termbase, as the segments from the TM are complete sentences, as opposed to 'disconnected' terms in the termbase. With pretranslation, therefore, you can focus on translating the rest of the text, saving you the time it takes to type some terms (especially long multiword terms) and ensuring that you enter them consistently by selecting each one from a list rather than by typing it. This would avoid making errors in selecting *cosmetic* synonyms (Warburton, 2015: 382) such as *check box, Checkbox, check-box,* etc. However, you should never rely on the correctness of the matches inserted by the CAT tool (Bowker, 2003: 57) and you should always discipline yourself to verify that there are no errors.

Importing and Exporting Terminological Data

Most CAT tools provide a range of formats in which you can import and export the data in your termbase. This will allow you to share your data with others, e.g. other translators, companies, clients, but it also allows you to move your data from one CAT tool to another. A typical import/export format for terminological data is MS Excel, although there are others. For example, **TBX** is an **XML**-based standard and it stands for 'TermBase eXchange' (Bowker, 2015: 315), although historically it has not been widely adopted. It was developed by LISA (the Localization Industry Standards Association), which existed from 1990 to 2011, so that termbases could be reusable across CAT tools (Di Nunzio & Vezzani, 2021: 183).

The main purpose of an exchange format such as TBX is to 'separate data and software' (Melby, 2015: 393). This separation 'provides multiple benefits to authoring and translation activities, including protection, consistency and interoperability' (Melby, 2015: 393). Of particular importance for translators is that it allows you to preserve the structure of your termbase when moving from one program to another, but it also allows you to design a termbase outside a terminology system and then import it into it (Popiolek, 2015: 346). Achieving this interoperability for termbases proved a major challenge for developers, who continue to face challenges in this respect (Melby, 2012; Popiolek, 2015: 346).

More immediately, exporting your terminological data can also be a way of backing up your data. Regularly exporting your data to Excel, for example, means that you could always reimport the data into a new termbase should your old one become corrupted or lost. It is especially important to have an efficient approach to backing up your terminological data, as this is very time-consuming to put together in the first place.

Finally, as technology evolves, we can expect that CAT tools will gradually increase access to terminological resources in real-time from within the CAT environment. This is already the case with some tools, such as Trados Studio, which offers real-time access to IATE, the European Union terminological database, through a plugin. This means that, conveniently, you can consult resources such as IATE directly from the editing environment of your CAT tool while you translate. Similarly, another expected trend is that more online collaborative terminological tools will emerge, allowing both translators and others who collaborate on translation projects to access and update online all the relevant terminological information for a particular project.

Follow-Up Tasks and Reflection

1. Both the translation memory and the termbase are databases, but how do they differ in the type of content they store? Why is it necessary to separate the two types of content?
2. Why is it important to organise a termbase entry around a *concept*, rather than around a *word*?
3. What would be the correct *canonical form* for the following terms?
   a. *Alzheimer's Disease*
   b. *fungi*
   c. *issued* [verb]
   d. *synovial Membrane*
   e. *cartilages*

4. How would you distinguish *reject* [noun] from *reject* [verb] in a termbase?
5. What fields should a termbase contain as a minimum to be useful for translators? Which ones should be made multiple and which ones mandatory?
6. What is the usefulness of definitions for translators?
7. What are the differences between 'Terminology Management Systems' and 'Translation Management Systems' (both abbreviated to 'TMS')?
8. In pretranslation, why are matches from the TM ranked above matches from the termbase?
9. Use the translation project you created (if you completed the tasks in Chapter 2 and Chapter 3) or create a new one following the same instructions in the tasks in Chapter 2. Now create a termbase of key terms in the same CAT tool and assign it to the project. Which fields will you use to create the termbase for this project and why? For example, does it need to be a comprehensive termbase because you plan to specialise in the topic, or does it only need to be a simple one because it is a topic you do not plan to work with professionally? Or something in between?
10. Extract some terms (e.g. six to eight terms) manually from the source text and add them to your termbase. Are there any words and phrases which make you doubt whether they are relevant terms for this project? Why?
11. If your chosen CAT tool has a term extraction component, run the source text through it and compare the results to the results of your manual term extraction. To what extent do they differ?
12. Now extract another three to four terms and store them with their translations in an Excel spreadsheet. Next, find out how to import this Excel spreadsheet into your termbase.
13. Now run the pretranslation feature of your chosen CAT tool (if it has one) and analyse the results. How useful was pretranslation in this case?
14. Make sure the active terminology lookup feature is activated in your CAT tool, then start to translate the text while making use of the termbase. Do you get matches for all the terms in the ST? If not, consider changing the fuzzy settings of the termbase.
15. What would you need to do if you needed this termbase to be available in another CAT tool? How would you do this?

Further Reading

Authoritative publications on terminology include the influential work of Cabré (1999, 2003). More recently, Alcina (2011) is an edited volume, aimed specifically at lecturers and students in university degrees and postgraduate courses and takes into account the 'drastic' changes the discipline has undergone in recent times. Olohan (2016) provides a general overview of the place of terminology in scientific and technical translation with relevant cross-references to CAT and MT, as well as Sketch Engine. Warburton has published extensively and recently (e.g. 2021) on the corporate aspects of terminology (e.g. 2008, 2010, 2011, 2014, 2015). For more on term extraction, as well as terminology management, as pertinent to specialised translation, it is worth reading Kageura and Marshman's (2020) chapter in the *Routledge handbook of translation and technology.*

For all-round reference, Bowker (2019) in the *Routledge encyclopedia of translation studies,* the two-volume *Handbook of terminology management* (Wright & Budin 2001), and the more recent *Handbook of terminology* (Kockaert & Steurs 2015) are valuable reference resources for lecturers, professionals and trainee translators. Other tools that can support the terminological work of translators include visualisation tools, mind-mapping tools and concept-mapping tools (e.g. Austermühl 2012). Concordancing can be used for a variety of term extraction and phraseological functions from corpora. Corpora provide access to a vast wealth of examples, but this can be both an advantage and a disadvantage (Bowker, 2019: 582). In the following chapter, we explore corpora in more detail.

5   Electronic Corpora

Introduction

Translation is a process of permanent decision-making. The same is, of course, true for interpreting, where the speed of decision-making is even more intense. As a translator, you are constantly asking yourself questions such as what does this word mean and what does it mean in this particular context, how can it be translated into the target language, which of the different options that the dictionary or **termbase** proposes is the correct one, and how do I express this in the target language, is it OK to say this, does this sound natural?

As we can see throughout this book, translators have access to a wide range of digital resources to help answer these questions – in addition, of course, to their own knowledge and experience. Yet, despite all these resources, there will always be questions that cannot be answered satisfactorily, problems that cannot be solved fully, and situations where we as translators are simply not entirely sure that we have chosen is indeed the correct solution. This permanent self-doubt is a hallmark of the translation profession, and at the same time it is also the mark of a good professional translator.

DOI: 10.4324/9781003160793-5

Translation doubts tend to appear more frequently and often with greater weight at the production stage of the translation, i.e. when we are creating and revising the target text based on our analysis and understanding of the source text, our research, our **domain** knowledge, and taking into consideration translation proposals presented to us by termbases, TMs, and MT systems. It is at this stage of finalising and optimising the target text that we can make excellent use of another type of translation tool, the parallel text, especially collections of parallel texts made available in the form of an electronic corpus (*corpora* in the plural).

The terminology around parallel texts and corpora can sometimes be confusing. The notion of a parallel corpus, for example, generally refers to a bi- or multilingual corpus containing translated texts and their source texts (see below, where we discuss the use of Sketch Engine's parallel concordancer feature). For the purpose of this chapter, we define parallel texts as non-translated texts in the target language that represent the same text type, domain, function, and time of publication as the target text to be produced and which thus can serve as textual role models for the translation. (Similarly, a text in the same source language as the one you are working on if referred to as a comparable text.) If, for example, you are working on the translation of an annual company report from Spanish to Japanese, annual reports from Japanese companies working in the same industry could serve as your parallel texts, showing you, for example, how annual reports of Japanese companies are generally structured (and how this might differ from how things are done in the source culture), how the different sections are named, what level of style is being used, etc. You will also be able to get a first impression of what terms are used and what word combinations are typical in annual reports (and whether they match your own ideas). In a sense, parallel texts are the textual replacement of your favourite native, or L1, speaker, i.e. instead of asking a person if it is OK to use, for example, a certain specialised term, a particular adjective-noun combination, a specific preposition, or whether your word order is acceptable, you ask the same questions of a collection of (quality) texts in the form of a search query. Looking at parallel texts for guidance is particularly relevant when you are not familiar with the norms for a specific text type and domain in your target language and culture, e.g. when working into a language that is not your language of habitual use (i.e. an L2 or L3), and/or when working within a specialised domain or even with specific clients that you are not entirely familiar with.

Let's illustrate these points with two simple, yet typical translation challenges: prepositions and specialised collocations. We'll start with a few questions on English prepositions. Which option would you chose as the appropriate one: 'This is a good example *for* the use of parallel texts in translation', or 'This is a good example *of* the use of parallel texts in translation'? Native speakers of some languages (e.g. German, Spanish) will probably recognise this problem as there is quite a bit of interference from their respective L1s. Other tricky English preposition decisions include, for example, constructions such as 'amid/among/in the audience', 'amid/during/in the current crisis', or 'I have serious doubts about/of/over this'.

So how can you solve these problems and how can parallel texts help? A quick phrase search on Google for the phrase 'example for' will bring you more than 200 million hits, and if you are just looking to check if the phrase is commonly used, you might just use 'for', not realising that 'example of' appears much more frequently (more than nine billion times at the time of writing). Now, change your Google search to the following – 'example for' site:nytimes .com – and see what happens. By adding the 'site' operator and the URL (i.e. the internet address) for *The New York Times*, you are adding an important quality filter. Now, all the examples illustrating the use of the two options that you are testing will come from texts published by a high-quality newspaper.

Let's make one more modification to your search, i.e. we will add the search operator 'intitle' in front of the search phrase. This modified query – intitle:'example of' site:nytimes.com – only retrieves search results that contain 'example of' in the title of NYT articles. You can now repeat the modified query for the second preposition (intitle:'example for' site:nytimes.com). This will allow you to scan the use of both the two options more easily and see how they are used in their natural textual context. You will see that 'example of' is much more frequent than 'example for', but by seeing your search phrase, or keywords, in context, you will also start to learn about the different ways in which the two options are used (e.g. you will begin to see differences in the type of objects that follow the two prepositions). In doing so, you will be not only able to answer the question above and decide what translation solution to choose, but you will learn about language use more generally.

By the way, and in case you hadn't already noticed, you have just done your first corpus analysis, where the World Wide Web represented your corpus (admittedly a really big and messy one) and where the search engine Google (Baidu, Bing, or DuckDuckGo would also do the trick) served as a so-called concordancer, i.e. a tool to access and exploit the texts available in a corpus. More on this later.

This chapter focuses on and aims at showing how translators can use electronic corpora and concordance tools to increase the quality of their work, especially with regard to producing target texts that are idiomatic and conform to the domain and text type norms of the target culture. To better understand the benefits of using corpora for translation, we will first discuss what a corpus is, what types of corpora exist, and for what general purposes they can be used. We will then explore how to access texts stored in a corpus, consider what kind of queries or questions we can ask of corpora, and learn how these queries can support translation activities. Finally, we will show how corpora, including the World Wide Web itself, can support the decision-making process of translators and, going beyond this, how they can be employed to support data-driven learning (DDL) for translators.

What Is a Corpus?

In general language use, the term 'corpus', which derives from the Latin word for 'body', refers to 'a collection of written texts, especially the entire works of a particular author or a body of writing on a particular subject' (www.dictionary.com/browse/corpus). In a more restricted sense, linguists refer to a corpus as 'a systematic collection of naturally occurring texts (of both written and spoken language)' (Nesselhauf, 2015: n.p.) or as a 'principled collection of naturally occurring texts which are stored on a computer to permit investigation using special software' (Evans, no date). The words 'systematic' and 'principled' in these definitions underline the fact that the texts included in the corpus have been compiled in a deliberate and replicable manner and 'according to pre-defined research purposes' (ibid.). While this might sound rather technical (the above definitions do refer to the use of corpora in linguistic research), we can see a number of parallels with how translators can, and indeed should, go about building and using corpora (e.g. having a clear idea of what the corpus should do, selecting appropriate texts, etc.). This is especially important with regard to the quality of the texts that are part of the corpora we use for translation purposes.

The strength of corpus applications in linguistics in general, and in language learning and translation in particular, lies in the *empirical* nature of the data they contain. This data 'pools together the intuitions of a great number of speakers and makes linguistic analysis more objective' (McEnery & Xiao, 2010: 364). For translators, this means that instead of relying on the subjective opinion of one or two L1 speakers (who might not be experts in a certain domain or may use their own language in idiosyncratic, unusual, or marked ways), we use corpora which bring together the outputs of a large virtual network of linguistic informants that is readily accessible at any time. We just need to make sure that these informants and the texts they provide meet our quality standards and fit our purposes.

In this chapter, we focus exclusively on corpora that are digital and that can be accessed electronically (either online or *offline*). McEnery, Xiao, and Tono (2006: 5) stress the electronic nature of modern corpora by referring to them as 'collection[s] of *machine-readable* authentic texts (including transcripts of spoken data) that [are] sampled to be representative of a particular natural language or language variety'. Two aspects of this definition are particularly important. First, corpora are composed of *authentic* texts and thus reflect real-life language use. Second, the texts contained in the corpus are *representative* of other texts of the same kind. While 'representativeness' is a complex and 'fluid concept' (Xiao, 2010: 147) in corpus linguistics and not without controversy, it is nevertheless an important feature for translators, as the authentic texts compiled in the corpus need to reflect, for example, the text type, subject area, and time of publication of the texts that the learners and translators themselves are dealing with (i.e. they have to be proper parallel texts).

Types of Corpora

Corpora come in all shapes and sizes, and their exact composition reflects their purpose or purposes. The following list shows the most frequent types of corpora that we find in linguistics. The dichotomies employed represent the most typical criteria used to distinguish between certain types of corpora, but the pairings are not meant to be exclusive, i.e. a corpus can, for example, be specialised, reflecting current (synchronic) texts in multiple languages, and can be annotated for grammatical information.

- General/reference vs. specialised;
- Synchronic vs. diachronic (historic);
- Monolingual vs. bilingual/multilingual;
- Comparable vs. parallel;
- Annotated/tagged vs. raw/plain/orthographic;
- General language vs. sublanguage (regional, youth language);
- Written vs. spoken (vs. mixed);
- Monomodal vs. multimodal;
- Native vs. learner;
- Developmental vs. learner/interlanguage;
- Static/sample vs. dynamic/monitor;
- Control vs. target.

Most of these corpus types and their potential uses are self-explanatory, but some might need further clarification (for a more in-depth discussion of different corpus types, see www.sketchengine.eu/corpora-and-languages /corpus-types). A multimodal corpus, for example, is defined as an annotated collection of 'language and communication-related material drawing on more than one modality' (Allwood, 2009: 208). Examples of multimodal corpora include 'digitized collection of texts illustrated with pictures and/or diagrams or a digitized collection of films with associated transcriptions of the talk in the films' (Allwood 2009: 207). More powerful technologies have recently enabled the development of corpora of sign languages such as the British Sign Language Corpus with 'associated systematic analysis of gesture patterning' (Knight & Adolphs, 2020: 354).

Monitor corpora are dynamic, constantly updated collections of texts, which, among other things, 'allow [...] lexicographers to track subtle change in the meaning and usage of a lexical item so as to keep their dictionaries up-to-date' (McEnery & Xiao, 2010: 365). A control corpus, often a general reference corpus, is used to double-check the results derived from the analysis of a smaller corpus.

In Translation Studies, the use of corpora as a research tool has led to the creation of the term Corpus-based Translation Studies (CBTS), which Laviosa & Liu (2021: 5) define as 'an area of research that adopts and develops the methodologies of Corpus Linguistics to analyse translation practices for theoretical, descriptive and applied purposes' (see Laviosa & Liu, 2021 for an overview of CBTS).

For the practising translator seeking to harness the benefits of corpora, general reference corpora and multilingual parallel corpora, i.e. corpora containing original texts and their translations in one or more languages, are the most relevant corpus types.

Corpus Applications for Translators

There are all kinds of things that one can do with a corpus, yet as translators and smart technology users we need to be aware of the tail-wagging-the-dog syndrome, and make sure that we tell the tool what to do, and not the other way around.

A corpus is of rather limited use if it cannot be accessed and analysed electronically. Thus, specialised software is needed to exploit, analyse, and query a corpus. This type of corpus analysis software is generally referred to as a concordancer. Concordancers can be stand-alone applications, such as AntConc (see below), MonoConc, or WordSmith, which can work with any collection of texts, or they can be part of an online or offline corpus package, such as Brigham Young University's corpus site, WebCorp's Linguistic Search Engine, or Sketch Engine (see below). As we have seen, we can also consider search engines such as Google as concordancers.

Despite their at times complex-looking interfaces, concordancers are rather straightforward in the functions and processes they offer to users. For translators (and language learners in general), the main features of a concordancer are:

1) Frequency lists (usually of a single word);
2) KWICs (Keyword in Context concordances);
3) **n-grams** (frequency list of a sequence of words where the n stands for the number of words in the sequence, e.g. a 3-gram would show the most frequent three-word strings in a corpus – see Chapter 6 for more on n-grams);
4) Collocate tables, which show a matrix of collocates, i.e. words that frequently appear to the right or left of a keyword and their frequencies.

We will illustrate these features below. For a comprehensive discussion of corpus tools and their features, see Anthony (2013), as well as Paquot & Gries (2020).

To use, or exploit, a corpus for translation purposes, you will need two things. First, you need to have a piece of software that allows you to ask questions of your corpus, i.e. a concordancer, which, as mentioned above can be a stand-alone, offline solution or implemented online. Second, you will need the corpus itself, i.e. a collection of parallel texts reflecting your information needs. You can create your own corpus or access existing corpora.

In this chapter, we will prepare our own corpus, i.e. we are starting the compilation process from scratch. This is different to (and more cumbersome than) approaches where you use existing corpora, available online. Online corpora will be discussed later. While creating your own corpus can be time-consuming, it has the advantage that you control the contents of your corpus and the quality of the texts it contains.

There are two basic ways of creating your own corpus. The first approach is to browse expert websites, identify relevant texts, and download the texts into a dedicated folder on your own computer. Let's assume that you are getting ready to translate a textbook on, say, kidney stone treatment, or, if you are an interpreter, that you are preparing for a conference on the same subject. You can also imagine that you are collecting relevant texts to produce a bilingual **glossary** or a termbase on the topic of kidney stone treatment. The way you compile your corpus, and the sources and types of texts that you select, will need to be informed by your own expertise in a given domain, in this case medicine, and take into consideration what you already know about high-quality sources of domain-specific information. For medical purposes, for example, and if you are working with American English, you will know that there are a number of U.S. institutions that provide reliable, accessible, and up-to-date information about the topic that you are working on. These include, for example, university medical schools (e.g. Harvard Medical School), research and other hospitals (e.g. the Mayo Clinic), and governmental public health agencies. So you could start your search for kidney stone treatment material on the website of the U.S. National Institutes of Health at nih.gov. On their homepage, you can hover over Health Information (the second item in the blue banner) and click on 'Kidney Disease' webpages and other documents with information, e.g. on the 'Treatment for Kidney Stones'. Many of these sites offer a Print view of the webpage or document that you will find on the screen. This Print format is usually 'cleaner' than the webpage, i.e. it will have no advertisements and fewer or no links, and will therefore make for better corpus material. Choose this Print option (or simply click CTRL+P if there is no option), before downloading the web document as a PDF file.

While browsing a number of webpages and then downloading individual files is not the easiest of processes, especially if you are planning to download a lot of files, it does have the advantage that the documents that in your corpus will have been carefully chosen and show a high degree of representativeness, meaning you have compiled a high-quality corpus that is fit for purpose. In addition, and as a kind of by-product, you will most certainly find additional useful information relevant to your translation task as you are browsing the expert website or scanning the search results, so deepening your knowledge.

A second, quicker way of compiling a corpus would be to start the document identification and selection process with a well-defined internet search. To better understand what we mean by well-defined search, we need to talk a bit about search engine algebra, how search engine operators work, and how you can use them to increase the reliability and usefulness of your search results to quickly compile a high-quality corpus. In addition to this technical knowledge (in particular of search operators), our wider cultural and domain knowledge will be important. Our cultural knowledge will allow us to identify relevant and reliable sources prior to carrying out a search, for example, *The New York Times* or *The Guardian*, for general English-language queries, or, in the field of medicine, the NIH or specialised journals, such as *The New England Journal of Medicine*. Combining this cultural knowledge with knowledge about the address (URL) structures of websites and familiarity with various search operators will then allow you to restrict searches to these preselected sources (e.g. site:nejm.org).

Additional useful operators include *filetype* (e.g. filetype:PDF), which restricts search results to documents (e.g. research reports, technical articles) published in a specific file format; *intitle* (e.g. intitle:'kidney stones'), which as mentioned limits search results to documents that contain the keyword(s) in their title, thus (likely) reflecting a greater thematic relevance of the document; and the *minus* sign, which allows users to exclude certain keywords or sites from the search. Adding '-letters' to a search in an online newspaper search would, for example, filter out letters written by newspaper readers and sent to the editors, just as adding '-blog' will exclude blogs, i.e. texts that might not necessarily follow standard writing conventions.

To restrict your search results, and hence the documents entering your corpus, to those containing up-to-date (current) information, you can further apply a *time* filter. In Google, you can use the Tools option to do so, or you can use the Before and After search operators. The latter use the format YYYY/MM/DD, so, if you only want search results published or updated from 2020 onwards, you can add 'after:2020/01/01' to your search query.

For our purposes, i.e. finding information about kidney stones and their treatment, a phrase search ('…') combined with *filetype* and *site* operators connected by the Boolean OR will suffice:

'kidney stone?' intitle:treatment site:edu OR site:org OR site:gov

The question mark (?) at the end of 'stone' is a so-called **wildcard** and will return search results containing the search term in both the singular and plural forms. The OR operator will increase the number of results by extending your search to any of the three listed top-level domains, i.e. higher education institutions, non-profit organisations, and governmental agencies.

A search such as this will provide you with a long list of relevant candidates for your corpus. You can now open search results that appear relevant (right-click and select Open in new tab to keep the original results tab). Open, for example, the first five documents and then scan them one by one before deciding if they are a good fit for your purpose and then downloading them into a dedicated folder (e.g. named Corpus_Kidney_Stones). Try to download ten documents, which you will then be able to analyse with a concordancer. You can also use the sample corpus on the book's companion website.

Enter AntConc – Using a Concordancer

Now that you have built yourself a small, specialised corpus, it is time to see what types of analysis you can perform. For this purpose, we will be using AntConc, a freeware concordancer that can be downloaded from the website of its developer (www.laurenceanthony.net/software/antconc/). AntConc runs on Windows, Mac, and Linux. The screenshots in this chapter are based on the Mac version of AntConc (version 4.1.0).

We will first load our kidney stone corpus, and carry out a number of corpus analysis tasks, starting with a simple frequency list. To load the corpus into AntConc, open AntConc and go to File/Create Quick Corpus. Browse to the folder where you saved your corpus, open it, select your files, and click Open. Note that while AntConc is able to deal with PDF files, other tools might need you to convert them into text-only format.

Once loaded, the files in your corpus will show up in the left-side part, or pane, of AntConc, along with information about the size of the corpus (i.e. number of files and total number of words [tokens]; see Figure 5.1).

Figure 5.1 AntConc with loaded corpus files.

The right pane of the screen shows the available analysis options and their results. Let's start with the command Word (the second option from the right). Click on Word and then on Start to create a list of all words in the corpus, including parts of hyphenated words or abbreviations with periods (e.g. Ph.D.), hence the high number of individual letters. Any frequency list such as this will be dominated by function words such as 'and', 'the', or 'to.' To exclude non-relevant terms, you will need to use a **stoplist**, i.e. a text file containing all words and single letters that you do not wish to show up in your search (including words and abbreviation typically found on webpages, such as 'URL', 'DOI', 'page', 'copyright', etc.). You will find a ready-made English stoplist on the companion site of this book, but you can also easily create one yourself in any language using Word and then save it in text-only format).

Here is how you add a stop list in AntConc:

- Open the Settings menu;
- Click on Global Settings;
- Select the Category Tool Filters;
- Select Cluster > N-Gram > Collocate > Word > Keyword Results;
- Select Hide words in file;
- Click Add File;
- Select your file(s) and click Open;
- Once done, click Apply;
- On the Word tab, click Start.

Basic Frequency List

You will see that you now have a much cleaner list of terms from your corpus. To see all results, selected Page Size, All Hits (by default, only 100 hits are shown). Now you can scroll through the list, which by default is sorted by frequency. This will give you a good idea of the **terminology** contained in your corpus (Figure 5.2).

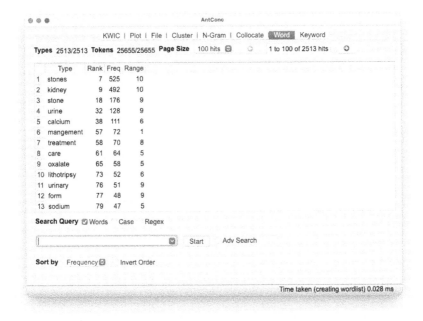

Figure 5.2 Frequency list (AntConc).

Unsurprisingly, 'kidney' and 'stone' appear at the top of the list, but the rest of the terms give us a gist of the main topics. We see words such as 'urine', 'calcium', 'oxalate', or 'sodium', which seem to indicate the chemical make-up of different types of stones. We also note that 'treatment' and 'care' are important, and that 'lithotripsy' might be one way of dealing with stones once they have formed.

KWICs

Let's investigate this a bit further and look at how the search phrase 'kidney stone' appears in its natural textual habitat. For that, we move to the KWIC (Keyword in Context) tab (Figure 5.3), which allows us to show our keyword as it appears in the texts of our corpus. Under Search Query, enter 'kidney stone', and click Start.

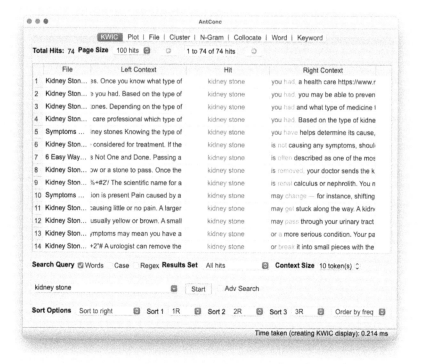

Figure 5.3 AntConc's KWIC feature.

The results show the text immediately before and after 'kidney stone.' By default, this search is sorted by the frequency of the word appearing to the immediate right (1R) of the keyword.

As you scan the list, you will start to understand that there are different types of kidney stones, which relates back to our initial findings from the simple keyword list, where words such as 'calcium' or 'oxalate' had already featured prominently.

N-Grams

Another query option will allow us to dig deeper into these types. For that, let's move to the N-Gram tab (Figure 5.4). As mentioned before, n-grams are sequences, or chains, of words where n stands for the length of these chains in words. On the N-Gram tab, select N-Gram Size 3, Page Size All hits, and click Start. Again, we are not using any keywords, as we want to capture 3-grams for the entire corpus.

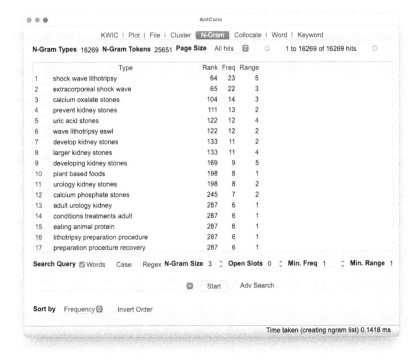

Figure 5.4 n-grams (AntConc).

Lines 5, 6, and 12 provide examples of the different types of kidney stones, while 'lithotripsy' appears again, here as part of the most frequent 3-gram 'shock wave lithotripsy.' Line 2 also contains 'shock wave', so clearly this seems to be an important multiword term in our corpus. To learn more about the most frequent 3-gram, double-click on it. This will trigger a KWIC search for 'shock wave lithotripsy', the results of which are displayed on the KWIC tab (Figure 5.5), with the right side of the results providing us with a first quick explanation of the term's meaning.

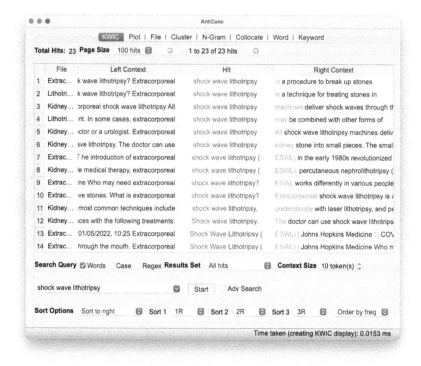

Figure 5.5 KWIC feature for 3-gram.

Our stoplist includes prepositions, so they are excluded from the results of our corpus queries. If you remove prepositions from the stoplist (see the separate sample file on the companion website), you will find potentially useful phraseology, such as 'break stones *into* smaller pieces' or 'stones *broken up* by ESWL may need to be *extracted with* an endoscope'.

Collocate Tables

A final useful feature in AntConc is a Collocate table (via the Collocate tab). A 'collocate', sometimes also referred to as 'collocator', is one of two parts of a collocation, a typical word combination. The other part is called a base, or node. So, for example, in the collocation 'to remove a kidney stone', 'remove' would be the collocate and 'kidney stone' the base.

Collocate tables allow you to identify these typical word combinations – 'You shall know a word by the company it keeps', to quote Firth (1957: 11) – in your corpus. If you enter the keyword (base) 'stone?', (the question mark serves as a wildcard, so that results will include 'stones' as well), AntConc will show you a list of the most typical words that appear in the immediate vicinity of 'stone' or 'stones'. The table also indicates how often these collocates appear to the left (FreqL) or to the right (FreqR) of the search word (Figure 5.6). This way, you can see that 'stone(s)' is often preceded by adjectives such as 'cystine', 'calcium', or 'struvite', which indicate different types of kidney stones and their composition. This not only allows you to identify specialised terms in the field and confirm your tentative translation solutions, but it also enables you to start building a concept map of the domain represented in your corpus (see Austermuehl 2012 for a detailed discussion of concept maps).

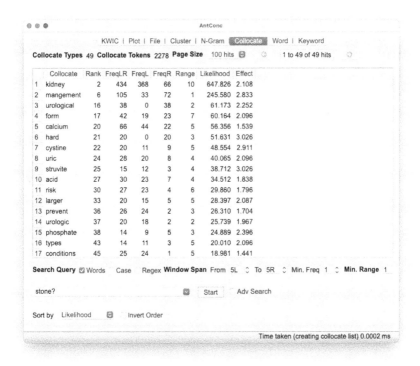

Figure 5.6 Collocate table (AntConc).

Additional Concordance Features – Sketch Engine

For some more advanced concordance features, and to see what online corpus analysis tools have to offer, we can turn to Sketch Engine (Figure 5.7). Sketch Engine is an online concordancer interface which also offers access to a number of existing online corpora. Some of these corpora are free, but others require a subscription to Sketch Engine. The same goes for some of the features of Sketch Engine itself. Many educational institutions already have access to Sketch Engine. For free access, you can also sign up for the

30-day trial option or use the 'Or try open corpora' option on the login page. Among the freely accessible corpora, you will find, for example, parts of the Europarl corpus, which is based on proceedings of the European Parliament from 1996 to 2012 (www.statmt.org/europarl).

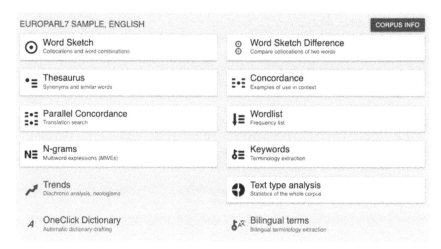

EUROPARL7 SAMPLE, ENGLISH   CORPUS INFO

Word Sketch
Collocations and word combinations

Word Sketch Difference
Compare collocations of two words

Thesaurus
Synonyms and similar words

Concordance
Examples of use in context

Parallel Concordance
Translation search

Wordlist
Frequency list

N-grams
Multiword expressions (MWEs)

Keywords
Terminology extraction

Trends
Diachronic analysis, neologisms

Text type analysis
Statistics of the whole corpus

OneClick Dictionary
Automatic dictionary drafting

Bilingual terms
Bilingual terminology extraction

Figure 5.7 Overview of Sketch Engine features.

Sketch Engine offers a whole suite of features – accessible via the application's Dashboard – including some that we have already seen in AntConc: frequency lists (via the Wordlist option), KWICs (Concordance), Collocate tables (Word Sketch), and n-grams.

Sketch Engine offers some features that go beyond typical concordancer options. The next section looks at these and particularly at ways in which they support data-driven learning (DDL).

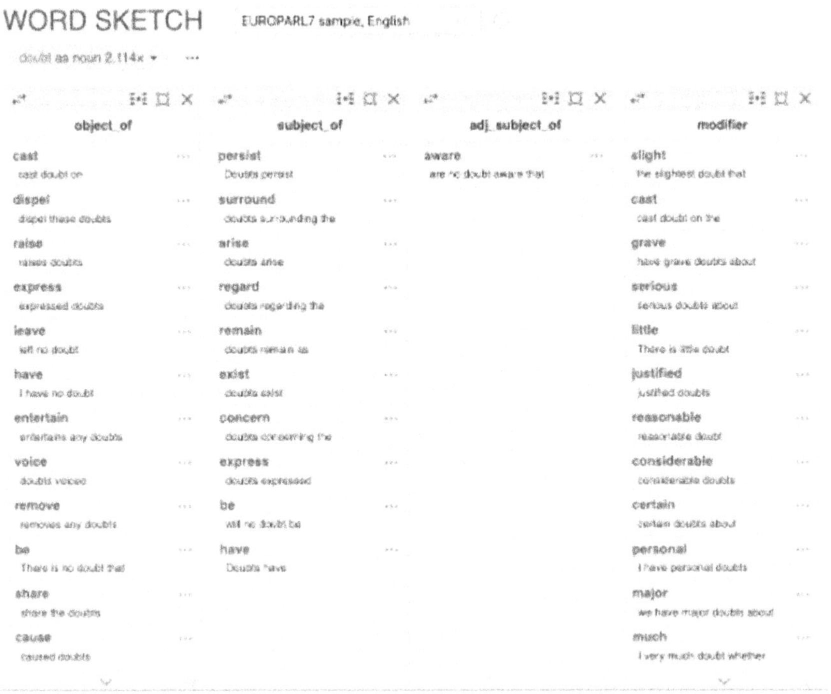

WORD SKETCH   EUROPARL7 sample, English

doubt as noun 2,114× ▾   ···

object_of	subject_of	adj_subject_of	modifier
cast cast doubt on	persist Doubts persist	aware are no doubt aware that	slight the slightest doubt that
dispel dispel these doubts	surround doubts surrounding the		cast cast doubt on the
raise raises doubts	arise doubts arise		grave have grave doubts about
express expressed doubts	regard doubts regarding the		serious serious doubts about
leave left no doubt	remain doubts remain as		little There is little doubt
have I have no doubt	exist doubts exist		justified justified doubts
entertain entertains any doubts	concern doubts concerning the		reasonable reasonable doubt
voice doubts voiced	express doubts expressed		considerable considerable doubts
remove removes any doubts	be will no doubt be		certain certain doubts about
be There is no doubt that	have Doubts have		personal I have personal doubts
share share the doubts			major we have major doubts about
cause caused doubts			much I very much doubt whether

Figure 5.8 Word Sketch (Sketch Engine).

Let's start with Word Sketch. Figure 5.8 shows the results of a search for the noun 'doubt' in the English version of the Europarl corpus. (Collocations involving the base 'doubts' can pose some rather challenging translation problems; see next section). As you can see, Word Sketch uses automatically generated grammatical information contained in the corpus to represent the 'grammatical relations' that exist between keywords and their collocates. The 'modifier' category, for example, offers a list of options that allows language learners and translators alike to enrich their language production and increase the range of collocations they use (for more details on the Word Sketch feature, see www.sketchengine.eu/guide/word-sketch-collocations -and-word-combinations).

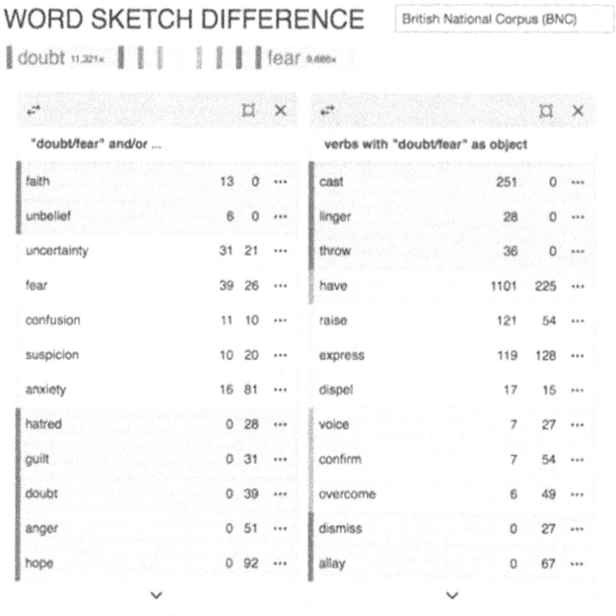

WORD SKETCH DIFFERENCE   British National Corpus (BNC)

|doubt 11,321× | | | | | | |fear 9,488×

"doubt/fear" and/or ...				verbs with "doubt/fear" as object		
faith	13	0	···	cast	251	0 ···
unbelief	6	0	···	linger	28	0 ···
uncertainty	31	21	···	throw	36	0 ···
fear	39	26	···	have	1101	225 ···
confusion	11	10	···	raise	121	54 ···
suspicion	10	20	···	express	119	128 ···
anxiety	16	81	···	dispel	17	15 ···
hatred	0	28	···	voice	7	27 ···
guilt	0	31	···	confirm	7	54 ···
doubt	0	39	···	overcome	6	49 ···
anger	0	51	···	dismiss	0	27 ···
hope	0	92	···	allay	0	67 ···

Figure 5.9 Word Sketch Difference (SketchEngine).

Sketch Engine's Word Sketch Difference feature (Figure 5.9) allows users to compare the collocates of two keywords. Coming back to our chosen example of the word 'doubts', dictionaries often provide numerous, yet context-less alternatives for a keyword, such as 'allay' and 'dispel' *doubts* for the German *Zweifel* 'zerstreuen'. In a case like this, Word Sketch Difference allows for comparison of the company of the two words to identify their different combinatory patterns, using a green-and-red colouring system, as you can see in the right column in Figure 5.8, while you can 'dispel' both doubts and fears you can only 'allay' fears, not doubts.

Additional Sketch Engine Features

In addition to the concordancer options discussed above, Sketch Engine offers some more features that might be useful for translators, interpreters, and language learners in general, but that are more complex and require deeper engagement than we can provide in this chapter. These features include a parallel concordancer, which allows you to perform a KWIC search in one language and see the translations of the keyword(s) in their respective target language contexts (a bit like the Concordance Search in Trados Studio or indeed like the popular website Linguee). Sketch Engine also offers tools that can be applied to extracting terminology from existing corpora. This can either be done for a single-language corpus (using the Keywords feature) or for a bilingual corpus (using the Bilingual terms option). Sketch Engine's user guide provides more details on these features (see www.sketchengine.eu/guide).

Using the Web as a Corpus

So far, we have discussed two main approaches to using corpora for translation (and language learning) purposes: the use of specialised concordancing software either offline (in our case with AntConc) or online (using Sketch Engine). The corpora accessed were either created by us or already existed and were accessible through a third-party application. These two approaches reflect more or less traditional ways of doing corpus linguistics.

In the following, we will go beyond these approaches and discuss how translators can use the Word Wide Web as a corpus and find answers to translation problems by creating customised internet search queries.

The Web as Corpus

The idea of the Web as Corpus (WaC) starts from the assumption that 'the web could serve as a substitute corpus, and Google or another search engine as a substitute concordancer' (Boulton 2015: 267). WaC thus refers to seeing the entire web as one 'megacorpus', from which data is retrieved through direct search engine queries. At the beginning of this chapter, we briefly discussed this idea of exploiting the billions of potential parallel texts that the web offers. In the following, we will show how we can use web-based parallel texts in a more strategic and critical manner.

Using the web as a corpus means that our search purpose is not to download search hits (as we have done above when creating our DIY corpus on kidney stones) but to find answers to our linguistic questions directly, ideally on the first SERP, or search engine results page. This approach is particularly relevant for the solution of concrete translation problems. In this sense, WaC becomes a heuristic tool that supports translators in their decision-making process, helping us to confirm and verify our tentative translation solutions (or to discard them). Using the web in this way, we move from the focus on pattern identification associated with a DDL approach to corpus use to a technique of data-driven decision-making (DDDM). For translators, the need for support in decision-making is particularly prominent at the text production stage, even more so when working into a foreign language or a highly specialised language.

As already mentioned, one problem that translators often face is finding appropriate word combinations, identifying correctly what words collocate with other words. Finding the right collocates is often particularly challenging for L2 learners, who tend to use more inaccurate collocations than L1 speakers or writers. 'Inaccurate' here generally refers to the selection of an 'unusual' collocate, a mistake that is very often linked to interference from the users' L1. Attempting to translate the two (or more) parts of the collocation not as a unit but individually, represents a veritable lexical minefield.

In the previous sections of this chapter, we have already seen how we can use AntConc's Collocate Table or Sketch Engine's Word Sketch feature or n-grams to identify the most frequent collocates for a given keyword. However, building a corpus or accessing existing corpora with a dedicated concordancer might not always be an efficient approach to solving your translation problems quickly. A Google search would indeed be quicker, but how do we ensure that the search results from such a query are as reliable as possible?

To illustrate this, let's go back to the example of the English plural noun 'doubts' and its potential company. Remember that collocations consist of two parts, the base and the collocate. The word 'doubt' or 'doubts' will usually represent the base of a collocation and, like noun bases in general, should not provide too much of a challenge. The collocate, however, is often much trickier to handle. Would, for example, the expression 'They got rid of doubts over their qualification for the job' be correct or acceptable in English? Does one 'get rid of' doubts in English? If not, what other options does one have? In Chinese, you 'eliminate doubts', Spaniards 'dissipate' them, Germans 'disperse' them, Japanese 'dispose of' them. Simple Google phrase searches will return thousands of results seemingly supporting these literal solutions, as will a search in Linguee. Dictionaries aren't always helpful either. While they generally show potential collocates, they do not always explicitly mention these options in the context of doubts (referring instead to fears, concerns, or worries). Langenscheidt's German-to-English online dictionary, for example, offers a total of six English equivalents for the German collocate *zerstreuen* ('disperse'). Three of these options – 'dispel', 'allay', 'dissipate' – are mentioned in relation to both *Argwohn* (suspicion, distrust) and *Zweifel* (doubt), but none of them is identified as a preferred translation solution or supported by contextual information. Cobuild's English-to-Spanish dictionary offers two options for *disipar dudas* – 'dispel' and 'remove' – but does not provide additional usage information or example sentences to help us come to a decision either. In cases where dictionaries do provide corpus-based example sentences, these are often more confusing than helpful, due to their sheer number and their unstructured random presentation.

In addition to the challenge of finding the correct verb, L2 users will also face questions regarding the grammatical company of 'doubts', in this case, the prepositions that typically follow the word. Potential candidates include 'about', 'at', 'of', 'over', 'regarding', etc.

Using the web as a corpus and Google, Bing, or Baidu as an analysis tool will allow language users in general and L2 learners and translators in particular to find answers to these questions, especially since, in many cases, users will already have a number of potential solutions, or hypotheses, which now need testing and confirmation or falsification. When it comes to translating collocations,

> translators usually do not have to start from scratch [...]. The bases
> will be available or easily retrievable from reference works, and there

will be a limited number of possible options for the collocator. What a translator needs at this point is above all reassurance, i.e. confirmation that one of the tentative solutions is, qualitatively, indeed the correct one and that, quantitatively, it appears, in high quality sources, with dominant frequency

(Austermuehl, 2012: 76)

Using the Best Search Operators

To successfully find collocational solutions in reliable sources, the use of search operators becomes absolutely essential. In our experience, the three most relevant operators for the verification of tentative collocation solutions are: 1) the phrase search ('...'), 2) the site: operator, and 3) the wildcard character (*). We have discussed the first two already. Let us take a look at the following example where we are looking for confirmation of our tentative translation solutions, or hypotheses (to dispel doubts):

'dispel * doubts' site:thetimes.co.uk

This search query retrieves web pages from the website of the UK newspaper *The Times*. As mentioned above, the 'site' operator represents an easy way of identifying a specific stratum of the web, a sub-corpus, so to speak, and allows users to restrict their searches to high-quality resources. The quotations marks, i.e. applying a phrase search, avoids searches for both keywords, 'dispel' and 'doubts', restricting the search instead to the strings of characters, including the space, indicated in the search, thus reducing the search to the two potential components of the collocation in the order in which they appear in the search query. The asterisk (*) functions as a wildcard and instructs the search engine to retrieve results that feature any number of words between the two keywords 'dispel' and 'doubts'. Such a search increases the so-called collocational span, i.e. the distance between the collocate and the base, and allows for results showing adjective-noun combinations such as 'lingering doubts' or 'growing doubts' and usage examples including articles, pronouns, or determiners, such as 'dispel any doubts' or 'dispel those doubts'.

Conclusion

Electronic corpora can be very powerful tools for translators, interpreters, and language learners in general. Using the web as a corpus can be a very quick way to confirm translation solutions that you have in mind, or indeed help you to discard these options and look for and identify other, more accurate solutions. Used in this way, a search engine becomes a substitute concordancer and provides an empirical basis for translation decision-making. More traditional corpus analysis approaches, either using a stand-alone offline solution such as AntConc or an online interface such as Sketch

Engine, is a less instantaneous approach to solving language problems (although once the right corpus is in place, they can perform these functions too, usually with more useful, focused results). The features of the more traditional tools and approaches, and the way linguistic data are presented (e.g. as KWICs or in Collocate tables) allow users to go beyond a focus on immediate language problems and thus serve as facilitators of data-driven language learning, offering translators and interpreters extremely useful ways to maintain and update their language knowledge more generally.

Follow-Up Tasks and Reflection

1. Create a corpus for a specific domain (e.g. climate change or food) in your L2 containing at least ten parallel texts (see definition at beginning of chapter).
2. Create a stoplist for this specific domain or (if your L2 is English) adjust the stoplist provided on the companion website for your purpose.
3. Using AntConc or a different concordancer, create a frequency list of terms (words) and multiword terms (2-grams and 3-grams) appearing in your corpus. Export all results into an Excel file, revise and clean the list, and import them into MultiTerm (see Chapter 4).
4. Study the search engine syntax of your preferred search engine and identify the search operators that allow you to filter by origin (site), filetype, and date ranges.
5. Use the United Nations Parallel Corpus website (conferences.unite.un.org/uncorpus) to create a bilingual table in Excel (with the language names in English showing in the first row of the table). You can then upload this file to Sketch Engine to the parallel concordancer feature mentioned above. Similarly, use the sample kidney stone corpus or your own DIY corpus to extract a list of terms using the Sketch Engine Keyword feature.

Further Reading

The *Routledge handbook of corpus linguistics* (Eds. O'Keeffe & McCarthy, 2022) offers several informative, introductory articles on corpus applications. Chapters 4 (Building a written corpus: what are the basics?), 9 (What can corpus software do?), 15 (What can a corpus tell us about multi-word units?), 29 (What is data-driven learning?), and 34 (How to use corpora for translation) are particularly relevant to the content of this chapter.

Using the web as a corpus and combining this approach with concept-oriented terminology work in the translation classroom is discussed in Austermuehl (2012). Enriquez Raido (2014) and Gough (2019) provide a good basis for understanding and developing web search strategies applicable to professional translators.

For those interested in learning more about DDL, Leńko-Szymańska & Boulton's (2015) *Multiple affordances of language corpora for data-driven learning* contains a range of application ideas, including in translator training.

6 Current Machine Translation Technologies

Key Questions

- What are the main types of machine translation in current use and how do they differ?
- How does neural machine translation work?
- What quality of output can we expect from neural machine translation?
- How can translators use machine translation?
- How does machine translation affect translation cost, quality, and speed?
- Will machine translation make human translators redundant?

Introduction

Machine translation (MT) is the term used for the automatic translation of text by computer software. It has moved from being a fringe pursuit of early digital computer enthusiasts to one of the most visible and widely available applications of **artificial intelligence (AI)** and a key part of many translation production workflows. When MT is produced as the final translation, perhaps to give a gist of a source text's meaning, we call this **MT for assimilation**. When MT is produced as part of a translation workflow and is subsequently adapted or **post-edited**, we call this **MT for dissemination**. In the latter scenario, MT may be integrated into a translator's CAT environment in several different ways, as we will see in Chapter 7. As with TM technology (see Chapter 3), contemporary **neural MT (NMT)** also follows the principle of reuse, whereby repositories of human translations are used to train MT systems. This has not always been the case. The arc of MT history has developed, following the increasing availability of data, storage capacities and computing power available over time, as we saw in Chapter 1.

In the following sections, we will look at the principles of different **paradigms** or methods behind MT in the sequence that they appeared (see

DOI: 10.4324/9781003160793-6

Chapter 1 and also Box 6.1). Then we will focus on NMT, the dominant paradigm at the time of writing, looking at how systems are trained, the data used for training, and different ways to evaluate MT quality. Finally, we will consider preprocessing of text for MT and the ways that MT can be integrated into a translation workflow. This is usually done by **post-editing**, the term used for editing the output of MT to produce a publishable translation.

Legacy MT Paradigms

Box 6.1: MT Dichotomies – Rules vs. Data

There are two ways to differentiate the various MT paradigms. The first is whether the system is based on rules or data. As we shall see, early systems translated using a series of rules and dictionary entries, whereas later systems propose solutions based on **translation data**, following the same basic principle as TM technology that 'existing translations contain more solutions to more translation problems than any other existing resource' (Isabelle, 1993: 8). As data-driven systems became the dominant MT paradigms, system developers no longer needed to have the linguistic expertise that had previously been a key requirement for hand-coding rules.

Rule-Based MT

The most popular MT paradigm during the 20th century became known as **rule-based MT (RBMT)**, and although now rarely employed as the sole MT method, RBMT is still used for translation between languages that are closely related and for which there is little training data available. System design for RBMT can be categorised within one of three types, known as *direct*, *transfer*, and *interlingua*. The earliest systems, such as the one used for the Georgetown-IBM experiment described in Chapter 1, used bilingual dictionary entries and a set of rules to translate in one direction from a source language (SL) to a target language (TL). After swapping SL words for TL words, the MT program used its rules to adapt the output to the syntax of the TL. This became known as the *direct translation* approach, and while the results were often rudimentary, such systems were quite satisfactory for some uses. For example, a Georgetown University Russian-English system provided output that was of poor quality but useful enough to be deployed in a number of defence and energy organisations.

The following generation of RBMT systems often employed the *transfer* approach, which involved three stages. During the first stage, SL text is converted to abstract SL forms with the help of lexicons that contain morphological, semantic, and grammatical information. In the second stage these SL forms are transferred to TL forms with the help of a bilingual dictionary of base forms, from which the final TL text is produced in the third stage. These stages could become quite complex, but could also be *modular*, meaning that analysis and production modules could be swapped in and out. Transfer RBMT systems were capable of producing better quality output than direct systems, and thus were dominant for commercial MT until the end of the 1980s for general domain use (e.g. Systran and Logos) or for subject-specific domains (such as the Pan-American Health Organization's SPANAM system).

A third strategy was the more ambitious *interlingua* approach, based on the idea that there are neutral representations of texts that will be valid for several languages (see the discussion on language universals in Chapter 1). This approach was intended to be more efficient than others in a multilingual environment, where one system could replace many unidirectional systems. In practice, this proved to be more difficult than had been anticipated. In the first stage, SL text was to be analysed before being translated to an interlingual representation, from which a TL text could be produced. The interlingua could utilise base forms of words (a crossover with the transfer approach), a lingua franca, an artificial language such as Esperanto, or another notional universal vocabulary. The KANT system in Carnegie Mellon University, for example, was an ambitious attempt to analyse source texts and to map them to a highly complex set of interlingual concepts, from which a target text could be produced. The European Commission-funded Eurotra project created a design whereby three stages of parsing would produce an intermediate representation of the source text. While a working prototype was never completed, the work was influential as the first stage of a continuing effort to develop MT to support multilingualism in the EU.

However, by the end of the 1980s, what was then called 'corpus-based' MT research began to threaten the dominance of RBMT. Over time, as the scale of these corpora grew, we began to speak of 'data-driven' MT. The notion of human translations as data, as introduced in Chapters 1 and 2, represented a sea change for those anchored to RBMT, but by the early 1990s, two competing approaches to data-driven MT were beginning to look very promising.

Data-Driven Approaches: Example-Based and Statistical MT

Example-based MT (EBMT) originated with a 1981 conference paper by Nagao (1984), although research did not begin in earnest until the late 1980s. Despite years of development, contemporary RBMT systems still struggled with ambiguity and were limited by an inclination to 'see meaning as objective and residing in more-or-less discrete concepts' (Kenny 2018: 437) to be built into sentences based on a rigid set of rules. Nagao (1984:

176) felt that since language is dynamic, RBMT systems would date quickly, whereas 'language data and its usage do not change for a long time'. He also pointed out that RBMT was only useful for closely related languages but did not produce useful output for English to Japanese, for example, as different lexical and syntactic systems make mapping of rules impossibly complicated. His proposal was to utilise **parallel corpora** (source segments with their human translations) of translation data that have been aligned (by rule-based or statistical methods) and from which 'equivalent phrases or word groups' (Hutchins 1995: 439) may be extracted and recombined (an idea that has been taken on in sub-segment TM matching, as we shall see in Chapter 7).

The other approach that emerged in the late 1980s – and quickly began to dominate – was **statistical MT (SMT)**. SMT had been attempted without success in the 1960s, so its presentation by Brown et al. in 1988 was met with incredulity. However, results soon surpassed other methods. An SMT system produces the most statistically likely translation for a source text, segment by segment, based on a **translation model** learned from a large **parallel corpus** (see Chapter 5), and a **language model** trained on a large monolingual target text corpus. The translation model focuses on **adequacy** so that the translation candidate in the TL expresses the *meaning* of the SL segment, and the language model focuses on **fluency** so that the translation is *fluent*, irrespective of meaning. The language model is intended to ensure that the output segment is likely to appear in the TL. Early systems were word-based, but within a few years **phrase-based SMT (PBSMT)** was found to produce better results. PBSMT does not use linguistic phrases per se, but rather **n-grams**: a string of words/punctuation or grams in a sequence of length *n* (these were introduced in Chapter 5). So, for example, a translation model where n=3 will attempt to **align** (see Chapter 3) SL and TL words (unigrams) in the bilingual training data, SL and TL groups of two words (bigrams), and SL and TL groups of three words (trigrams). If desired, a PBSMT system can continue to align longer n-grams. For example, it has been found useful for English-Irish systems to work with up to 6-gram language models (Dowling et al., 2018). This idea was similar to, and superceded, EBMT. The alternative model of syntax-based SMT, parsing sentences into syntactic units rather than n-grams, was less widely used than PBSMT (Figure 6.1).

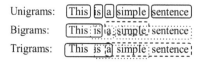

Figure 6.1 A visual representation of n-grams.

An SMT process involves three phases. In the 'training' stage, the system learns from the corpora of training data; in the 'tuning' phase, output preferences or *weights* are adjusted; and in the 'decoding' phase the system produces several potential outputs from the translation model, chooses the most probable one based on the language model, and outputs a translated segment that maximises the product of the two models (it is also possible to 'force' SMT to make one particular choice, which might be useful for consistency of terminology, for example). As time went on, a number of pre- and post-processing steps were added to improve SMT quality, often based on rules. For example, **controlled language** involved constraints to the source segments, limiting the complexity of sentences and prioritising active rather than passive verb formulations (among many other rules), to improve the final output quality.

Despite the addition of these preprocessing steps, SMT quality seemed to plateau by the early 2010s for *well-supported* language pairs, i.e. those for which there were rule-based preprocessing tools and sufficient bilingual and monolingual training data (for example, the English to German SMT system in Castilho et al. (2018) was trained on a parallel corpus of 24 million sentence pairs and 159 million monolingual German sentences: most of the parallel data came from publicly available sources such as the European institutions and other open corpora available from opus.nlpl .eu). Output could be very good for languages that are syntactically similar, but word reordering often presented problems and common output errors included mistranslations, additions, and omissions of words. Experiments with hybrid systems brought statistical techniques to RBMT and vice versa, without producing output that could compete with state-of-the-art SMT.

Since it first appeared, increases in computing power and memory, widespread use of PCs as consumer products, and the availability of translation data enabled huge growth in the use of SMT (see Chapter 2). The free and open-source Moses system (Koehn et al., 2007) made SMT accessible to those with the necessary technical skills, but free online SMT from Google, Microsoft, and others was a huge change that suddenly made MT ubiquitous (Gaspari & Hutchins, 2007). However, by 2016 these free online systems began to move to a new paradigm that offered hugely improved translation quality and differed from SMT in some notable ways (see Box 6.2).

Neural MT

Box 6.2: MT Dichotomies – Symbolic vs. Subsymbolic MT

The second way to differentiate MT paradigms is whether they are *symbolic* or *subsymbolic*, terms that draw from literature on AI that describe whether or not computer representations are human-readable. A symbolic system uses words, phrases, or symbols that humans can understand to perform its task. We can see why an RBMT system produces its output and makes manual changes if necessary. An SMT system will carry out operations on words and text that is legible throughout. As NMT is subsymbolic, its operations cannot be easily understood, which is why NMT is often referred to as a 'black box'. Words (or chunks of words) are *encoded* to a sequence of numbers, on which hundreds and thousands of operations are performed before they are *decoded*. There is a growing area of research that attempts to explain the decisions within a subsymbolic **machine learning** system such as NMT known as explainable AI (xAI). This field hopes to be able to explain choices made by the system to users without this causing any detriment to performance.

Neural Networks for Translation

The notion of 'neural networks', based loosely on theories at that time about how the brain works, was proposed in the 1940s and 1950s, the idea being that from multiple inputs, a *simulated* or *artificial neuron* could evaluate and choose a single output. The input connections could be *weighted* to help with this choice. By 1969, Minsky and Papert proposed that by adding layers of these neurons to create a multilayer neural network (see Figure 6.2 for a unidirectional neural network) in which the output from one neuron would feed into another, then another, before the final 'output layer' produces an output, it might be useful for a broader range of applications. It was some time before computing power and data availability caught up with these ideas, but by the early 2010s there were working artificial neural networks that could successfully classify data and make predictions based on existing training data. This brought about a jump in the performance of **automatic speech recognition (ASR)** systems in the early 2010s, for example.

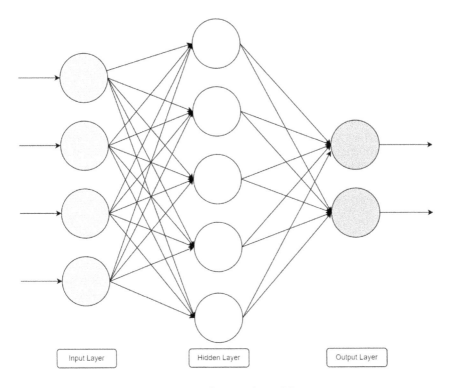

Input Layer   Hidden Layer   Output Layer

Figure 6.2 A simple perceptron neural network model.

When applying artificial neural networks to translation, networks need to be trained with examples of training data from a parallel corpus. This is similar to SMT, but NMT training requires far more data than SMT, usually numbered in millions of sentence pairs, although its effectiveness will depend on how representative it is of the material to be translated. The NMT system breaks segments from the training data into *tokens*, which are usually a word, and *encodes* words and sentences as numbers (see Box 6.2). This training data provides examples for the system of expected inputs and outputs, and it sets about iteratively making adjustments to the weighted connections between artificial neurons so that, for an input, it will produce the expected output. Initially, the weights between neuron connections are random or perhaps taken from a previous similar task, but by making repeated corrections, by comparing the network's output to a reference translation, these are *trained* to produce the appropriate output. During this training process, each layer of neurons will build a representation of the words in the training data, a little like a word cloud. These representations are known as **word embeddings**.

Word embeddings are numerical representations of a word and its connections to other words: Do they regularly co-occur? Are they translated as the same word? If so, the embedding will be similar. Relationships between words should also be similar, so that the numerical difference between the names Tokyo and Japan should be similar to Reykjavík and Iceland, or we should see that Prince relates to King as Princess relates to Queen. This lattice of weighted connections also crosses between SL and TL, building a dynamic model of how embeddings map between languages. Kalchbrenner and Blunsom (2013), in one of the earliest publications on the topic, refer to mapping between 'continuous representations' rather than 'alignment', which might imply something static. When an NMT system has been trained, an additional calculation takes place to adjust the **attention** that the system should pay to each word in a source segment, as the meaning – and thus translation – of a word is likely to change depending on its context (Bahdanau et al. 2016).

Following each iteration of training (an 'epoch'), the NMT system is tested using automatic evaluation (see the section on this later in the chapter) with segments from a **test set** of data (sometimes known as a development corpus), a small parallel corpus that was not included in the training data. If the target segment produced shows an improvement from the previous iteration, appearing more similar to the human translation from the test set, training is allowed to continue. If there appears to be no improvement as results appear to have *converged* to the same automatic evaluation score on repeated iterations, training is stopped. Otherwise, the quality of output will begin to deteriorate as the capacity of the system to *generalise* or produce translations for unseen source segments will deteriorate. This tendency is known as *overfitting*.

So, in summary, an NMT system runs a huge number of operations to build a representation of words from a large set of training data. This representation takes into account the proximity of words of the same language and the words that regularly co-occur in the other language so that it can produce the best possible predicted translation when given a new input segment to translate. NMT can usually produce fluent-sounding output that takes account of context (usually only within a sentence rather than a whole document), but that output is not always consistent, and might change depending on the sentence to be translated, the training data, and the words produced so far.

NMT Processes

At the time of writing, the most popular NMT architecture is the *Transformer* model. This model comprises an encoder to compute word embeddings for each source token (as mentioned, usually a word), using the attention mechanism to adjust for context, and a decoder to output each token, one by one, in the target segment. The decoder also makes use of word embeddings and attention to determine its best prediction for each output token, considering those already produced, ending with a sentence ending token, such as a full stop or exclamation mark. The *recurrent encoder–decoder* model is similar but prioritises the tokens nearest to the one being output, ignoring those more distant.

While tokens are usually words, many NMT systems include a preprocessing step of breaking words down into chunks and using these as tokens. Such systems can better translate variations of words, particularly for morphologically rich languages, or compound words that did not appear in training data. Rather than using rules to do this, a process known as **byte pair encoding** (Sennrich et al., 2016) scans the data to identify commonly occurring chunks such as, for example, an *-ing* ending. This will usually result in better translation of words that do not appear, or occur infrequently, in the training data, but can also result in some output errors, such as compound words that do not appear in any dictionary or the translation of 'I trained' into Spanish, French, and Dutch as 'It rained' (Vanmassenhove, 2019). Of course, we can only *assume* that this error is due to byte pair encoding, as it is currently impossible to interrogate where the problem occurred. An NMT system is an example of blackbox AI: a look inside will only reveal a barrage of numbers and mathematical operations. It should also be said that these sorts of errors are usually quite rare, as NMT can produce remarkably fluent output in many languages.

NMT Quality

Within months of the first proposal of NMT, Bahdanau et al. (2016) found that performance was comparable with state-of-the-art English to French SMT systems. By 2018, after a great deal of research and development, Microsoft claimed to have achieved parity between Chinese to English news translation by their NMT systems and human translators based on crowdsourced comparisons, despite finding more errors in NMT output (Hassan Awadalla et al., 2018; for a critical response to this claim, see Läubli et al., 2020). What we can conclude from looking at many studies of NMT output is that the quality is better than that of SMT. There are far fewer errors overall, and fluency has improved for most TLs. There are still mistranslations in MT output, but NMT fluency can make this difficult to spot. At the time of writing, there is no way to force NMT to produce fully consistent terminology – the use of word embeddings permits variability, although there has been some success in increasing term accuracy by annotating source terms with their target translations (see Exel et al., 2020). There can also be problems with register, and it can be difficult to train a domain-specific NMT system due to the amount of in-domain data required.

NMT output also tends to be less lexically diverse than its training data, with the most frequently occurring words being chosen. There are problems with bias, whereby professions, attributes, and adjectives are associated with one or other binary gender, and the grammatical gender output may be incorrect and may change from one sentence to the next, or even within a sentence (Vanmassenhove, 2019). For instance, Nissim et al. (2020) received results of the query 'man is to doctor as woman is to X' ranging from 'doctor' to 'gynaecologist' to 'nurse_midwife'. Other less obvious biases may also appear based on the content of training data. Very occasionally the output may have no relation to the source segment or to the target tokens produced previously and may even be completely ungrammatical, producing what is sometimes called a *hallucination* (Lee et al., 2018). Hallucinations and untranslated words in NMT output may be down to **data sparsity** – either the system has been trained on insufficient data, the training data contains infrequently-occurring formulations, the training data domain is not appropriate for the text to be translated, or the data contains parallel segments in SL and TL that are unrelated.

In order to avoid problems of data sparsity, it has become common to augment training data with **back-translated** parallel data – i.e. monolingual TL data that has been machine translated to the SL. While this tends to improve the overall output quality, it does mean adding training data that is probably less trustworthy than human translations and that contains errors. That said, not all human translation used for training is perfect, and NMT training data often includes data scraped from web pages, which may not be of good quality and has possibly been machine translated. It can be difficult to decide whether quality or quantity is better for NMT training. Ideally, we would have both.

One other solution for data sparsity is multilingual NMT. A multilingual system would save on the effort, computing time, and power requirements of many bilingual NMT systems, and could also help with poorly supported languages for which there is little bilingual data available. Johnson et al. (2017) made the interesting discovery that 'zero-shot' NMT worked within their multilingual system, i.e. that they could translate between languages for which they had no parallel corpus at all. In their experiment, a system trained on English to Portuguese and English to Spanish data could translate from Portuguese to Spanish and vice versa. Based on this discovery, Johnson et al. (2017) proposed that the system must create a sort of interlingua, an idea that you might recall from RBMT. In time, there seemed to be a quality boost for poorly supported language pairs within a multilingual system, and a multilingual system developed by Tran et al. (2021) and that can translate in 14 language directions was found to beat bilingual systems for news translations into ten of those languages. This test was, however, carried out using automatic evaluation, and as we will discover in the following section, there are pros and cons to each one of the many ways to measure MT quality. At the time of writing, research continues on massively multilingual systems, with NLLB Team et al. (2022) reporting on a system that supports 210 languages and Bapna et al. (2022) supporting over 1,500 languages. The resources required to build such systems are only available to the best-resourced research teams, but despite their huge resources they are faced with problems related to data sparsity.

MT Quality Evaluation

Human Evaluation

If we are to use MT, we will want to have some sort of assurance that it will be good enough for our needs. Over time, many different methods to measure MT quality have been developed, giving us lots of options (see Moorkens et al., 2018). Ranking exercises involve human evaluators comparing one output segment to one or more others, so that we can build up a picture of which system is preferred. Fluency and adequacy measures involve evaluators being asked to score fluency ('How natural does this segment sound in the TL?') and adequacy ('To what extent does the target segment reflect the meaning of the source segment?') across a scale, usually from one to five. Evaluators can also be tasked with post-editing the MT output, making the edits required to reach publishable quality, in which case we can measure their temporal effort (time spent), technical effort (edits made, although a shortcut often used is **edit distance**, as described in Chapter 3: measuring the minimum number of single-character edits to change one string to another), and even cognitive effort (Krings and Koby, 2001), which can be a valuable measure even if the MT is not expected to be post-edited. While these measures can tell us a lot about MT quality, there are often problems with inter-evaluator agreement. In research articles you'll usually see this referred to as IAA or inter-annotator agreement. One person's 'five' for adequacy might be another person's 'three'. This is also a problem for human evaluation based on error categories. There are many typologies that have been created for translation errors, with MQM (Multidimensional Quality Metrics) probably the most widely used at the time of writing for both MT and human translation (Lommel, 2018b). These typologies offer the opportunity to identify in detail the sorts of errors produced by MT systems, although again differentiating one particular type of error from another can prove tricky and the entire effort very laborious.

Human evaluation of MT tends to be time-consuming and expensive, quite aside from problems with inconsistent evaluations. In some competitive 'shared tasks', where MT developers pit their systems against one another, using the same training data, direct assessment is used (Graham et al., 2016). This method involves crowdsourced evaluators using a 100-point rating scale to judge the adequacy of a translated segment. Crowdsourcing saves on cost and allows access to a high number of evaluators, mitigating problems of IAA and reliability. There have been questions about the quality of the test data used for these shared tasks, and crowdsourcing is notoriously open to malicious behaviour, so while this method is useful for comparative purposes within shared tasks, it might be best avoided elsewhere (Läubli et al., 2020). In an effort to improve IAA for these sorts of large-scale evaluations, Licht et al. (2022) propose a return to one-to-five scales using their Cross-Lingual Semantic Textual Similarity (XSTS) score. Two crucial elements to this are a focus on adequacy rather than fluency (in response to the strengths of NMT systems in fluency) and a calibration phase, when scores are calibrated against previously-rated segments in a *calibration set* of agreed scores from multiple evaluators.

If translations are to be used for a specific purpose, task-based evaluation can be a better option. Evaluators can be asked to complete a task using machine-translated instructions, with task completion time measured (if they manage to complete the task at all). For creative and literary texts, Guerberof and Toral (2020) measured narrative engagement, comprehension, and enjoyment of MT output, comparing this with human translation or post-edited MT.

Whether using judgement metrics, error annotation, or task-based evaluation, human evaluation of MT is often inconsistent due to quality being subjective, and it is time-consuming to organise, carry out, and to analyse its results. It can often be expensive and using a cost-reducing shortcut such as crowdsourcing will hinder reliability. For this reason, automatic evaluation of MT is widely used. Popular automatic methods are described in the following section.

Automatic Evaluation

Koehn (2009: 220–221) sets out the goals for **automatic evaluation metrics** (**AEMs**) for MT: they should be *inexpensive*, requiring less time and money than human evaluations; they should be *consistent*, with repeated uses of a metric producing the same results; scores should be *meaningful* at a glance; and results should be *correct*, ranking better MT output higher. Not all AEMs conform to these goals, but the stated target is useful.

The first generation of AEMs, such as **BLEU** (**Bilingual Evaluation Understudy**) (Papineni et al., 2002) and NIST (Doddington, 2002), are still widely used. They look solely at the target segment and measure similarity between the MT output, usually comparing n-grams, and one or more reference translations, (i.e. human translations that are considered the 'gold standard'). This reference translation might be a portion of the training data – the test set – held back for system tuning or testing purposes (Way, 2018). A problem here is that there is more than one way to correctly translate even a short segment. Koehn (2009) provides examples of individual translator variation. However, AEMs encourage system developers to see a single translation as a gold standard, with the corollary that when the system produces a translated segment that is judged (often by non-expert crowd evaluators) to be better than the gold standard human translation, unhelpful terms such as 'human parity' and 'superhuman performance' are bandied about (Toral, 2020).

At the time of writing, BLEU is still the most popular AEM, comparing n-grams (usually up to four) between a reference and MT segment, with modifications for repeated words and averaging results over a corpus. It is used to measure whether quality improves or *converges* in NMT training and will appear in most MT research publications. It is reported using either a decimal formulation (zero to one, where one is perfect), but sometimes whole numbers or percentages, which does not always make the score meaningful for readers. BLEU can be useful as a rough measure of quality, or to demonstrate that output has changed, but does not differentiate between important words (e.g. 'not') and less important words (e.g. 'the'), and has rarely been found to correlate with human judgement. BLEU also does not constrain word order, so that the word order improvements from SMT to NMT will not alone lead to better scores.

HTER (**Human-Targeted Translation Edit Rate**; Snover et al., 2006: 223) is also used to measure the 'number of edits needed to fix the output so that it semantically matches a correct translation', often comparing the MT output with a post-edited version. The metric suffers from similar problems of variability to BLEU, without measuring the relative importance of words. One other problematic usage is to measure post-editing effort as a basis for payment to translators, as the HTER measure of the minimal possible number of edits rarely equates to the actual effort put into post-editing a segment.

Neural Evaluation

First generation AEMs are sometimes (perhaps derisively) referred to as string-based or surface-level metrics, as they are based on a somewhat superficial similarity to a reference translation. A newer generation of metrics such as COMET (Rei et al., 2020) uses pretrained neural models to evaluate MT output, considering *both* the source segment and a reference translation. As these neural models incorporate word embeddings, a **neural AEM** can judge the proximity of synonyms or paraphrases to the word used in the human reference, and is thus more generous to variation in translation, as long as it has been used in the training data. Importantly, they seem to show a far improved correlation with human judgement when compared with string-based metrics (Kocmi et al., 2021). Neural AEMs are also better able to judge the relative importance of words and penalise scoring accordingly. As with NMT more generally, neural AEMs are black boxes in that it is very difficult to interrogate the reason for a score produced, and there is a chance that there is bias baked into the training data.

Neural AEMs are closely related to automatic MT quality estimation (QE). There are lots of reasons to accurately gauge MT quality, such as for end users to know whether they should consider MT output trustworthy or for use cases where 'good enough' quality will fulfil a communicative purpose. A translator using a CAT tool will receive an indication of how useful a TM match will be, but for MT without any indicator, the output could be very useful or worthless (see Chapter 7). The field of QE tended to use lexical features of source segments and translations as proxy judgements of quality, but contemporary measures again use pretrained neural models to make a judgement without the aid of a human reference translation. Using neural models, QE has finally reached a stage where it is deployed in the industry, albeit on a limited basis.

MT Post-Editing

Post-editing has been applied to the output of MT to produce a publishable translation since the RBMT era, becoming a consideration for more text types as MT quality has gradually improved. The nature of the task and the amount of editing required has changed over time and will vary depending on the quality requirement for the translation and the 'raw' MT quality. According to the harmonised guidelines published by TAUS (Translation Automation User Society) in 2010, developed with Sharon O'Brien at CNGL (see https://info.taus.net/mt-post-editing-guidelines), there are two main types of post-editing: **light post-editing** for 'good enough' quality, and **full post-editing** for publishable quality (for dissemination), equivalent to a human translation. Light post-editing aims to produce a sort of minimum viable (translation) product, removing offensive material and aiming for a semantically correct translation, without making stylistic changes. Full post-editing adds consideration of grammar (including hyphens and punctuation), syntax, formatting, and terminology. However, both guidelines recommend making the fewest possible changes to the raw MT output.

Post-editing can take place within a word processor or text editor tool, a CAT tool (as described in Chapter 2), or a dedicated tool or platform. It might involve MT *propagated* within a target text window or an MT suggestion appearing as just another proposal within the CAT interface. MT can otherwise be used as a suggested starting point for a translation without being actually edited within the target text window, or as a predictive typing tool, such as in an interactive, adaptive MT workflow (see Chapter 7). Post-editing makes up a sizeable portion of the global translation market, and as such is now an expected skill for translators in many fields. There have been occasional suggestions that translators are overqualified for post-editing as the linguistic transfer is carried out by MT rather than a human, but research has not supported the notion of monolingual post-editing.

The main incentive for post-editing, from the perspective of translation buyers, is speed and cost. The ISO standard for post-editing calls it a 'viable solution for translating projects that need to be completed within a very tight time frame and/or with a reduced budget (ISO 2017: v)'. This is where post-editing becomes contentious. Some translators do not like revising at all, but many do not like correcting MT output in particular, especially if they consider MT a risk to their job. Some translators like post-editing, whereas others say that it limits their opportunity to create quality content. Post-editing is usually paid at a reduced rate when compared to translation from scratch, potentially making it more difficult to earn a good wage, on the assumption that MT output is always useful, and that post-editing is easier than translation. However, as noted previously, NMT errors can be difficult to detect and to resolve.

Research on SMT post-editing found a disconnect between post-editing speed, almost always faster than translation from scratch or even with TM assistance, and translators' *perceived* post-editing speed. In the NMT era, this appears to have realigned, and increased productivity (albeit not much increased from SMT) usually matches translators' perceptions. Quality expectations of post-editing are less clear-cut. Post-edited text has been found to be of publishable quality, but with a tendency to particular characteristics. NMT output, while more fluent than previous paradigms, will stick closely to the source text without any creative divergence. As post-editors are encouraged to use as much of the raw MT as possible, post-edited text will also tend to retain this close relationship: translators often say that once they see an MT proposal, it can be difficult to think of another way to express the same sentiment. Research by Toral (2019: 273) using several parallel corpora and language pairs identified common elements of what he calls 'post-editese': a tendency for simpler translations than those by humans that retain similar length to the source segment, with 'a higher degree of interference from the source language' than human translation.

Sociotechnical Issues with MT

The standard orthodoxy for the use of MT in a translation workflow is that the level of automation should equate to the shelf-life, risk, and value of the text (Way, 2018). If, for example, an online review will only be read for a few hours and for which a mistranslation will cause no harm beyond possible confusion, raw MT might be the best option. For a report with few readers that will be superseded within months, as long as there are no legal repercussions for mistranslation, perhaps post-editing is a good choice. For many printed materials, high-value marketing texts, literature, medicinal instructions, and corporate reports, for example, perhaps automation should be minimised. Some translators claim that at the upper end of the market, for those with the skill and specialisation, word rates are high and MT is little-used (Durban, 2022). They recommend that translation graduates aim for this market for making a good living with little risk of technological unemployment. Mainstream subtitling (see Chapter 9), where for some language pairs rates have dropped, MT use is commonplace, and work is constrained by templates and proprietary platforms, shows the danger of overreliance on automation without due consideration of job satisfaction and motivation.

There are a number of other issues regarding MT, and in particular data-driven MT. We mentioned problems of bias in training data, drawn from previous translations and 'scraped' from the internet, where online opinion is often polarised. There are currently no perfect ways to de-bias language data. Ownership of translation data is also a controversial issue. The Berne Convention considers translations to be derivative work that can hold copyright, subject to the rights of the original author. Troussel and Debussche (2014) and Cabanellas (2014) believe there is some potential for retention of copyright on the part of translators, depending on their jurisdiction, for both the translated text and TMs as databases. However, in practice, translations are handed over to clients and can be reused for MT training, even if the translator is opposed to the use of MT. Translation data usually has attributes removed prior to MT training, meaning that authorship is not ascribable, even if this were possible at the scale of NMT training data. Legal restrictions to personal data such as the European General Data Protection Regulation make this more likely, as translation metadata that contains the name of the translator could be considered personal data.

Growing use of **cloud-based** software in general and neural models in particular are associated with high energy consumption. NMT requires expensive, power-hungry graphical processing units (GPUs) and lots of training time. Strubell et al. (2019) found that large transformer neural models emit the same amount of carbon dioxide as the lifetime emissions of five cars. Thankfully not all models are of this size, and some researchers are actively looking for ways to make NMT more energy efficient, but there is also greater use of large language models for NMT and for other tasks such as monolingual text generation, pushing emissions in the wrong direction (see Dodge et al. (2022) for discussions of measures to mitigate emissions from AI training).

Conclusion

MT quality has greatly improved since the advent of NMT, with fluent output in well-supported languages (at the time of writing, Google NMT is available for 133 languages – a fraction of over 6,000 non-endangered languages worldwide). Adding MT to translation workflows can improve speed, but (as Chapter 7 will show) there is no single best method of translator interaction with MT. Although NMT can produce impressive quality, there are still many error types prevalent and biases inherent in its output. Eradicating these problems can be difficult as NMT is currently a 'black box', and it is therefore difficult to find the source of problems. Measuring quality and identifying errors in MT can also be difficult. It is important to use the appropriate measure of human or automatic evaluation to support a claim about MT quality. The amount of effort required for post-editing will depend on MT quality and the intended final text quality. Post-editing is part of the skill set expected of translators, but to empower them to be involved in decisions about when and where it is appropriate to use MT and with what training data, it is important to be aware of how MT works and to have reasonable quality expectations of MT.

Follow-Up Tasks and Reflection

1. Choose two MT systems for your language pair, translating into your first language. Include at least one well-resourced general domain NMT system such as DeepL, Google Translate, or Bing Translator and perhaps another system such as Google Sheets (using the Translate formula), Yandex, Tilde Translate, Apertium RBMT, or one of the stock systems on MutNMT (ntradumatica.uab.cat). Choose two comparable documents to translate, with similar segment lengths and complexity. To what extent does the output of both reflect the meaning of the

source text? Is the output fluent? Post-edit both to produce a high-quality, publishable translation, noting the amount of time taken for both documents. What does this tell you about the MT output quality? Was it better or worse than expected? Were you faster for the second document because you became accustomed to post-editing?

2. Look at the MT errors that you fixed and try to categorise them, perhaps looking at mistranslations, register errors (to do with politeness or choice of pronoun), word order errors, and words added or omitted in the raw target text MT output. How many errors appear in total? What type of errors do you see most often?

3. Look for a text that might cause gender difficulties in the MT output: perhaps about a female Prime Minister, a female doctor, an intersex or transgender sportsperson, or a male nurse. Ideally, the text will sometimes refer to the person by their role rather than using gendered pronouns. Do both MT systems translate these texts accurately and consistently? What might be the effect of static MT output as our language and terminology changes?

4. Using MutNMT or LetsMT.eu, carry out an automatic evaluation of the MT output from Step 1. Use the templates provided if using MutNMT, adding source text, raw MT output, and your post-edited text as a reference translation (although post-edited text tends to be closer to the MT than human translation without the aid of MT). What do the results tell you about the automatic evaluation of MT quality? Do segments where you found fewer errors or which you found to be more fluent and accurate fare better in this automatic evaluation than those that you considered worse? Are these scores useful and how might you explain them to someone who knows nothing about translation?

Further Reading

The work of W. John Hutchins (e.g. 'Machine translation: A brief history' from 1995) on MT history and different paradigms is always useful and informative. For readable introductions to SMT and NMT, see Mary Hearne and Andy Way's Statistical Machine Translation: A Guide for Linguists and Translators (2011) and Juan Antonio Pérez-Ortiz et al. How neural machine translation works (2022). For detailed technical information on SMT and NMT, their uses, evaluation, and training, the books by Philipp Koehn *Statistical machine translation* from 2009 and *Neural machine translation* from 2020 are excellent sources. Finally, the book *Machine translation for multilingual citizens*, edited by Dorothy Kenny (2022a), is available for no charge in e-book format and provides a highly readable introduction to NMT and many surrounding issues.

7   Advanced Leveraging in CAT Tools

> **Key Questions**
>
> - What are the main limitations of conventional CAT tool retrieval?
> - Beyond full segment and terminology matches, what other types of leverage would be useful?
> - What approaches (manual and automated) have been developed to enable **sub-segment matching**, and which tools use them?
> - How is sub-segment leverage exploited by CAT tools?
> - How can CAT tools be connected to MT systems in a shared environment?
> - What different uses can CAT tools make of MT proposals and other information?
> - What are **interactive and adaptive MT**, and how does using them differ from standard post-editing?
> - How far has the distinction between CAT and MT become blurred in modern tools?

Introduction

CAT tools as presented in Chapter 2 have contributed to increasing the speed and consistency of many types of translation by **leveraging** legacy information from two main data sources: a **translation memory** (**TM**) (or a **fuzzy index**) containing whole **source language** (**SL**) segments from previous projects **aligned** with their **target language** (**TL**) equivalents, and a **termbase** (**TB**) containing (usually) hand-crafted information about how to translate single or multiword **terms** in the relevant domain (see also Chapter 4). However, there are two main weaknesses in this standard approach which developers have been working to overcome, or at least mitigate, to make their tools more productive.

The first major weakness is that basic CAT tools waste a lot of useful translation information. Standard TM technology is unable to identify and

DOI: 10.4324/9781003160793-7

reuse (**leverage**) the large amount of fine-grained equivalence data contained *inside* each **translation unit** (**TU**). Between the two levels of equivalence represented by TM and TB, corresponding broadly to sentences and words respectively, lie *phrases*, meaningful fragments or chunks of text which can extend from a couple of words to whole clauses. A typical SL segment of any significant length may contain several such units of meaning, each of which will probably have an equivalent on the TL side that it would be potentially useful to identify for reuse, yet standard TM technology is unable to drill down into a TU and identify which SL fragment is translated by which words in the TL. If such sub-segment matches could be identified and extracted, they could be very useful in improving the leverage (and value) of the TM database. The following section of the present chapter will discuss the different ways in which CAT tools have been enhanced to leverage this otherwise wasted level of equivalence.

The second and most obvious weakness of CAT is that when no useful matches are found in either the TM or the TB, the standard tool can provide no leverage at all, leaving the translator to translate the new segment from scratch. The extraction of sub-segment matches can go some way towards filling this gap, supplying the translator with useful fragments of the unfound segment, but an overall solution to this problem that may be more productive is to send unmatched SL segments out to an external **machine translation** (**MT**) system, then pull the results back into the CAT environment to give the translator at least the possibility of some useful TL text to work with (i.e. **post-edit**). Part 2 of this chapter will look at some of the ways in which MT has been combined with CAT tools, to the point of significantly blurring the boundary between these two technologies.

Increasing Leverage from Existing Translation Data

To illustrate the types of equivalence that standard TM technology is unable to leverage, consider the following pair of segments, S1 and S2:

S1: A scroll compressor is a spiral-shaped pump that compresses the refrigerant.
S2: A spiral-shaped scroll pump compresses the refrigerant.

Assume now that English is the SL of a translation project about refrigeration techniques, you find S1 in the new **source text** (**ST**) that you are working on, while S2 is present in your active TM, aligned in a TU with its translation. On the surface the two sentences are very different, and a conventional string-matching algorithm (see Chapter 3) will not identify S2 as a useful match for S1. However, they have many semantic and orthographic elements in common, which would undoubtedly be helpful to you if the CAT tool could extract them from project databases or reference materials and propose them for reuse. In a basic CAT tool, you might expect 'refrigerant' to be in your TB alongside its translation, and perhaps also the verb 'compress', so you should see a couple of terminology proposals. But you won't get any help with 'scroll pump' unless both it and 'scroll compressor' have been included in the TB, either as separate entries, or with one as a **synonym** of the other (domain knowledge is of course required to make this semantic connection). The recurrent expression 'spiral-shaped' is non-terminological, so would not normally be included in the TB (on these distinctions, see Chapter 4).

However, thinking of translation leverage here solely in terms of hand-crafted TB entries is to neglect the obvious point (to a domain-informed human) that the meanings of S1 and S2 are much more similar than their surface strings suggest, so they can be translated in similar ways. To reduce work and ensure consistency in the TT, you would ideally want an enhanced CAT tool to identify this similarity of meaning and propose the translation of S2 as a potentially useful TL match for S1. This is a hard requirement to meet using current technology, but it would at least be helpful to the trans-lator if reliable translations for common fragments such as 'spiral-shaped pump' and 'compresses the refrigerant' could be extracted and presented automatically, alongside any proposals from the TB. In the sub-sections that follow, we shall start by looking at two tools which take essentially opposite approaches to this problem: Star Transit NXT, which tries to identify the similarity of meaning between different SL strings such as S1 and S2 by also searching the TL side of its reference fuzzy index, and Déjà Vu X3 (DVX), which has an additional (third) database where you can store manually cre-ated translations of frequently-occurring but non-terminological text frag-ments from the ST, such as 'spiral-shaped'. Part 1 will then conclude with an examination of how some other tools perform automatic sub-segment matching, and the different uses to which they put it.

Star Transit NXT's 'Dual Fuzzy' Lookup

Star Transit NXT is the only CAT tool to address systematically in its design the problem of finding the whole TU of S2 as a fuzzy match for S1 (see above), i.e. of identifying a close similarity of meaning between two SL segments that have been expressed in different (non-matching) strings. Saying 'the same thing' using different words, and/or a different word order, is a surprisingly common, if in principle undesirable, phenomenon in technical writing (see e.g. Rathjens (1985: 45) who defines consistency in technical writing as referencing 'the same thing with the same word(s)'), and a CAT tool that could detect and resolve at least some such cases would clearly be advantageous to the translator. The approach implemented by Transit is a 'Dual Fuzzy' lookup which extends the method of string matching to the TL side of the project: the program makes a continually updated index of *both* the SL and TL sides of the ongoing transla-tion job (the working folder) and associated reference materials (Star, 2018). If the normal SL fuzzy index can find no match for the **active segment** (S1 in our example), the system takes the first word(s) of the TL text string that the translator is typing manually and runs an automated concordance search on it in the TL fuzzy index, narrowing its search as you type more words of the translation until it finds a match, or matches (in our example, this might include the TL translation of S2). Any TL matches of this type are presented in a Target Fuzzy pop-up window in much the same way as conventional matches from the SL index, except that they are enclosed in red-outlined boxes rather than green ones (Figure 7.1).

Figure 7.1 Target Fuzzy matching in Star Transit NXT (reproduced with permission from Díaz & Zetzsche, 2022: 181).

If the list contains a suitable match, you can insert and, if necessary, edit it in just the same way as a match from the SL fuzzy index. This should not only save typing (and so time), it may also reduce spelling errors and can potentially increase the consistency of the TT. It also gives you the opportunity to edit the ST to make the new SL segment consistent with the reference segment that expresses the same content. It is worth noting at this point that a similar principle of automatic target-side concordance searching is implemented in the different versions of TL predictive typing offered by several other CAT tools (see below), although they do not normally produce whole segments as match proposals in the way that Transit aims to do.

Déjà Vu's 'Lexicon'

Atril's Déjà Vu X3 (and earlier versions) takes a different approach to creating translation leverage for segments for which no useful proposal is found in the TM. Rather than looking for full segments on the TL side that have a similar meaning to the current SL segment, DVX introduces a third database, additional to the TM and TB that most other CAT tools also offer, that it calls the Lexicon (see also Chapter 4). In translation technology *lexicon* normally designates the special kinds of dictionary used in rule-based MT systems (see Chapter 6), but here the Lexicon provides a manual method of enriching translation leverage with SL-TL equivalent text fragments (short expressions etc. such as 'spiral-shaped' in the example above) that are neither full segments, nor existing entries in a termbase, but are identified as recurring in the new ST and so are worth taking the time to translate as part of the preparations for the new job. When you take the optional step of creating a Lexicon (which can happen at any point in the project workflow but is normally done at the start), DVX takes the new project ST(s) and breaks it/them up into all **n-grams** of user-specified maximum length, giving you the opportunity to translate useful recurrent fragments. Some n-grams are more independently meaningful (and therefore potentially worth pre-translating) than others: of the bigrams contained in

S3: A short test sentence

the **string** 'test sentence' is likely to require the same translation in every case, whereas the adjectival 'A short' is not, particularly if the TL is marked for gender.

To look at these translation decisions in more detail, we can return to the same small English to Arabic translation project about solar water purification that we used as an example in Chapter 2. After switching to the Lexicon tab on the DVX ribbon and clicking the Create Lexicon button, we see a new 'Lexicon' item appear in the Project Explorer tree, and double-clicking it opens a tabbed translation grid with the SL n-grams from the ST displayed in the second column (Figure 7.2).

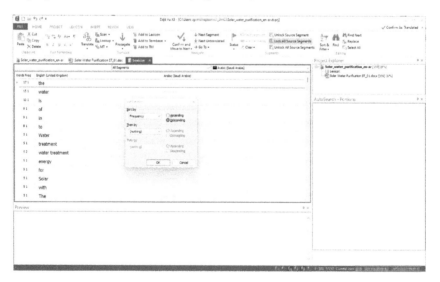

Figure 7.2 Sort Lexicon dialog in Déjà Vu X3.

With the Sort Lexicon dialog open we can see that the n-grams have been sorted in descending order of frequency (usually more useful than alphabetical order). Many of the most frequent fragments are single function words (e.g. 'the' at the top occurs 17 times in this short text), but these may well be unsuitable for translation because, depending on the TL, they might not correspond to a single translation or might be subject to morphological modification. However, 'water' (15 times, plus five more in capitalised form), 'treatment', 'water treatment', 'energy', and 'Solar' (five times each) could well be worth translating, and along with other words lower down the list, such as 'osmosis' (three times) and 'contaminated water' (twice), you might in fact judge them to be valid and useful terms in this domain. If so, DVX allows you to send them and their translation straight to the TB, either individually or in bulk, using the Add to Termbase button, which means that the Lexicon can be used as a **term extraction** tool, allowing you to inspect the new ST for terms in a more thorough way than simply reading through it. Any other non-terminological n-grams that you subsequently decide to translate can be left in the Lexicon, or you may decide to send some of the longer fragments to the TM using the Add to TM button. Once you have finished translating the Lexicon, you can bulk-delete all the untranslated rows, then export your data to Excel or as a text file, for reuse in subsequent translation projects or to pass on to another translator, etc.

Déjà Vu is the only CAT tool with an extra database dedicated to storing non-terminological fragments in this way, and while you are translating, you may receive proposals in the Autosearch Portions window (see Figure 7.3) not just from the TM (no. 1, red) and TB (nos. 2 & 3, blue), but also the Lexicon (nos. 4 & 5, white):

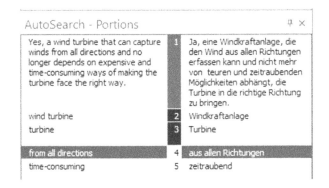

Figure 7.3 AutoSearch proposals in Déjà Vu X3.

However, its usefulness does not end there: a populated Lexicon can be used alongside the TB, during Pretranslation, to attempt to 'Assemble' a translation for any segment for which there is no good TM proposal. It can also be used, again alongside the TB, as a data source for **fuzzy match repair** (see below).

Automatic Sub-segment Matching

The DVX Lexicon, which aims to deliver sub-segment translation leverage through manual pretranslation of useful fragments of the ST, has the advantage that the translations produced are of known human quality. However, the obvious disadvantage is that working through the Lexicon generated by a long ST is likely to be time-consuming, and only worthwhile if more texts of a similar type are expected to come up for translation in the future: this explains why it might not be used in every translation project. It would really help the CAT user if potentially useful fragments in the active segment could be looked up automatically in the TM/fuzzy index, and any TUs containing them were selected and then searched for the corresponding TL equivalents. Beginning with the first version of Trados Studio in 2009 (Zetzsche, 2016), several of the major tools now offer a version of automatic sub-segment recall, using the results in a variety of ways to offer the translator additional proposals, although the details of the different methods used by each tool, like those of their segment-matching algorithms (see Chapter 3), remain commercially confidential.

Kevin Flanagan's (2015) article on sub-segment retrieval identified four types of recall strategy that had already been implemented in CAT tools (a development of his own new method, first developed for his PhD at Swansea University, would later be incorporated into Studio 2017 as its new upLIFT feature). The first and simplest approach is to search the project TM(s) for complete shorter segments (e.g. document headings) that translate part(s) of the longer active SL segment, essentially using the TM like a TB (Flanagan, 2015: 68). This is likely to produce significant extra leverage only when the active or reference TMs contain many relevant short segments, such as those with TUs originating from spreadsheets, software interfaces etc. Phrase's 'Subsegment match' implementation works in this way: 'If a smaller part of the original text was previously translated as a short segment, the CAT pane will display it even though the match is lower than the threshold set in the Editor's Preference' (Phrase, n.d.(a)). In the second type, automatic concordance search (Flanagan, 2015: 68), the tool breaks up the active segment into contiguous substantial portions, rather like Déjà Vu's Lexicon but with a greater (user-configurable) minimum and maximum fragment length to avoid presenting numerous non-meaningful text fragments. It then looks up each selected portion in the TM(s) and any reference documents, extracts all TUs containing it, and attempts to identify the translation from the TL data; if it is unable to do so (when there are too few examples to analyse), the translator can open a concordance window to display the whole of any corresponding TL segment(s) and search for the translation manually. This approach, exemplified in memoQ's Longest Substring Concordance (LSC) feature, is more efficient than the translator running a manual concordance search to look up one phrase at a time, but it may produce substantial amounts of TL data for inspection, which can be cognitively costly.

What would be even more helpful is if the tool could reliably find and highlight the phrase's translation automatically, and Flanagan (2015: 69) identifies two approaches to achieving that, both of which use statistical extraction techniques originally developed for **phrase-based statistical machine translation (PBSMT**, see Chapter 6) – an important example of the convergence of CAT and MT technologies. The bilingual fragment extraction approach, used most notably by the AutoSuggest feature incorporated into Trados Studio 2009 and later versions, requires a TM of at least 10,000 TUs which is analysed for statistically significant correspondences between SL and TL segment fragments. These are then compiled into an AutoSuggest dictionary which can be configured to contribute predictive typing proposals as the translator works. MemoQ's 'Muse' is similar, requiring 'a few thousand segments' to 'train' its predictive typing capability (memoQ, n.d.(b)). This approach has two main limitations: it only works with a large existing TM, and its dictionary is static, so to incorporate new data from the ongoing translation, the extraction routine needs to be run again ('retraining' the Muse). The other statistical method identified by Flanagan, dynamic TM analysis (DTA), largely overcomes both limitations by making on-the-fly use of all available TM and reference document resources, but its extracted proposals are typically less numerous and less accurate; Déjà Vu's 'Deepminer' feature works in this way. UpLIFT significantly improves on this approach, requiring a minimum corpus of only 1,000 TUs (5,000 for optimum performance; see RWS (n.d.)) with on-the-fly updating and offering greater sub-segment coverage with more reliable translations, giving Trados Studio the advantage in this aspect of TM retrieval (Avila, 2018).

Having found, by whatever method, one or more TL sub-segment matches for the active SL segment, CAT tools use that additional leverage in two main ways. The first, mentioned in the previous paragraph, is an enhanced predictive typing capability. Many tools, including OmegaT with its AutoCompleter and Wordfast Pro with its AutoSuggest, can 'guess' from the ST segment and one or more newly typed TL characters (the number is sometimes user-configurable) the next word(s) the translator is likely to want, prompting them with suggestions (with or without fuzzy matching) from a TB or glossary. Those with sub-segment leverage such as Trados Studio's AutoSuggest extend this capability by including fragment matches, while Déjà Vu's AutoWrite can additionally use manually translated Lexicon fragments for this purpose (Atril, n.d.). The biggest limitation of these predictive typing routines, aside from the variable availability of match data, is that for a proposal to appear, whether from the TB or a sub-segment match, you need to have started to type it – in other words, it tends not to act as a prompt towards a solution that you had not already thought of. For that reason, some tools (e.g. Phrase and memoQ) also display sub-segment matches in their match panes alongside those from TB and TM, as resources for the translator to select.

The other major benefit of sub-segment matching is its potential to improve fuzzy match repair. If the ST of a fuzzy match from the TM differs from the active segment by an item that is found in either the TB or a matched fragment, the correct translation can be inserted into the TL segment in place of the original fragment to improve the match quality, ideally turning it into a 100% match. In partnership with MT-provider Systran, XTM Cloud's TM tool now takes this process a step further: in a process they call Neural Fuzzy Adaptation, the whole of a fuzzy TU (both SL and TL segments) in the 75%–84% band may be sent out for machine translation, rather than just the non-matching part of the SL segment, as in other systems. The advantage of this 'AI-enhanced TM' (Systran, n.d.) approach is that Systran can compare the grammar of its own MT translation proposal with that of the original fuzzy match and make adjustments to ensure that the final output segment remains grammatically accurate – so that, for instance, if a masculine noun in the fuzzy target needs to be replaced by a feminine one, agreements elsewhere in the segment will be modified accordingly (Zetzsche, 2022).

MT Integration into CAT Tools

For a segment with no available matches from human-created data, the translator's only leverage option comes from MT – fortunately, NMT is likely to provide useful proposals in many language pairs and text domains (Chapter 6). The standard method is to connect the CAT tool via an **application programming interface** (**API**) to one or more online MT providers, using a paid-for access key and/or other authentication token which validates your subscription (see Figure 7.4).

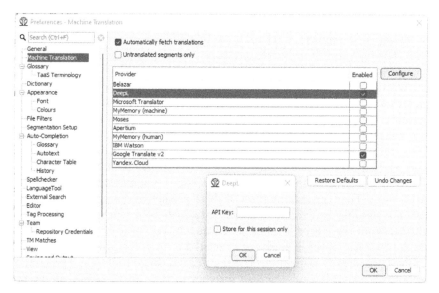

Figure 7.4 Configuring OmegaT to use MT proposals from DeepL and Google Translate.

Many tools let you decide whether to send all SL segments out to MT in this way, supplying an alternative to TM proposals (at the cognitive expense of more data for the translator to scan), or just segments with a low, or no, TM match. The almost instant MT result will typically appear in the CAT pane as a proposal for you to accept and **post-edit** in much the same way as you would correct a fuzzy match. If you generally prefer to post-edit rather than start from an empty TL segment, many CAT tools can be configured to use MT during pretranslation (see Chapter 2), for any segment without an exact or high fuzzy match – you can still see any available TM proposals, but the MT would typically be inserted by default, giving you a fully populated translation grid to work with. Additionally, some tools can use MT, either interactively or during pretranslation, for fuzzy match repair (see above) whenever a solution cannot be found in the project databases. MT can even (e.g. in Trados Studio) be configured to contribute predictive typing proposals, alongside those coming from the CAT databases and sub-segment matching routines (see above).

Not all CAT tools require paid subscriptions to integrate MT into their editing environments. Matecat, originally created as an open-source research project with EU funding and now maintained and developed by the Translated company, offers free MT 'out of the box', as well as a premium subscription service to its ModernMT engine. Free proposals come from its slightly confusingly named MyMemory repository (originally just a very large public TM, MyMemory now also sends segment queries to Google Translate and Microsoft Translator). MT from MyMemory is also offered by Wordfast Anywhere alongside free MT from WorldLingo, together with the option to integrate paid MT services via API key. In addition to the integration methods already discussed, Matecat is able to use MT in many language pairs in combination with AI-processed data in both its public MyMemory TM and any user-specific TMs, to save translators the effort of placing inline tags (e.g. to mark the scope of a format change or the location of a footnote reference or hyperlink) manually in the TL segment. To illustrate the subtle way in which its Guess Tags feature seems able to combine MT with TM (Matecat, n.d.), notice in Figure 7.5 that the SL string 'Minor Injury Unit' (on the left) is enclosed between tags (which in fact mark a hyperlink), and the corresponding TL string in the MT proposal on the right, 'Unité des Blessures Légères', is also within the same tags.

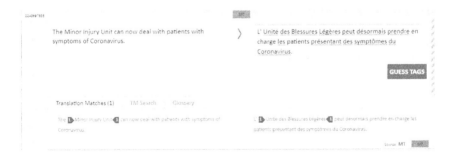

Figure 7.5 Matecat's 'Guess Tags' feature.

However, after clicking the Guess Tags button (Figure 7.5), the placement of the opening tag in the translation proposal has been correctly moved forward to include the leading definite article 'L', apparently because the AI has 'learnt' from its vast TMs that this is required for capitalised named entities in French (Figure 7.6).

Figure 7.6 Matecat – after clicking 'Guess Tags'.

Details of how the AI algorithm works are, like much to do with modern CAT tools, kept confidential, but the important thing from the translator's point of view is that it potentially saves time compared with, for instance, using the Placeables system of Trados Studio (see Chapter 2) to position each tag manually.

Phrase has developed another original approach to integrating free MT: a paid-for add-on called Phrase Translate which by default sends the active segment to a range of free MT systems (it can also be configured to use paid MT via API key) and return the result as a translation proposal for post-editing. It uses an AI-powered Autoselect process to identify the best engine for the active language pair and, for some languages (currently around a dozen) the domain of the text, which it establishes by scanning it for terminology. The AI system works by recording the post-edit corrections to MT proposals made by large numbers of users, then ranking engines so that segments are sent to the engine that has typically required the lowest proportion of corrections. While it is not certain that Phrase also passes this data on to the MT providers, the usual caution about sending confidential information to free MT services clearly applies here too – Microsoft's 'Terms of use', for instance, stipulate that by submitting data to any of their websites, including Bing Translator, you automatically license the company to 'copy, distribute, transmit, publicly display, publicly perform, reproduce, edit, translate and reformat your Submission' (Microsoft, 2022). Phrase has been clever to monetise the free MT systems provided by other organisations in this way, adding value for its users by training the AI system that selects the best provider for them using their own post-editing work.

Another useful Phrase feature is that in some cases the AI can perform a Quality Estimate on the MT proposals returned, which allows them to be compared with and ranked hierarchically against TM fuzzy matches, thereby seamlessly integrating MT and TM as information sources which look similar to the translator (for similar reasons, Wordfast Anywhere ranks all its MyMemory proposals at 76% and those from WorldLingo at 75%, although it does not attempt any quality analysis). For example, in the English to Welsh Phrase project shown in Figure 7.7, the active SL segment has a fuzzy TM match of 77%, with tracked changes beneath showing the differences, but in between is a MTQE (MT Quality Estimation) proposal ranked at <u>75</u>%, signifying a 'Good MT match, but likely to require some post-editing' (Phrase, n.d.(b)) – a proposal with a higher confidence score would be ranked at either <u>99</u>% or <u>100</u>%. The MTQE proposal has the same orange-brown colour coding as the fuzzy TM match, and the only indication that it comes from MT is the dotted underline beneath the number <u>75</u> (in contrast, a proposal for which no quality estimation is available would be marked 'MT' against a blue background).

Figure 7.7 Phrase MTQE proposal.

This implies that Phrase is deliberately blurring the distinction between CAT and MT technologies, presenting MTQE and fuzzy match proposals in very similar ways within the same editing environment. This also happens during project preparation, as MTQE can optionally be enabled for both ST analysis (when <u>75</u>% and <u>99</u>% MT-scored proposals are counted in the corresponding fuzzy match bands), and pretranslation (see Chapter 2 for a description of these processes). Finally, when translation is complete you can use the 'Analyze MT' option to run a Post-Editing Analysis and show how many keystrokes have been used to correct the MT proposals (this is the same data that Phrase uses to assess and compare the MT engine performance).

All these advanced capabilities can provide useful additional translation leverage, but the 'standard' method of integrating MT into the CAT environment has one significant limitation: the proposal received from the MT system is static. When you send a sentence to Google Translate via the web interface, however, you often receive alternative proposals for the full sentence, while even the free version of DeepL takes this further, in many cases offering alternative translations for the whole segment, and also allowing you to click on any word to see different possible translations (often near synonyms, but also different syntactic options) which came slightly lower down its list of probable candidates. Selecting one of these word-level alternatives from the drop-down list (Figure 7.8) will often modify the rest of the MT proposal to fit.

Figure 7.8 Alternative translations in DeepL.

Making such an alternative selection also activates the 'Glossary' function, allowing you to specify whether you want the alternative translation to be applied to future occurrences of the SL word, which is thus an opportunity for limited customisation of 'your' MT system. This useful interactivity is lost when such MT proposals are pulled directly into a conventional CAT editing environment, limiting the translator's interaction with them to the mode of post-editing. Having to correct errors in such static MT-originated TT segments can be a frustrating experience for the translator – depending, of course, on the initial quality of the proposals. The problem is made worse because the same errors are likely to recur and need post-editing repeatedly throughout the document: conventional MT does not 'learn from its mistakes' until it has been retrained on updated data.

These limitations are all addressed in an innovative way by translation company Lilt, whose Lilt Translate online CAT tool has offered since 2015 'Interactive, Adaptive MT' (Lilt, n.d.) in around 100 language pairs. Lilt offers a streamlined, browser-based translation environment similar to those of Smartcat and Matecat, and like the other browser-based tools, Lilt encourages you to upload relevant TM and TB data into your project which is leveraged in the usual way to provide segment matches, down to 75% similarity, that you can accept or edit. However, this legacy data is also used for an initial customisation of Lilt's 'baseline MT', an in-house system that is constantly being adapted (retrained) on the fly every time you confirm a newly completed segment or add an entry to the TB, so that it 'learns' through this **feedback loop** the preferred translations it should be proposing for your specific document(s). This overall adaptive capability, which should avoid the need to correct the same MT errors multiple times, is complemented at segment level by the ability of the system to interact with input from the translator, which takes away much of the frustration associated with static post-editing. When you start working with a Lilt MT proposal, you can accept it one word at a time by clicking on it or hitting the Enter key, until you reach a point in the segment where you want to modify the proposal. As you type out the next word, Lilt immediately uses the context you have added to recalculate and update its proposal from that point until the end of the segment, and you can either accept the whole of the new proposal with Shift+Enter, then edit it as necessary, or continue typing your own solution until Lilt's proposal coincides more closely with what you wanted. If you do not like the original proposal, you can type the first word(s) of your translation and watch Lilt adapt its text, as in Figure 7.9. Here, the upper screenshot shows segment 59 of a French ST with Lilt's original English translation proposal, while in the lower box the translator has decided to modify the syntax and typed the first word, the auxiliary 'Having', leading Lilt to react immediately and update the syntax of the whole segment by modifying not just the immediate verb form, but the following one ('discussed') as well:

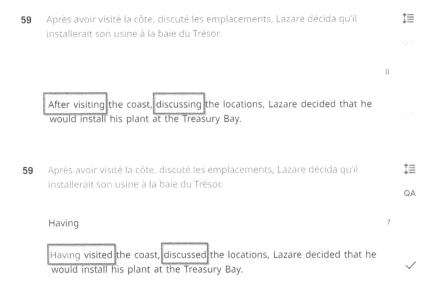

Figure 7.9 Lilt's MT adapts its proposal to the translator's input.

Again, once you are happy with the product of your interaction with the MT system and confirm the segment, it immediately becomes part of your personal TM, which Lilt undertakes not to share with other system users.

Conclusion

Getting more value out of the human-quality data in TMs through sub-segment matching is one well-tried approach to advanced leveraging, while bringing in MT for unmatched segments is another, yet despite treating them in separate sections, this chapter has shown that they are in fact highly complementary. In modern CAT tools they work together to provide the translator with more, and more accurate, proposals, also saving time by enabling predictive typing, fuzzy match repair, and even automatic tag placement, thanks to commercially confidential algorithms, some of which apparently use machine learning. Further improvements in NMT quality, but also in the scope and accuracy of TM retrieval, are to be expected in the near future. With regard to the latter, Ruslan Mitkov offers a tantalising glimpse of research into 'intelligent TM systems' (Mitkov, 2022: 376) which can perform semantic rather than just string-based matching. His team has experimented with using 'novel semantic similarity methods' (ibid.) includ-ing paraphrase dictionaries, clause-splitting, and the kinds of deep learning techniques on which NMT is based, to extract more and better information from TMs. This suggests that future-generation CAT tools and MT systems are homing in on the all-important goal of capturing similarities of mean-ing, rather than just between the surface forms of words. In fact, the very distinction between CAT and MT is already becoming blurred, when MT proposals can be given a percentage quality score and ranked in the editing environment among TM matches, while user-generated TM and TB data (this distinction too is becoming less clear-cut in some tools) can be used on the fly to adapt and retrain a baseline MT system, and make it responsive to the project context. As NMT becomes even more accurate, and methods of integrating it with CAT in the same interactive environment improve, we may wonder whether, before long, the translator will still care much whether proposals come from TM or MT, so long as they are useful and speed up the work.

Follow-Up Tasks and Reflection

1. Explore the advanced database recall and MT integration features of the CAT tools you used for the tasks that follow Chapters 2, 3, and 4. How easy is it to find out from the program documentation what they are and how they work? What contribution (positive or negative) would you expect them to make to your translation workflow?

2. Return to the Practice translation project you constructed at the end of Chapter 2. Experimentally retranslate your Practice ST using the same tools, this time with all their advanced leverage features enabled. How much additional help do they provide?
3. Now select an MT-enabled cloud-based tool that you have not previously used and configure it to provide MT-based proposals for all segments. Retranslate your Practice ST once more: how good are the MT proposals, and how easy are they to post-edit (the answers to both questions may depend on your language pair)? Do you prefer to translate with TM only, MT only, or a combination of both?
4. Thinking about the different ways in which MT and TM have been combined to date, which approach do you think is the most helpful to a translator, and what additional MT-related functionalities would you like to see CAT tools acquire?

Further Reading

A clear overview of sub-segment TM matching techniques can be found in Kevin Flanagan's (2015) article 'Subsegment recall in translation memory – perceptions, expectations and reality'. 'The translator's extended mind', by Yuri Balashov (2020) provides a worked example of CAT tool use by a translator from a cognitive perspective, including advanced features such as fuzzy match repair. 'Integration of machine translation in CAT tools: state of the art, evaluation and user attitudes' (Zaretskaya et al., 2015) contains a useful classification of approaches to integrating MT with CAT just prior to the dawn of the NMT era, as well as a survey of translator attitudes to MT-enhanced tools. Ruslan Mitkov's (2022) entry on 'Translation memory systems' in the *Routledge handbook of translation and memory* gives a succinct, if rather technical, account of experimental enhancements to TM retrieval which may soon find their way into commercial CAT tools. As ever, the best way to dig down into the advanced functionalities of the different tools available is to study their user documentation, and there are also useful explanations and demonstrations available on YouTube.

8 Translation Project Management

Key Questions

- What is a translation management system (TMS)?
- How does a TMS differ from a standard CAT tool?
- What are the key requirements of a TMS?
- How does a modern TMS exploit cloud-based architectures?
- How does it support LSPs?
- How does it support project managers?
- How do translators interact with the project manager and reviser in a TMS?
- How does a TMS influence the working pattern of translators?
- To what extent is project management becoming automated?

Introduction

As presented in Chapter 2, the most basic form of project implemented by CAT tools and typically used by translators working alone is designed to link together the different parts of a translation job – the ST and the resources (TM/fuzzy index, TB) that will be leveraged to translate it – inside a single editing environment. For translation companies (LSPs), however, projects are often more complex and may involve many documents in different formats and/or multiple source and/or target languages, teams of translators and revisers, reviewers, QA experts, desktop publishing (DTP) and web designers, and data managers, often working in different parts of the world (time zones), as well as tight deadlines. Jobs may come as many small fragments needing urgent turn-around, and documents are increasingly updated while translation is already underway, requiring a so-called **agile workflow** and careful use of leverage. Keeping track of the financials (freelancer rates, quotes and invoices to the client, software subscriptions, etc.) adds a further layer of complexity:

DOI: 10.4324/9781003160793-8

Translations have become projects and translation is only one component in the workflow. The translation project requires management of communications and accounts in addition to the actual translation process. Sheer volume demands a different approach to how we translate and deal with demands.

(Mitchell-Schuitevoerder, 2020: 16)

These growing demands have led to the expansion inside LSPs of the role of the professional project manager (PM), whose job is to ensure effective communications and timely delivery of the project, rather than work as a linguist (though a PM may also do some linguistic work in their language pair(s)).

In parallel, CAT tools have evolved dramatically, taking advantage of cloud-based architectures (Chapter 2) to support complex projects and the PMs who manage them. Many have developed into fully-fledged translation management systems (TMS) – not to be confused with terminology management systems, with the same abbreviation (Chapter 4). The boundary between standard CAT tools and TMS is fuzzy – for instance, in its *Language Technology Atlas 2022* (Akhulkova et al, 2022), language industry specialist market research company Nimdzi lists all the CAT and TMS tools discussed in this book under the same heading of 'Generic TMS for Every Customer Profile', while the definition of TMS that it gives on its website is very broad:

A translation management system (TMS) is a solution for managing translation projects, large and small, and can integrate glossaries, translation software, and translation memories. There are a number of options on the market, and each solution has its own features and integrations. Some translation management systems include a CAT (computer-assisted translation) component, others don't and function as a BMS (business management system).

(Nimdzi, n.d.)

Nevertheless, we believe it is still useful to differentiate between tools focussed primarily on supporting the individual translator (CAT) and those of the kind described in this chapter which, while still offering a complete CAT environment, also provide sophisticated project management capabilities – the type of TMS that Shuttleworth (2015: 681) defines as 'language-centric'. Nimdzi's category of business management systems that do not support actual translation lies outside the scope of this book.

The first TMS systems in our sense of the term were arguably the server-based team editions of workstation-based CAT tools such as Trados Teamworks that came along in the early 2000s, but the arrival later in the decade of cloud-based tools with a **software-as-a-service** (**SaaS**) charging model (Shuttleworth, 2015: 680) led to a great advance in their power and flexibility. Box 8.1 summarises the main tasks a modern TMS can be expected to support:

**Box 8.1: Main Requirements of a Translation
Management System (TMS)**

- Project setup, management, and delivery in the cloud, by one or more project managers (PMs);
- Centralised setup and management of project workflow stages (e.g. Translation, Revision, Review, Sign-Off);
- Centralised setup, management, and allocation of translation resources (TMs, terminology, reference documents);
- Centralised creation and management of linguist (translator/reviser, terminologist) accounts;
- Centralised allocation to linguists of workflow tasks and deadlines;
- Collaborative translation editing workspace, including real-time sharing of translation resources;
- Centralised overview and control of project progress and financials;
- Automated routine email communications (e.g. generation and sending of Purchase Orders) between PMs and other project participants.

At the heart of any language-centric TMS there still lies a translation editing environment of the kind familiar from earlier chapters, which is the place where linguists do their work for the project. A key difference is in their experience of data sharing: multiple translators may be using and updating the same cloud-based TM and TB at the same time, potentially receiving proposals from TUs that another translator has only just confirmed. Another difference is centralised oversight by the PM, usually manifested in automated communications from the system to initiate and complete workflow stages. How this works, from the perspectives of both the PM and the linguist, will be the main topic of the present chapter. The first part will give a detailed description of the workflow of a small multilingual project using a basic but still powerful TMS, Wordfast Anywhere (WFA). The second part will then examine the extra features of a more complex TMS interface, that of Phrase TMS (formerly, Memsource Cloud), and show how such tools are evolving to become business platforms as much as translation environments.

TMS Essentials – Wordfast Anywhere 6

Imagine you are a project manager (PM) named Mary working for a small LSP and have been tasked with coordinating a multilingual project to translate an English language patient information website for a local Health Board in Wales, UK. The target languages are Welsh and Polish (one of the most widely spoken local community languages after English and Welsh).

The LSP is experimenting with the cloud-based tool Wordfast Anywhere 6 (WFA), already mentioned in earlier chapters, which offers a 30-day trial for $1 and a free Academic Program. WFA offers all the essential features of a cloud-based TMS: centralised project control, project workflow management, user management, shared data resources (TM and TB), and basic financials. We will explore the capabilities of WFA in some detail in this section because it offers a clear and conceptually transferable example of how complex, multi-agent translation projects can be constructed and managed.

Stage 1: Project Setup

You first need to set up your WFA account, then log in (wordfast.com/myaccount). Select the 'Project' tab on the ribbon, click 'New' and in the Project Setup dialog (Figure 8.1) click the Advanced button (Standard projects are for translators working on their own, in the scenario we described in Chapter 2). The project needs a name and can optionally be given a description; 'Currency' is used for calculating costs, paying linguists and invoicing the client, and the 'Decimals' box is ticked to ensure those figures include pence as well as pounds. The 'Auto' tick-box would automatically send the job to the next workflow step (e.g. revision) as soon as the first task (translation) is completed – the default, however, is for the PM to do this manually.

Figure 8.1 WFA Project Setup dialog.

Click the + button next to Language pair to select the first project TL and click Save (Figure 8.2).

Figure 8.2 WFA Add a language pair dialog.

If you do not already have a TM and **Glossary** (WFA's simplified form of TB) available, you are invited to create empty ones, and are then taken to the resources management dialog (Figure 8.3), which you can also use to add, edit etc. other resources as the project develops.

<table>
<tr><td colspan="5">Assign TMs and glossaries to a language pair</td><td colspan="5"></td></tr>
<tr><td colspan="4" align="center">Translation Memories</td><td></td><td colspan="4" align="center">Glossaries</td></tr>
<tr><td colspan="4">Create Add Upload Merge View/Edit</td><td></td><td colspan="4">Create Add Upload Merge View/Edit</td></tr>
<tr><td>Active</td><td>Description</td><td>Type</td><td>Read-Only</td><td></td><td>Active</td><td>Description</td><td>Type</td><td>Read-Only</td></tr>
<tr><td>✓</td><td>EN›PL (0)</td><td></td><td>☐</td><td></td><td>☑</td><td>EN›PL (0)</td><td>📖</td><td>☐</td></tr>
</table>

? Save

Figure 8.3 WFA's TMs and glossaries dialog.

After going through the same steps for the project's second language pair, you return to the Project Setup dialog with the language pair list now populated (Figure 8.4).

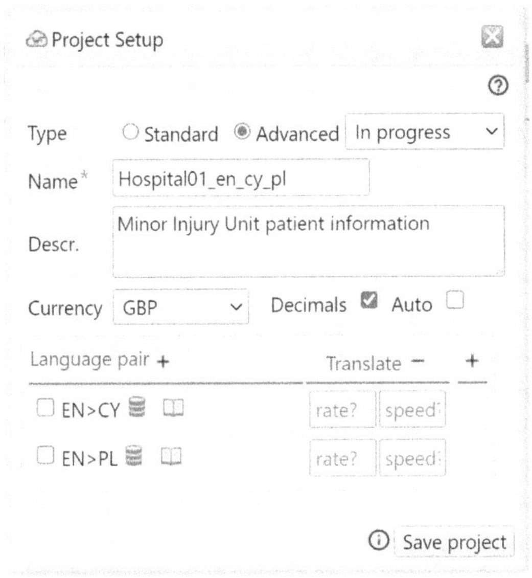

Figure 8.4 Project Setup dialog with two language pairs added.

Your project currently has only one workflow step, Translate, but the client has also asked for Revision and QA checking (see Chapter 2 and 11), so to add these tasks, click the + button to the right of Translate and type their titles in the dialog, which adds the corresponding columns to the Setup (Figure 8.5).

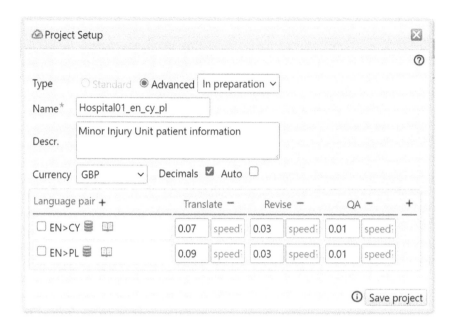

Figure 8.5 Project Setup with added tasks and rates.

Note that we have also added some figures representing the rate the LSP expects to pay, per word of translation/revision/QA, in each TL, with translation into Polish being more expensive (nine pence per word rather than seven) because there are fewer Polish linguists available. We have not set expected speeds (in thousands of words per day). Additional language pairs and resources can be added at any time by returning to the Project Setup dialog.

After saving the empty project structure, you can upload the text for translation into both language pairs by clicking the green '+' icon on the blue title bar and browsing to its storage location (to add a file to a single language pair, click the same icon inside that pair). Figure 8.6 shows the project with the same small ST in each language pair, comprising 31 segments, 231 words, and 1513 characters. The blue colour coding of the project title bar indicates that the project is still in preparation, hence the 0% progress figure in the Translate, Revise, and QA columns.

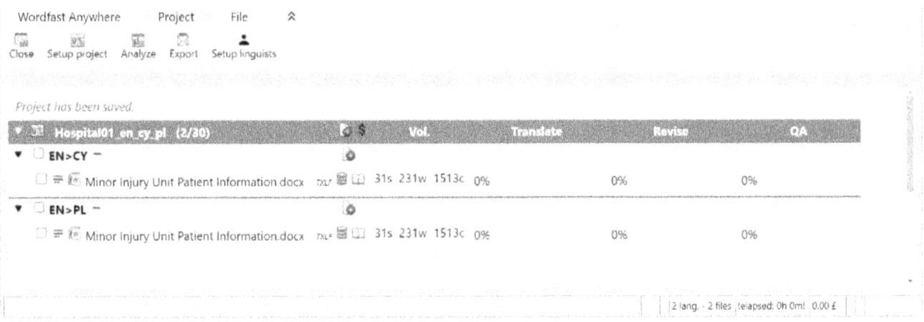

Figure 8.6 Language pairs, resources and tasks.

At this point you could add further files for translation if you wish. If you click on the TM icon in either language pair you will see Settings for project tasks: the TM is set to be shared by default, which gives the most complete leverage, but if you were concerned that it contained confidential material that you did not want to share with your linguists, you could select Create project TM instead, to make a new, empty TM that they would share, containing only matches from the main TM and any new translations added by them. The penalty for doing this, however, is that the PM would need to update the main TM afterwards with all the new TUs from the project. The main TM can also be set for use in pre-translating the ST (see Chapter 2). Finally, you can click the dollar sign button for a financial overview of the project (Figure 8.7).

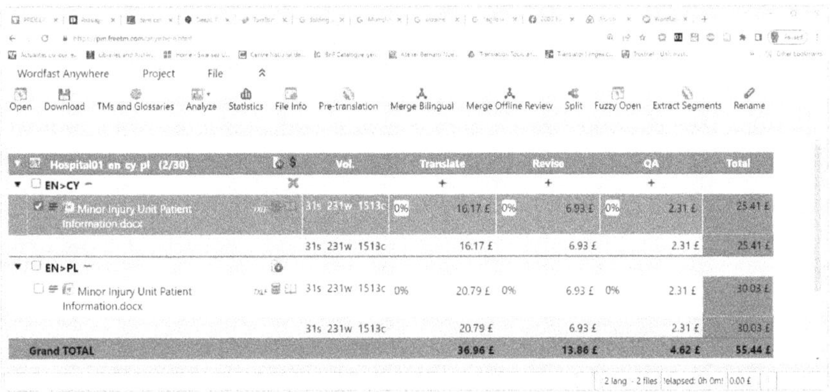

Figure 8.7 WFA project financial overview.

Here we see that the different per-word rates inserted earlier are reflected in the total costs of translation, revision, and QA for this small ST (£25.41 for Welsh, £30.03 for Polish). If the TMs were not empty, it would be sensible at this point for the PM to click the Analyze button and run a TM analysis on each language pair (see Chapter 2) to determine the degree of leverage available and whether any corresponding reduction in the quote to the client is possible.

Stage 2: Linguist Setup

Now that the project structure and ST are in place, you need to allocate the different tasks to suitable linguists (WFA's generic term for anyone who performs translation, revision, terminology, QA etc. work). Assuming your LSP already has a database of freelancers, often referred to as *suppliers* or *vendors* in the project management context, your first step is to select two suitable people for each TL (one translator/QA checker and one reviser) and set them up as linguists for your project. On the supplier database you find two suitable Welsh linguists, Jack and Jill, and two Polish linguists, Jacek and Jana. Before you can add them to your project, they must each create their own individual WFA account, after which they receive a Welcome email containing useful links to the program Start Guide, FAQ, User Manual etc. Now, with the current WFA project open, click the Setup linguists button on the Project tab to open the Linguist management window, then the Add icon to enter the details of the first person in the Edit Linguist dialog (Figure 8.8).

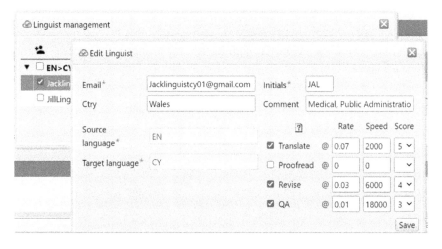

Figure 8.8 WFA – Edit Linguist dialog.

Jack's email address, initials, SL, and TL are mandatory information, but in addition we have given the country where he is based (this could be useful for time zone reasons) and, in the Comment field, his specialist domains. He can be used for all three project tasks (Translate, Revise, QA – the linguists will all be asked to proofread their own work, so that will not be a separate task in this project) and we have also entered the rates he charges, along with an estimate of his daily wordage capacity (speed) and a confidential competence score based on previous experience of his work, for each task. You can see immediately that his Translation rate is the same as the one we have quoted to the client, which would leave no profit margin for the LSP, but also that he scores more highly as a translator than as a reviser or QA checker. Once you have set up records for all four linguists, you are taken to the Linguist management window (Figure 8.9) which summarises the information about them and helps you decide to whom you will allocate each task.

Linguist management						
	Linguist	Ctry	TR	PR	RE	QA
▼ ☐ **EN>CY** –	+					
☐ Jacklinguistcy01@gmail.com (JAL)		Wales	0.07-2000-5		0.03-6000-4	0.01-18000-3
☐ JillLinguistcy02@gmail.com (JBL)		England	0.05-2500-4		0.03-7000-4	0.01-20000-5
▼ ☐ **EN>PL** –	+					
☐ JacekLinguistpl02@gmail.com (JCL)		PL	0.06-3000-5		0.03-8000-5	
☐ JanaLinguistpl01@gmail.com (JDL)		PL	0.06-2500-5		0.03-5000-4	0.01-15000-4

Figure 8.9 Summary of available linguists for the project.

On the Welsh side, it seems Jill is less good than Jack at translating, and her first domain is Automotive rather than Medical, so even though her rate falls within the project's budget, it would probably be best to use Jack as the translator, ideally after negotiating a slight discount with him, and Jill as the reviser and QA checker, since she scores more highly in those tasks. For Polish, Jacek offers reasonable rates, high quality and good speed but his domains (Environment, Legal) are not ideal, and he does not do QA checking, while Jana has similar rates but is slightly less good and slower at translating, has Medical as a second domain and does offer QA checking – so, on balance, she will be first choice as translator and QA checker for this language pair.

Stage 3: Task Allocation

Now the team of linguists for the project is also in place, the next step is to allocate the different tasks to them in their language pairs. With the project open as in Figure 8.6, select the file for translation into Welsh (if there were several STs, you could select more than one by holding down the CTRL key or all of them by ticking the checkbox to the left of the language pair designation), and note that a small '+' appears in each task column. To allocate the Welsh translation to Jack, click the '+' under Translate: a dialog appears listing the linguists able to perform that task. Select Jack's row and note that the cost of using him appears in the summary box above: Mary has negotiated a discounted rate of six pence/word, so she enters that figure and adds a Note of confirmation below, as well as setting a Deadline (Figure 8.10).

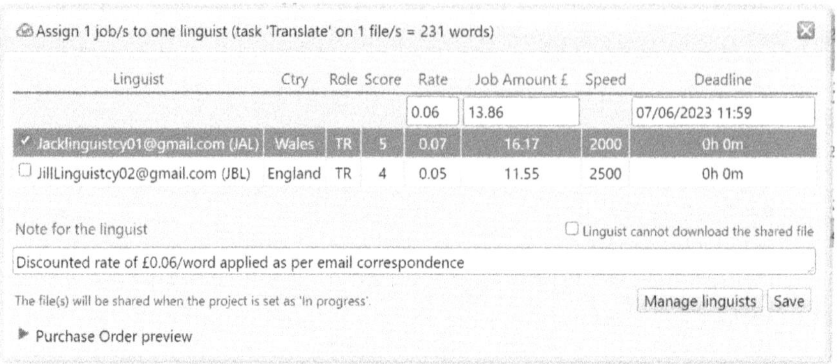

Linguist	Ctry	Role	Score	Rate	Job Amount £	Speed	Deadline
				0.06	13.86		07/06/2023 11:59
✓ Jacklinguistcy01@gmail.com (JAL)	Wales	TR	5	0.07	16.17	2000	0h 0m
☐ JillLinguistcy02@gmail.com (JBL)	England	TR	4	0.05	11.55	2500	0h 0m

⚙ Assign 1 job/s to one linguist (task 'Translate' on 1 file/s = 231 words)   ☒

Note for the linguist   ☐ Linguist cannot download the shared file

Discounted rate of £0.06/word applied as per email correspondence

The file(s) will be shared when the project is set as 'In progress'.   Manage linguists | Save

▶ Purchase Order preview

Figure 8.10 Allocating a job to a linguist.

Note the option to tick the box 'Linguist cannot download the shared file', useful for sensitive or confidential material, and the option to preview the Purchase Order (PO) that will be automatically emailed to Jack once the project status has been changed to 'In progress' – by default, the PO text is a template that Mary needs to edit in her user profile to contain the name and contact details of the LSP and the PM, etc.

After clicking the Save button to complete the assignment of the translation task to Jack (initials JAL), you return to the Project view where you can allocate the Revision and QA tasks to Jill (JBL) in the same way, with tight deadlines after the translation is complete, then follow the same procedure on the Polish side (note that because Janek (JCL) does not offer QA, only Jana's name (JDL) is listed for that task). Now that all tasks have been allocated, we can click on the project's title to return to the Project Setup dialog (Figure 8.6, above), change its status to 'In progress' and 'Save' it. Figure 8.11 shows the results: the project colour has turned from blue to orange, all the tasks have been allocated with deadlines (indicated by the clock icon), a PO (see below) has been emailed (with copy to the PM) to each of the linguists who will do the translations, and both the ST and the resources (TMs and Glossaries) are now shared between the two linguists in each language pair, as indicated by the three little figures now superimposed on the original icons.

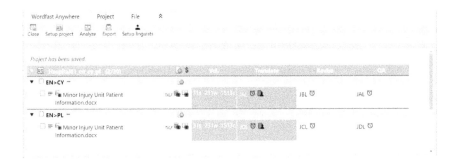

Figure 8.11 Project in progress dashboard.

The Translate column is highlighted in orange to indicate that this is the currently active stage of the project, and a red document icon has appeared next to the initials of each translator, which in the event of a problem (such as the translator failing to deliver on time) would allow the PM to 'revoke' (i.e. terminate) their participation, including removing their access to all data.

Stage 4: The Linguist's Experience

When Mary the PM set the project to 'In progress', Polish linguist Jana received an automated Purchase Order email giving full details of her task including remuneration – note that translation resources are shared only 'for the duration of this job' (Figure 8.12).

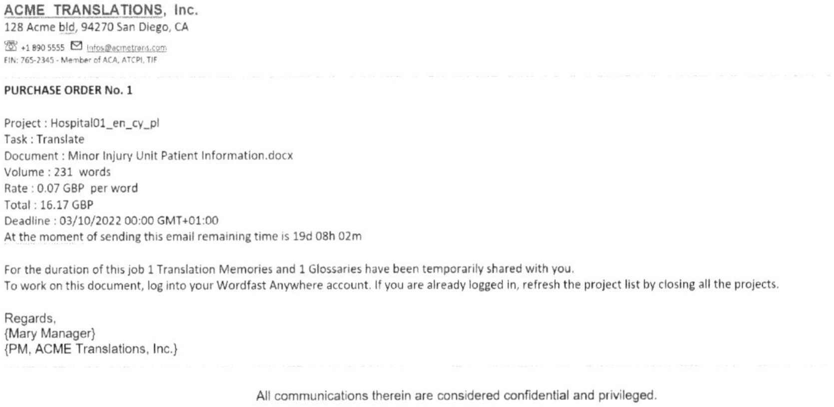

ACME TRANSLATIONS, Inc.
128 Acme bld, 94270 San Diego, CA
☎ +1 890 5555 ✉ info@acmetrans.com
FIN: 765-2345 - Member of ACA, ATCPI, TIF

PURCHASE ORDER No. 1

Project : Hospital01_en_cy_pl
Task : Translate
Document : Minor Injury Unit Patient Information.docx
Volume : 231 words
Rate : 0.07 GBP per word
Total : 16.17 GBP
Deadline : 03/10/2022 00:00 GMT+01:00
At the moment of sending this email remaining time is 19d 08h 02m

For the duration of this job 1 Translation Memories and 1 Glossaries have been temporarily shared with you.
To work on this document, log into your Wordfast Anywhere account. If you are already logged in, refresh the project list by closing all the projects.

Regards,
{Mary Manager}
{PM, ACME Translations, Inc.}

All communications therein are considered confidential and privileged.

Figure 8.12 WFA Automated Purchase Order.

When she logs in to her WFA account, in the list of Projects Jana sees a 'Standard Share' link containing the email address of the PM, and when she clicks on it the translation job opens in exactly the same interface as if it were her own individual project, with an MT proposal from MyMemory (scored as a 75% match) provisionally inserted in the first row (Figure 8.13).

Figure 8.13 Jana starts to translate.

Meanwhile, Mary the PM can monitor progress on her project dashboard through the completion percentages that appear next to Jana's initials: in Figure 8.14, Jana has completed 61% of the Polish translation and Jack just 35% of the Welsh.

Figure 8.14 Project translation progress (PM view).

Mary can even open the bilingual file in her own WFA editor while Jana is working on it and observe her editing actions segment by segment in almost real time, which some linguists might regard as an unwanted level of intrusion. In any event, once Jana is satisfied that she has finished translating, she needs to select the File tab on the ribbon and click the Close button to close the file and return to her project dashboard, which now shows the file as 100% translated (title bar in green). She inspects the project resources by clicking on the TM icon and finds that the TM contains the correct number of TUs (31): similar statistics would be available for the Glossary if she had added any terms.

Finally, to return the translated file to Mary, Jana selects the File tab again and clicks the Revoke button to remove the completed task from the list, at which point both the file and the resources also disappear from her dashboard: her task is complete, and *she no longer has access to the work (TT, TM, Glossary) she has just submitted* (this loss of control over your own translation work may be one of the downsides of working in a TMS, and it also means you must be very sure that the version you are submitting is complete and correct). Meanwhile, Mary PM has received an automated email telling her the document has been 'revoked' and is pleased to see her own dashboard updating to show that the Polish translation is now complete (flashing light and dark green) and ready to be sent to the reviser, Jacek, by clicking on the right-facing green chevrons – if 'Auto' had been selected in the Project Setup, this would be done automatically. Now Jacek receives an automated PO tasking him to revise the translation, which he opens from his own dashboard using the Review ribbon. He works through the text, making any necessary changes and automatically updating the shared TM, and when he has finished, he again revokes the document, which becomes available for Mary to allocate as a final task, QA checking, i.e. a careful proofread by Jana. After performing this last task, Jana might choose to click the Download button to keep a copy of the final documents and the TM data for her own future use (since Mary did not disable this option in the project setup). At this point Mary can see from her own dashboard that the Polish translation is well ahead of the Welsh version, with all three Polish tasks showing green and 100% complete (the overall multilingual project completion stands at 58%), so she may want to contact the Welsh team to ask how things are going. She can now download the Polish TT for onward transmission to the client, along with any other data that might be useful to the LSP in the future, while she waits for the Welsh project to catch up.

Comparing the translator's overall experience in a cloud-based TMS such as WFA with that of a stand-alone, workstation-based CAT tool, there are both positive and negative points to note. On the positive side, the burden of setting up and managing the project and its linguistic resources is carried by the PM: linguists do not need to create their own TMs or glossaries, they can spend their whole working time on translating, revising, and QA tasks. They have no software to download, install, troubleshoot, or upgrade, and can collaborate easily in the cloud with other linguists, taking advantage of shared TMs and glossaries and using MT without needing their own API key (see Chapter 7), sharing data in real time and progressing to the next workflow step without needing to exchange packages by email. Perhaps less positively, the PM has significant managerial control over the conditions, deadlines, and remuneration rates of participating linguists, and has the power to observe their work in almost real time, as well as prevent them from accessing their 'own' work for future leverage purposes (a security measure often appreciated by clients but experienced by linguists as frustrating). For some translators, this can lead to a sense of lost professional autonomy, and they may see a TMS as a system of control as much as a tool to aid their productivity (see Chapter 12). The reality of the market, however, is that the TMS is very much here to stay, with more and more work coming through such platforms.

Advanced TMS Features – Phrase TMS

Unlike WFA, Phrase TMS (developed as Memsource Cloud from 2010 to 2022) was designed from the start as a collaborative TMS with a strong focus on the LSP's administrative requirements and the project manager role. Four subscription-based plans are available (https://phrase.com/pricing), priced by a combination of the number of PMs (linked to variable numbers of free linguist accounts) and the range of advanced features provided (including, for instance, 'integrations', i.e. API-based connectors to external systems and tools such as WordPress and Microsoft SharePoint). All but the custom Enterprise plan come with a free one-month trial, which allows the advanced features to be explored by anyone, including individual freelancers. Phrase TMS also has a well-developed, cost-free Academic edition (https://phrase.com/roles/academia) designed to give students project management as well as CAT and MT experience, along with certification programmes for both students and their lecturers. In the description that follows, we will present only the features of Phrase (Team edition) that are additional to those offered by WFA. Other TMS systems (e.g. Lionbridge Translation Workspace, Wordbee, XTM Cloud) offer comparable functionalities to the ones described below, so as with WFA, the conceptual understanding you gain by experimenting with Phrase TMS will be largely transferrable.

User Management

Phrase TMS is built around a hierarchy of three main user categories (Administrator, Project Manager, Linguist) and a sophisticated and customisable system of permissions in which each role can do everything a lower-category user can do, plus some role-specific higher-level capabilities. At the top of the tree is the Administrator (a role WFA lacks), who runs the whole Phrase TMS account on behalf of the company and is responsible for creating PM accounts (the number allowed depends on the subscription plan). PMs can then create and manage projects, resources (TMs, TBs) and linguist accounts, and linguists are notified of jobs, with resources ready set up, by automated email, and do their translation work in a familiar online editor (see Chapter 3), much as in WFA but with more fine-grained control options.

The Administrator's Home page displays a (configurable) dashboard showing graphical data for different aspects of the LSP's use of the system (Figure 8.15), which gives quite a full picture of the performance of the business.

Figure 8.15 Phrase TMS Administrator dashboard.

The Administrator can select data for a specific time period and each default tile (other charts can be added) can be clicked to expand information about the LSP's overall *Jobs* (by language pair, domain, status, client, file type); *Issues* (jobs overdue by project, language pair, workflow step, linguist); *Costs* (by date, language pair, client, project, linguist); *Leverage* (by date, client, language pair); *Machine translation* (jobs by MT engine, MT savings and leverage); and *Words* (by date, language pair, client, and domain).

Whenever a new User is created in Phrase TMS, mandatory information includes Names, Email, Username, Role, and Time zone (a fully-fledged TMS must be able to manage global projects). The least powerful of the three roles is Linguist, which can be created by either an Administrator or a PM, who can determine whether the linguist can make changes to the TB and TM, and whether they are allowed to use MT (Figure 8.16).

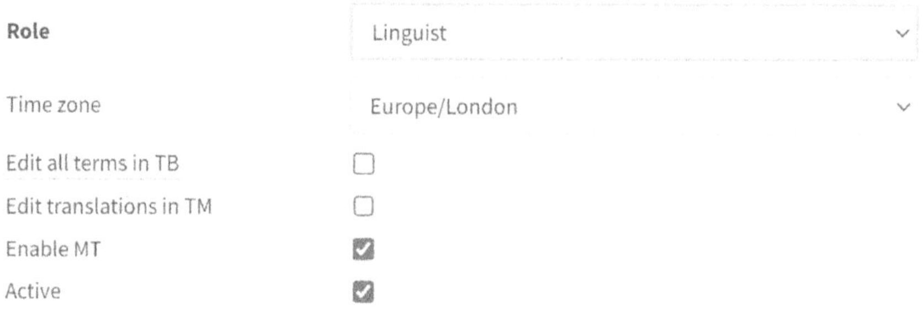

Role	Linguist	⌄

Time zone	Europe/London	⌄

Edit all terms in TB	☐
Edit translations in TM	☐
Enable MT	☑
Active	☑

Figure 8.16 Phrase TMS Linguist role options.

They can also apply a Price List to a Linguist's work and a Net Rate Scheme, a more sophisticated version of WFA's Rate option, which sets out what percentage of the full price will be paid for different types of TM match and degrees of MT post-editing (see Chapter 3). Another powerful concept which can be applied to all PM and Linguist accounts is *Relevancy*, which allows the creator to specify the user's SL(s) and TL(s), specialist domain(s) and subdomain(s), the client(s) they can work for and the workflow steps (Translation, Revision, Client Review, or any custom steps) they are able to undertake. If all these parameters are set for all users in the database, a PM can easily filter it to shortlist linguists able to work on a new project in a specific domain and language pair.

In addition to these Linguist settings, when a PM user is being created many further parameters need to be set which determine the exact scope of their powers over projects and other users. All options are active by default, which is potentially dangerous because, for instance, unless the relevant options are *deselected*, a new PM would have the right to see, modify, and delete data (Projects, TMs, TBs) owned by other PMs, in addition to creating and managing their own data: though there may be circumstances in which this is desirable for a senior PM, it would be inappropriate to give such wide access to most PMs. The categories for which decisions on these permissions need to be made are: *Projects, Project templates, Translation memories, Term bases,* and *Users,* and some of the options need to be handled with care – for example allowing a new PM user to 'View all data' or 'Modify Setup's server settings' (see Figure 8.17).

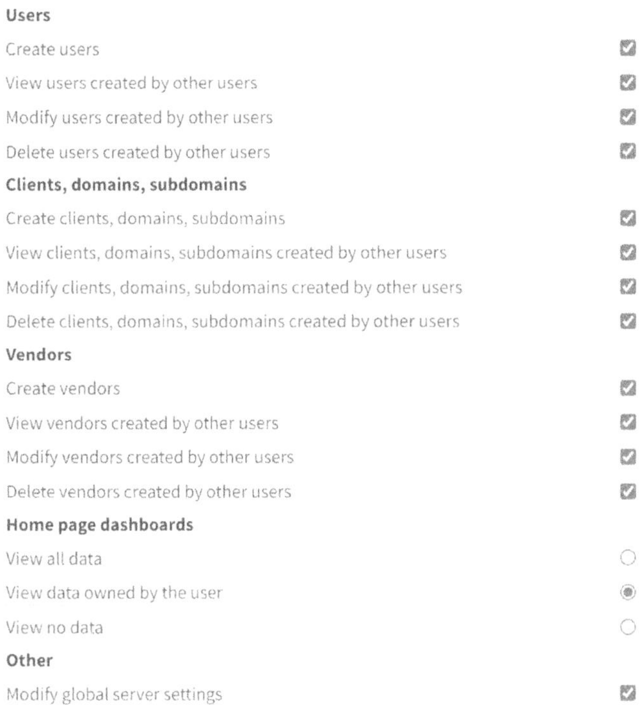

Users

Create users	☑
View users created by other users	☑
Modify users created by other users	☑
Delete users created by other users	☑

Clients, domains, subdomains

Create clients, domains, subdomains	☑
View clients, domains, subdomains created by other users	☑
Modify clients, domains, subdomains created by other users	☑
Delete clients, domains, subdomains created by other users	☑

Vendors

Create vendors	☑
View vendors created by other users	☑
Modify vendors created by other users	☑
Delete vendors created by other users	☑

Home page dashboards

View all data	○
View data owned by the user	◉
View no data	○

Other

Modify global server settings	☑

Figure 8.17 Phrase TMS default PM permissions.

These many settings serve to control very tightly which users have access to which parts of which of the many projects that an LSP may be working on at any time, but they also simplify management of large projects by providing the basis of semi-automated linguist selection, financials, and communications between team members.

Project Setup and Workflow

In Phrase TMS, Projects can only be set up by PMs or (less commonly) Administrators. They may be based on a previous project structure (using a template) or created from scratch. *Name*, *SL*, and *TL* (may be multiple) are mandatory; optional parameters include *Client* (selected from a list set up by the PM or Administrator), *Domain*, and *Subdomain*, *Due date*, *Status* (New – Assigned – Completed – Cancelled), and Purchase Order number. There is then a tabbed list of advanced options for the PM to set, or at least review, before creating the project (Figure 8.18).

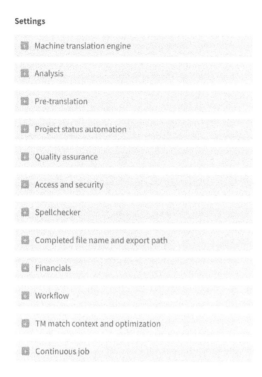

Settings

- Machine translation engine
- Analysis
- Pre-translation
- Project status automation
- Quality assurance
- Access and security
- Spellchecker
- Completed file name and export path
- Financials
- Workflow
- TM match context and optimization
- Continuous job

Figure 8.18 Phrase TMS Advanced Project Setting tabs.

Among the most important of these, *Pre-translation* determines whether the linguist will start work on a file automatically pre-translated from the TM (down to a configurable fuzzy threshold) and/or MT; *Access and Security* turns email notifications on or off, determines whether external vendors can be used, and sets linguists' rights to download the job for translation in the optional off-line editor, whether they can edit the source segment, tags etc.; *Workflow* determines whether the project will include Revision and/or Client review steps (custom steps can also be added); and *Continuous Job* enables scheduled review of source files to check for any changes, allowing the project to operate in **agile** mode.

At this point in the project setup, the PM can select the source of MT proposals for the project (on Phrase Translate, see Chapter 7), and one or more TM(s), TB(s) and existing reference translations that can contribute to pre-translation and will be used by linguists as they work, and/or create new ones. When creating a new TM, the PM, in addition to mandatory **metadata** fields for *Name, SL,* and *TL(s)* – TMs can be multilingual – may choose to select *client, domain* and *subdomain* from the same drop-down lists as for the overall project. TBs are created in the same way, and legacy data can be imported into the TM via TMX and into the TB via Excel or TBX (see https://support.phrase.com/hc/en-us/articles/5709733407772, and Chapters 3 and 4 of this book) – but again, only PMs can do this. Linguists can only update the databases (if they have the relevant permissions) by adding TUs and term records: they cannot create or upload them, or download them for their own future use (unlike in WFA, where, as we saw, this may be allowed).

Once the Phrase project structure has been set up and the project created, a new job is started for each ST, which can be split automatically between several linguists to save time if it is long. Each workflow step requires a new job. The ST(s) are uploaded and optionally pre-translated (determined by a tick box), a due date and time are set, and appropriate translation 'providers' (linguists) for each file and TL are selected in order of preference from the drop-down list(s) automatically populated from the Relevancy information in the linguist users database. They can then be notified automatically by a standardised 'New Work' email, either all at once or at set intervals (e.g. every ten minutes) (Figure 8.19) until one of them responds by accepting the job (so if you are a linguist looking for this type of work you need to monitor your email closely).

Figure 8.19 Phrase TMS Notify providers dialog.

The linguist accepts the job by clicking on a link in the notification email and is immediately taken to the linguist platform displaying the project and job details. The job opens in the standard Phrase environment (see Chapter 3), and the linguist works through it using all the resources (pre-translation, MT, TM, reference, and TB proposals) allocated by the PM. Once the job is complete, the linguist navigates back to the project and changes the job's status to 'Completed by linguist', which sends a notification to the PM and updates their project dashboard. At this point, the linguist can no longer open the job (as in WFA when the job is 'revoked'), so you need to be very sure that you have indeed finished; other stages (e.g. revision) will be done by somebody else and by default you will not see any changes they make. As with WFA, this can be experienced by translators as disempowering, and even unethical.

Conclusion

Whether designed from the start to use the cloud (Lionbridge Translation Workspace, Phrase TMS, POEditor, RWS Language Cloud, Wordbee, XTM Cloud, etc.) or introduced to add collaborative functionality to an established workstation tool (memoQ Server, Trados Live Team, Déjà Vu TEAMserver, etc.), a modern TMS is much more than just a translation environment. The collaboration and project management features explored in this chapter by reference to WFA and Phrase are implemented in different ways across all such tools to create working environments which translators today are likely to experience increasingly often. TMS tools undoubtedly present both advantages and challenges for translators, and understanding the concepts underlying how they work behind the scenes, not just in the immediate environment of the translation editor, should help to mitigate some of the less positive aspects such as a sense of compromised autonomy (see Chapter 12). As suggested in the Introduction to this chapter, the TMS concept is rapidly evolving in the direction of full-scale business manage-ment systems on the one hand, and client-facing purchasing platforms on the other. These allow translation jobs to be ordered, quoted for, routed to a suitable linguist and delivered entirely automatically, without the inter-vention of a project manager. In Chapters 3 and 7 we explored Matecat as a powerful (and free) translation environment for linguists, but if instead you click the Buy translation button after uploading a file, the platform can also outsource translations automatically to a suitably qualified freelance linguist. In Figure 8.20, a small English to French job has been routed auto-matically – and almost instantaneously – to a linguist called Audrey who has a five-star rating and apparently translates about 38,000 words each month on average:

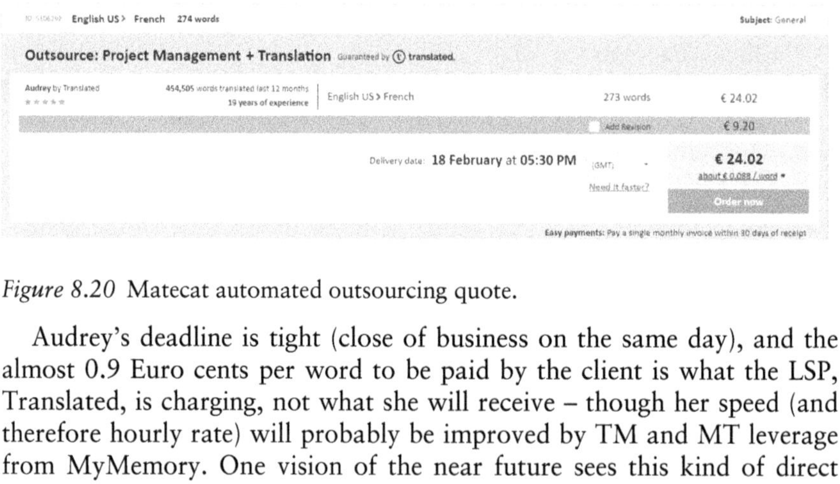

Figure 8.20 Matecat automated outsourcing quote.

Audrey's deadline is tight (close of business on the same day), and the almost 0.9 Euro cents per word to be paid by the client is what the LSP, Translated, is charging, not what she will receive – though her speed (and therefore hourly rate) will probably be improved by TM and MT leverage from MyMemory. One vision of the near future sees this kind of direct interaction between client and translator, mediated by an automatic system with no role (or costs) for a project manager in the middle, becoming the dominant model, and many larger LSPs have already developed automated client platforms of their own. However, it seems clear that big, complex projects will continue for the foreseeable future to require the experience of a human PM, not least to cope with the unpredictable vagaries introduced by all the other humans in the supply chain, so the role of project manager seems secure for some long time to come.

Follow-Up Tasks and Reflection

1. Create a trial project manager account for yourself in Wordfast Anywhere and use any translation data you have available to set up and manage a test project with one or more language pairs, following the steps outlined in the first part of this chapter. If you have friends or colleagues who are translators, ask some of them to become involved, but if not, you can create one or more dummy accounts that will allow you to view the project from the perspectives of both PM and linguist. How do the issues that preoccupy a PM differ from those familiar to you as a translator? Are there potential conflicts between the two roles, or do you feel the collaborative environment of a TMS is beneficial to either, or both? If you were able to work with other translators, how did they feel about the experience?

2. Now use the same data to set up the same project using a Phrase TMS trial account. What differences do you note compared to WFA, from the perspectives of both PM and linguist? Do you think the greater project management complexity of Phrase is justified by the enhanced flexibility it offers, and if so, for what type or size of translation project? As with WFA, assess any positive and negative aspects of working as part of a Phrase TMS project team.

3. Decide which tool you prefer to use in each role and list the reasons why (this will give you a useful perspective when it comes to assessing other tools in the future). Did you enjoy experimenting with project management, and if so, is it a role in which you might see yourself working?

Further Reading

Though written in 2012, Mark Shuttleworth's overview of TMS in the *Routledge encyclopedia of translation technology* (Shuttleworth, 2015) remains useful, especially on the topic of business systems. A succinct and reliable source of information about current individual TMS systems is the online 'TMS Feature Explorer' (Schipack, n.d.) hosted by Nimdzi Insights, which includes details of the history, design, and capabilities of many tools, along with links to YouTube videos about them. Nimdzi's online *Language technology atlas* (Akhulkova et al., 2022) is also a good way to monitor new developments, while Andrej Zito's (n.d.) 'Localization academy' YouTube channel offers informal 'first experience' video reviews of many TMS systems from a new user's perspective.

9   Subtitle Editing Tools

Key Questions

- How does subtitling relate to translation tools and technologies?
- What different purposes does subtitling fulfil?
- What is the difference between **open** and **closed subtitles**?
- What are the important constraints on translated subtitles?
- How is subtitle reading speed calculated?
- What are the main features of a subtitle editing application?
- How do workstation and cloud-based subtitling tools differ?
- How far can the on-screen appearance of subtitles be manipulated?
- What are some of the main subtitle file formats?
- In what ways can subtitles be displayed with video files?

Introduction

Until recently, the activity of subtitling and the computerised tools that support it might not have appeared to have a natural place in a book about translation technology: subtitling was traditionally regarded as a specialised type of video editing. After all, a high proportion of subtitling does not involve translation at all but is done for reasons of inclusion and access, in the same language as the original audiovisual (AV) production. However, the ongoing global explosion of both amateur and 'official' AV content makes translated subtitles an increasingly important mode of intercultural communication, now widely researched in the expanding discipline of Audiovisual Translation (AVT) Studies (see for example Pérez González, 2018). The opportunities for translators to work in the broad field of subtitling are correspondingly extensive:

> the gamut of audiovisual genres that are translated nowadays is virtually limitless, whether for commercial, ludic or instructional purposes: films, TV series, cartoons, sports programmes, reality shows, documentaries,

DOI: 10.4324/9781003160793-9

cookery programmes, current affairs, edutainment material, commer-
cials, educational lectures and corporate videos to name but a few.

(Díaz Cintas & Remael, 2021: 3)

The process of producing subtitles, in any language, requires mastery of a
specialised type of software that stands in a similar relationship to 'standard' translation tools as software localisation applications (see Chapter 10):
'Would-be subtitlers are expected to demonstrate high technical know-how
and familiarity with increasingly more powerful subtitling software' (Díaz
Cintas, 2015: 634). The worldwide market for subtitling tools ('solutions')
is forecast to grow by 7.7% year on year, from USD$261 million in 2020
to around USD$441 million in 2027 (QYResearch, 2021: n.p.), with far
greater additional revenue generated from commercial use of such tools by
LSPs, so it should offer opportunities to translators well into the future.
However, as with terminology management (Chapter 4), effective subtitling
is not just a matter of technical competence; it also requires a clear understanding of the aims, challenges, and methods underlying the activity itself.
This chapter will therefore start by outlining some of the basic principles
of subtitling practice, before exploring how to implement them using two
different tools, selected from the wide range available for their conceptual
representativeness and the transferability of the user experience.

Different Subtitling Requirements

Different types of subtitles serve different purposes. Modern broadcast
media companies are subtitling more and more of their video content
for reasons of equal access, led in the UK by the BBC: 'The BBC subtitles 100% of its broadcast content, and some of its online-only content'
(BBC Academy, 2021a: n.p.). On the other hand, while the BBC produces
only same-language subtitles, online streaming services such as Disney+ and
Netflix offer a very wide range of content with human-translated subtitles
in many languages. Meanwhile, many videos on YouTube come with a
button to turn on automated 'subtitles' (more correctly, a word-by-word
transcription), generated by speech recognition software, which can then be
auto-translated by MT into many other languages (though often not very
accurately – see below for reasons why this is the case). All these cases
involve **closed subtitles** (also called **closed captions**), which are not part of
the video stream and are not displayed on screen by default, but need to
be switched on by the viewer. **Open subtitles** on the other hand, which are
often used for international film distribution, are *burnt* (or *hard coded*) into
the video file and cannot be switched off. The primary purpose of broadcast closed subtitles is disability access, with an intended (but not exclusive)
audience of viewers who are deaf or hearing impaired:

> Subtitles are primarily intended to serve viewers with loss of hearing,
> but they are used by a wide range of people: around 10% of broadcast

viewers use subtitles regularly, increasing to 35% for some online content. The majority of these viewers are not hard of hearing.

(BBC Academy, 2021b: n.p.)

Most broadcast subtitles are prepared in advance, but there are also live subtitles (e.g. for news broadcasts or sports events) which are generally produced by **respeaking**: in a manner somewhat similar to simultaneous interpreting, a same-language subtitler listens to the audio stream and respeaks the words, for clarity and to remove background noise, into a high-quality audio system, and this 'clean' input is then processed by speech-to-text software, with real-time corrections keyboarded by the subtitler as necessary, for display on screen with just a slight delay to account for the production time.

There are significant differences between *intra*lingual subtitles for accessibility purposes and *inter*lingual subtitles done by organisations such as Netflix for people who are not hearing impaired but cannot understand the original language. When equality of access to information is the goal, the speech content of the broadcast will as far as possible be transcribed verbatim: any alterations would be confusing for lip-readers, and this kind of subtitle can also support viewers with reading difficulties, as well as language learners. Key criteria for success are satisfactory user experience, and readability:

> Good subtitles convey to the viewer as much of the experience of watching with sound as possible. The text needs to be readable, match the dialogue as closely as possible, be well timed and not obscure important parts of the video. Achieving all of this at the same time isn't always possible, so the subtitler needs to make an editorial decision about the best balance.
>
> (BBC Academy, 2021a: n.p.)

Subtitling is always a matter of compromise between the conflicting requirements of *completeness* and *concision* of information. Accessibility subtitlers can use visual means to convey meta-information about the audio stream: for instance, changes of speaker may be indicated by different coloured text, and other significant audio elements (sound effects) annotated in CAPITALS or [square brackets]. On the other hand, a hearing viewer using translated subtitles will typically not need colours or indication of background sounds, but will want an easily assimilable, condensed version of the dialogue in their own language that they can read quickly and that distracts them as little as possible from following the video content. Particularly in a production with fast-paced and/or rapidly alternating dialogue, a completely satisfactory translation from the information perspective may well be impossible to read in the time it would be on screen. Available time and space impose strict constraints on the translator-subtitler which require more complex editorial decisions than those facing an intralingual subtitler who is basically transcribing. A key objective of subtitling tools is to support that decision-making by ensuring that information about the constraints is constantly available, helping the translator to focus on meeting the complex requirements of the job.

Box 9.1: Key Requirements for Translated Subtitles

They should aim to:

- Convey as much of the meaning of the speech as possible in a limited space/time;
- Also convey the meaning of any significant background music or on-screen text;
- Be as succinct as possible, to limit cognitive distraction from the video;
- Coincide in time with speech segments;
- Consist of meaningful and self-contained syntactic/semantic units;
- Appear in a legible font/size against a contrasting background;
- Remain on screen (only) long enough to be read at a reasonable speed;
- Be separated by a minimum gap (typically two frames/0.1 seconds) to avoid flashing effects.

They should normally not:

- Take up more screen space than strictly necessary (normally, max. two lines at the bottom);
- Exceed a maximum line length specified in language-specific guidelines;
- Break lines at an unnatural place (e.g. between article and noun);
- Run across a change of shot;
- Anticipate the on-screen action or what is about to be said.

The often-conflicting requirements set out in Box 9.1 mean that a strategy of transcribing the original audio verbatim, then translating it freely in the normal way, is unlikely to be effective. Instead, the translator will need to be *selective* (judging which meaning elements are essential and which can be omitted) and linguistically *creative* (finding shorter synonyms and alternative formulations, simplifying syntax) to *compress* the TT so that it conveys essential information in the on-screen time and space available. This is assessed by a measure of the reading speed of the subtitles, usually in units representing **characters per second (CPS)**, i.e. relating a subtitle's *length* in characters (including spaces) to its *duration* on screen. Different organisations, languages, and locales have different guidelines about maximum reading speed: for English, for instance, the range is normally 37–42 CPS, whereas for a non-alphabetic language such as Chinese it may be 16 CPS, and for Japanese as low as 13. For further details on compression constraints, see Díaz Cintas and Remael (2021), especially Chapters 4 and 6.

In order to help the subtitler to meet these complex requirements, any subtitle editing tool will need to include at least the following components (Box 9.2).

Box 9.2: Essential Components of a Subtitle Editor

- A video viewing window with the usual navigation controls;
- A timeline, graduated in either seconds or frames, to help with **spotting** (timing) the subtitles (a process also known as **cueing** or *timecoding*);
- A representation of the *audio waveform*, to help with precise identification of the start and end of each speech segment and the **in and out times** of the corresponding subtitle;
- A space in which to type, edit, and format subtitle text;
- A numbered subtitle list typically showing the text of each subtitle, its in and out times, and an automatic reading speed calculation in CPS.

What makes the subtitle editor special is that these components are *synchronised*, so that when the video plays, the timeline, waveform display, and draft subtitles also advance to give a real-time preview of how the subtitled clip will look, and allow detailed adjustments of timing, or edits to the text. A particularly useful aspect of this synchronisation is that clicking on a subtitle in the list will take you to the relevant point in the video and audio tracks, and vice versa.

Once the subtitling job is complete, the subtitle list and corresponding timecodes can be exported from the program in one or more text-based formats readable by video players. The simplest and most widely known of these, *SubRip Text*, produces by default **Unicode** (**UTF-8**)-encoded files with a .SRT extension, which saves each subtitle in three lines: its numerical identifier, start and end timecodes in hr:min:sec format, and the text itself (Figure 9.1).

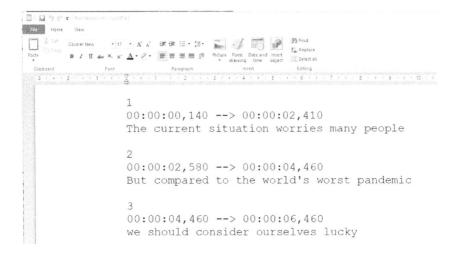

Figure 9.1 Exported SubRip (.SRT) file opened in Wordpad.

If the .SRT file is saved with the same filename and in the same location as the video file, a player will find it and automatically display the subtitles at the bottom of the screen, picking up the timecodes to synchronise them with those of the video. Alternatively, to create open (i.e. always-on) subtitles the file needs to be hard coded into the video file itself using a separate application such as the free, **open-source**, and **cross-platform** Handbrake video transcoder. Throughout this chapter we will use a short German-language documentary about pandemics as our example clip, which we will subtitle into English. Figure 9.2 shows Handbrake open in its 'Subtitles' tab, working to hard-encode into the video a subtitle file called Pandemics .srt, which it has identified as being in English and encoded in UTF-8. Note the check mark in the 'Burn in' box (the expression 'burning in' goes back to the days when subtitles were literally imprinted in celluloid film by heat), and the progress bar at bottom left indicating that it has taken just over four minutes to re-encode 62.3% of the clip with the subtitles (so this can be quite a lengthy process).

Figure 9.2 Handbrake 1.5 'burning in' a .SRT file.

Handbrake is capable of performing many types of video transcoding apart from subtitle burning and, unlike some otherwise similar tools, it works well with subtitle files in Arabic, Chinese, and other non-Latin scripts, so it is worth the effort of learning to use it.

Workstation-Based Subtitling – Aegisub

The leading professional workstation-based subtitling tool is WinCaps Q4, which has many advanced features and a seven-day free trial but is otherwise expensive and runs only under Windows. There are several free workstation tools which do essentially the same job as WinCaps in quite similar ways, including Open Subtitle Editor, Subtitle Edit, and Subtitle Workshop, but the one we will explore here is the open-source tool Aegisub 3.2.2. Aegisub is cross-platform, and is popular with **fansubbers** around the world because it offers rich formatting possibilities and provides all the key features and working techniques of a high-end commercial tool. It also has a special translation mode and is well served by the JTFREE series of video tutorials on YouTube (Ricks, 2020), though we should note that the official online Help files are no longer available. Aegisub is a sophisticated piece of software with a wide range of options, including many interface languages, so the presentation that follows will only be able to cover its core functionality, but it provides an excellent introduction to subtitling concepts and practice.

User Interface (UI) Basics

After launching Aegisub, opening a clip from the Video > Open Video…
menu and creating the first few subtitles, the main interface window looks
as in Figure 9.3. The (resizable) video viewer with navigation slider beneath
is at upper left, showing a preview of the current subtitle, while the audio
waveform viewer at upper right has a timeline in seconds above it and vertical lines marking the subtitle's start (in, red) and end (out, blue) times.

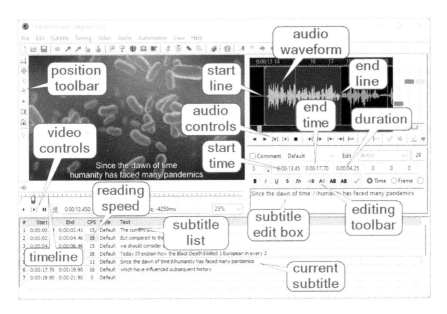

Figure 9.3 Aegisub main UI window.

Since this is primarily a graphical UI, spotting of subtitles is done by
clicking on the waveform (left mouse button to set the red start line, right to
set the blue end line): you can play just the audio in between by clicking the
'Play selection' icon on the audio controls toolbar, and adjust the subtitle
spotting by dragging the start and end lines until they exactly match the
speech segment you are subtitling. Once the segment has been accurately
timecoded, you can type the text in the edit box – in the case of the current
subtitle here (no. 5), the text has been split between two lines, the shorter
above to minimise visual intrusion into the video, by insertion of a *new line
code* ('\N'). When everything is correct, you click the green tick-mark icon
on the toolbar above the edit box, which confirms the subtitle, adds it to
the subtitle list in the lower portion of the window, and clears the box for
you to type the next subtitle. The same toolbar contains icons to toggle the
timeline between seconds and frames, along with some basic text formatting options (bold, italic etc., font name and size, fill colour, etc.). Note that

the reading speed for the currently selected subtitle (11 CPS) is well within normal limits, but the figure for nos. 4 and 6 (16 CPS) is rather high so it is shaded in light pink, while no. 2, at 18 CPS, is a darker pink – this clip has a rather fast voiceover. The visual CPS warning goes through several further shades before reaching red at around 26 CPS, to indicate that the subtitle text really must be further compressed.

Formatting, Styles, Position

Conventional subtitles tend to display as one or two lines of white text centred horizontally near the bottom of the screen, and if you save your Aegisub subtitles in .SRT format, that is what you will get. However, one of Aegisub's strengths is that it allows application of a very wide range of 'visual typesetting' formats, along with flexible positioning and orientation, all of which can be preserved by exporting the subtitle file in *Advanced SubStation Alpha (.ASS)* format – still a text file but containing much more information. Aegisub's more advanced formatting options only appear when you click the Edit button to open the Style Editor dialog (Figure 9.4).

Figure 9.4 Aegisub Style Editor – defining 'Wacky' style.

This not only gives you control of additional presentational features (font colour, outline and shadow width and colour, precise positioning, whether to place an opaque box behind the characters, even character encoding), it allows specific combinations of all these attributes to be defined as *styles*, much as in MS Word and other office programs. This can be useful if, for instance, you want to differentiate between two or more speakers by font colour: instead of resetting the colour each time the speaker changes, you simply create different styles, associate each with a different 'Actor', then select the relevant actor for each subtitle. Typesetting options can also be combined with the movement and rotation (including 3D) controls available from the position toolbar to make the kind of creative solutions beloved of fansubbers (Figure 9.5).

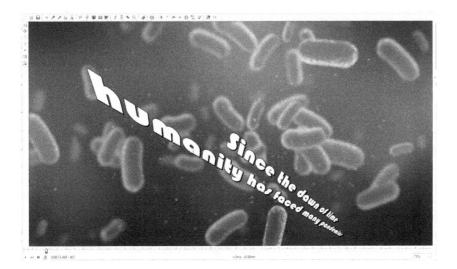

Figure 9.5 'Wacky' style applied to subtitle 5.

You may not want or need this kind of effect in your real subtitling work, but it is fun to explore the visual possibilities available in Aegisub, and many of the individual attributes are likely to prove useful. If you create styles that you want to reuse later, you can pull down the Subtitle menu, open the Style Manager dialog and copy them into a default or user-definable storage location, from where you can retrieve them for use in subsequent subtitling projects. Finally, the Styling Assistant, accessed from the same menu, allows you to preview the audio or video stream corresponding to the active subtitle with the current style applied, and optionally see how it will look with different styles that you may have created.

Translation Assistant

The same Subtitle menu gives access to another unusual feature of Aegisub, the Translation Assistant. This is useful if you already have a subtitle file for your video, perhaps because you have been sent one in the original language by the client or LSP. If that is the case, after opening the video, you load the existing subtitle file from the File menu and select the first subtitle you want to translate, then pull down the Subtitle menu and select 'Translation Assistant …', and type the translation into the lower box (Figure 9.6).

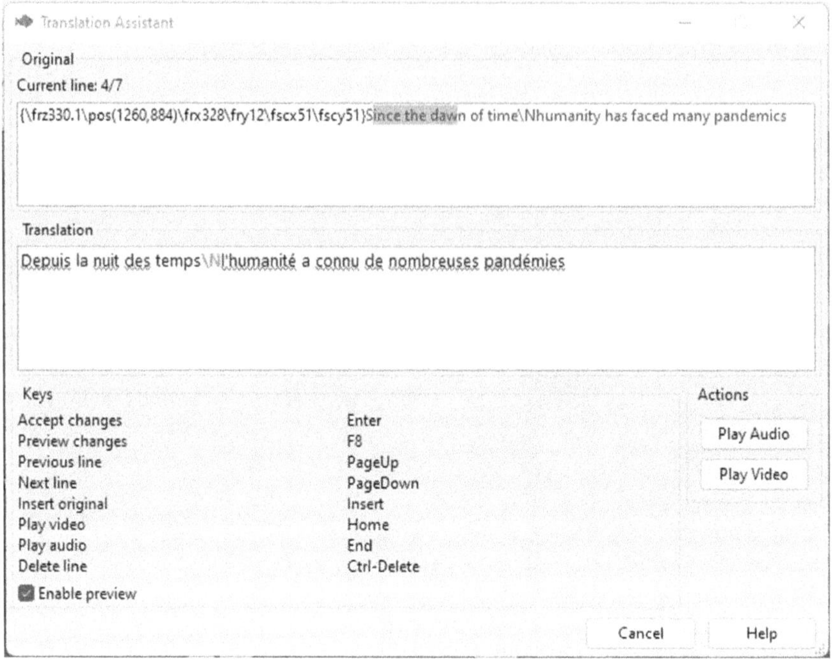

Figure 9.6 Aegisub Translation Assistant.

Since the original subtitles have already been spotted, you do not need to do this again, though you can preview the audio or the video corresponding to the subtitle timecodes and adjust them if necessary. Once you are happy with the translation, press 'Enter' to insert the translated subtitle in the place of the original in both the video preview (Figure 9.7) and the subtitle list, then move on to the next one.

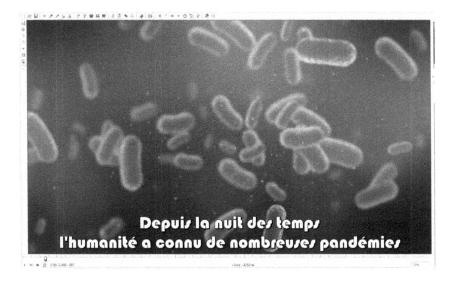

Figure 9.7 Subtitle 5 translated into French.

This is a convenient way to produce versions in potentially many TLs from a 'master' subtitle list, whether in the original language or in translation, which has already been spotted and adapted by the original subtitler to meet reading speed and other constraints.

Cloud-Based Subtitling – Matesub

As with CAT tools (Chapter 2) and TMSs (Chapter 7), there is a growing tendency for new subtitling and other AVT applications to be developed not for the workstation but in the cloud. A new generation of tools, including Ooona, Happyscribe, Kapwing, and Veed, are now exploiting the convenience of cross-platform access from anywhere via a slick web-based interface to sell subtitling apps and services to individual subtitlers, LSPs, and corporate clients. At the same time, a convergence is taking place online between subtitling, **automatic speech recognition** (**ASR**), and MT technologies which may well point to the future of the practice. We will explore this below by focusing on Matesub, by Translated, the developers of Matecat (see Chapter 7). At the time of writing, Matesub is in beta testing and free to access, but is due to become a subscription-based (**SaaS**) tool. Apart from a more modern-looking interface, Matesub's cloud-based architecture offers several key advantages. First, as with TMS systems such as Phrase TMS, XTM Cloud, or Wordbee (Chapter 7), there is no software for the user to download, install, maintain and upgrade: updates happen silently in the cloud. Secondly, Matesub can take advantage of cloud-based computing power to connect the subtitler to other services that would be beyond the capabilities of a workstation-based tool – most notably, an accurate *multilingual speech-to-text decoder*, as well as the same AI-based MyMemory TM and MT engine used by Matecat. This advanced connectivity allows Matesub to process the source video in ways that substantially automate some of the more routine and time-consuming aspects of subtitling, particularly spotting and transcription of the SL audio, as well as attempting to translate it automatically. In fact, Matesub's auto-generated subtitling design intentionally parallels the evolution of CAT tools in the direction of MT post-editing, on the assumption that it will be easier and quicker for the subtitler to post-edit its AI output than to translate from scratch. However, our experiments show this not to be reliably the case yet for complex content, so the workflow we illustrate below will not use the auto-generation option.

It is worth considering some of the constraining factors which in general make it extra difficult for MT to produce usable subtitles (Box 9.3).

Box 9.3: Constraints on MT for Subtitling

- Context and ambiguity: in a video production, especially a non-documentary one, much of the context needed to resolve potential ambiguities is visual, not verbal, and current AI translation systems have no access to this information;
- Unit/screen coherence: longer verbal strings (sentences) need to be divided into several separate subtitles, but these must make sense sequentially, both as partial sub-strings, and in combination as a coherent utterance;
- SL and TL syntactic differences: the wider the structural differences between the languages, the more difficult it becomes to achieve this coherence;
- Compliance with guidelines: each individual subtitle needs to meet the reading speed guidelines adopted for the project (see below), which puts further pressure on the AI's choice of a translation solution;
- Speed of delivery: when more is said than can be accommodated by a simple transcription/translation process (see above), subtitles need to be compressed by selective omission and rewording. This a significant challenge for expert humans and currently well beyond the capabilities of AI, because in addition to verbal tricks (using shorter synonyms, modifying syntax, and swapping parts of speech), it requires awareness of complex contexts (above), which may include narrative conventions and even the plot and characterisation of a whole video.

Each of these factors adds a constraint to the production of MT subtitle output that is absent from the 'free' translation of a single sentence in a document. While their individual effects will weigh differently in different language pairs and project types, their cumulative impact is such that, except in the simplest projects (basic, short sentences with unambiguous content, spoken slowly), it seems too much to expect Matesub, YouTube, or any other current platform to produce consistently usable automatically translated subtitles – but we suggest you experiment and make up your own mind. This does not, however, reduce the interest and usefulness of Matesub's other technologies, which we explore below.

Project Setup

Setting up a new project in Matesub is simply a matter of giving it a name, uploading the video, and selecting the appropriate SL (Figure 9.8).

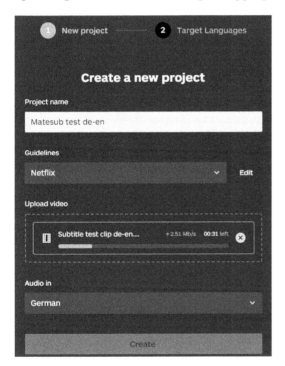

Figure 9.8 Matesub Create a new project dialog.

Like Aegisub, Matesub will automatically tell you as you write subtitles whether you are exceeding default limits on **characters per line** (**CPL**) or per second (**CPS**), but it has the additional ability to apply different sets of guidelines, which the user can select from the drop-down Guidelines menu (Figure 9.9).

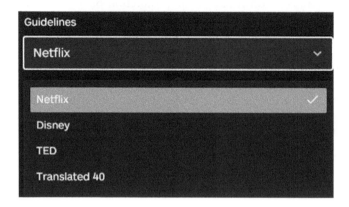

Figure 9.9 Selection of guidelines.

We will keep the default, Netflix, as it is the most complete and the figures are quite similar anyway, but a useful aspect of this choice is that if, for instance, you are subtitling a TED talk or a Disney production, you can be confident you are adhering to the correct standards. Clicking on the Edit button to the right of the Guidelines drop-down opens up a table listing details of the selected guidelines, which the user can customise into their own version if required, covering default text alignment and font name, as well as default spotting parameters: minimum and maximum subtitle duration (time on screen) and minimum interval between subtitles, each expressed in either frames or seconds; maximum number of lines; and reading speed, expressed as both maximum CPL and maximum CPS (Figure 9.10).

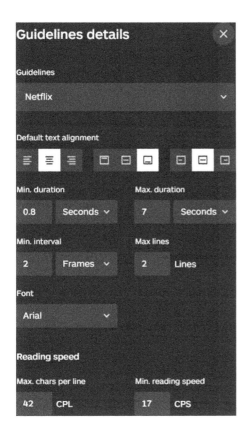

Figure 9.10 Netflix default guidelines.

Below this is a table of Exceptions giving alternative CPL and CPS settings for different languages and scripts which will be automatically applied if you select one of these as your TL (Figure 9.11).

English (Canada) ⌄	42	CPL	20	CPS	⊗
Serbian (Cyrillic) ⌄	39	CPL	17	CPS	⊗
Chinese (Simpl... ⌄	16	CPL	9	CPS	⊗
Chinese (Tradit... ⌄	16	CPL	9	CPS	⊗
Chinese (Tradit... ⌄	16	CPL	9	CPS	⊗
Japanese ⌄	13	CPL	4	CPS	⊗
Korean ⌄	16	CPL	12	CPS	⊗
Hindi ⌄	42	CPL	22	CPS	⊗

Figure 9.11 Some reading speed exceptions.

Once you have set the SL and other basic parameters for the project, clicking the big Create button takes you to the Target section of the setup (Figure 9.12), which is where you can select one or more TL(s) and decide whether to enable auto-generated subtitles.

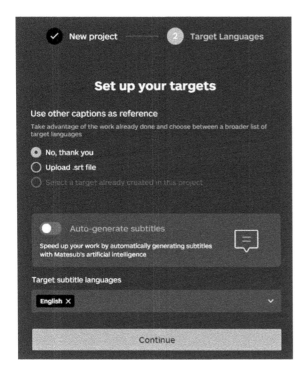

Figure 9.12 Matesub target setup.

A final interesting option here is to upload an existing subtitle file in .SRT format if you have one. The only reason Matesub gives for doing this is to broaden
the choice of TLs, perhaps by supplying text for an SL which its ASR cannot
handle, but if the .SRT file already contains a translation, it may also act as a
kind of subtitling **pivot language**, helping the AI create a translation in a third
language by creating the equivalent of a TM from the clip's original dialogue
aligned with a first set of human-translated subtitles, which capture solutions to
the complex constraint problems identified above. This would essentially allow
the AI to weight its auto-generated translation towards the existing subtitles,
rather than having only its own transcription (see below) to work with, which
might well produce improved results.

User Interface and Project Completion

Having finished the setup stage, we can now click 'Continue' and wait while the
program works on the video clip. Although this process is described as 'generating subtitles', we have said that we want to make our own and in fact Matesub
is only doing the first, but extremely useful, step in the process: converting the
SL speech in the audio track to text. When it has finished, clicking the Editor

button takes us into the main editing interface, most of the components of which are familiar from Aegisub, although the layout is different (Figure 9.13).

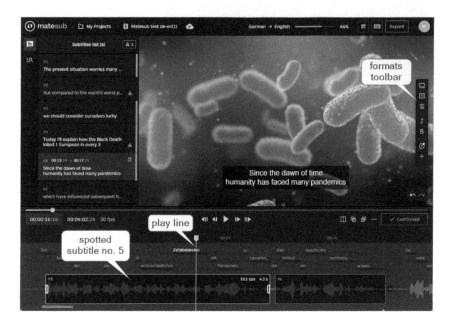

Figure 9.13 Matesub editor screen.

The subtitle list is to the left of the viewer, with the video controls centred below, while superimposed on the right side of the viewer window is a vertical strip of basic subtitle formatting controls (position, bold, italic, font colour) – these are much less extensive and flexible than those available in Aegisub's Style Editor. The most interesting element is at the bottom of the screen, where the vertical yellow play line synchronises not only the video and the audio waveform, but also an automated transcription of the SL narration, produced by the *speech-to-text* system and displayed word by word at the corresponding point in the timeline. You can download this transcription as a text file by clicking the Export button, which means that Matesub can be used just as an automatic transcription tool if required. In and out times can be set by clicking and dragging the mouse along the relevant part of the audio waveform (this spotting happens automatically when auto-generated subtitles are selected), with handles appearing at each end of the selected box for fine tuning (Figure 9.14).

Figure 9.14 Spotting with Matesub's synchronised transcript and waveform.

Another difference from Aegisub is that subtitles are typed directly into an expanding black box in the viewer window, and only added to the subtitle list when the Confirm Subtitle button is clicked. As the text being typed approaches the maximum CPS and CPL values allowed by the selected guidelines, alert boxes giving the current figures appear to the left (CPS) and right (CPL). In Figure 9.15, CPS is close to the maximum of 20 while CPL is in red because the 42-character maximum line length has been exceeded.

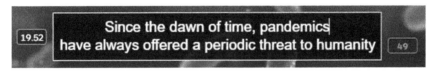

Figure 9.15 CPS and CPL figures for the active subtitle.

If the subtitle is confirmed despite this excessive length, a red warning triangle appears next to it in the subtitles list to encourage the user to revise it. Once all the subtitles have been spotted and translated, the Export button allows them to be written to various types of text files including .SRT and the similar, HTML5-based WebVTT (Web Video Text Tracks) supported by YouTube and most browsers, but not the rich .ASS format used by Aegisub to preserve positional and typesetting information. At that point the subtitles can be hard coded into the video if desired (see above).

Conclusion

Subtitling is a growth industry offering many opportunities to translators: Stasimioti (2022), for instance, describes the current shortage of media localisers, including subtitlers, as an industry-wide crisis amounting to a 'talent crunch' – though she also highlights the consequent conditions of 'stress and burnout' under which many practitioners find themselves working. To be employable in this field, you need not only a good conceptual overview of how subtitling tools work, but also extensive practice in the kind of *constrained* translation that subtitles typically require. Comparing the two types of tools discussed in this chapter, the 'traditional', workstation-based Aegisub has superior formatting capabilities and also offers a translation editor that facilitates the translation of existing subtitles. Matesub's AI-based auto-generated subtitles may not be of high enough quality to save you much time, but its automatic speech-to-text transcription and slick interface almost certainly will. The convergence of these different technologies in increasingly automated and user-friendly apps in the cloud seems to be the direction in which subtitling will continue to evolve, but the basic skills of spotting, information selection, and compressed translation will remain core to the subtitler's work, whether done professionally or as a fansubbing enthusiast.

Follow-Up Tasks and Reflection

1. Find the online Netflix Style Guide for your language(s) or locale(s) and compare its requirements to the English one (Netflix, 2021b). What are the most significant differences?
2. Open some YouTube videos belonging to different genres (e.g. documentary, children's cartoon, drama, etc.) in your first language and turn on automatic subtitles. How accurate is the transcription? What kinds of errors do you see? Are some types of clips more accurately transcribed than others?
3. Use a free subtitle download service such as Downsub (https://downsub .com) to download some auto-generated YouTube subtitles in your first language to a .SRT file. Open the file in Aegisub or another subtitling tool and edit a few transcribed lines to turn them into proper subtitles. What kinds of changes do you need to make?
4. Download some short clips of different genres in (one of) your foreign language(s) and test the quality of a) Matesub's automatic transcription of the SL speech; b) its automatic translation and production of subtitles in your first language. How useable are the subtitles? What kinds of errors do you find? Are some genres 'harder' than others for the system to cope with? Compare Matesub's transcription with those of other cloud-based subtitling tools that offer a free trial account.
5. Finally, select one of your downloaded clips and subtitle (part of) it properly in your first language using Aegisub. What kinds of decisions about spotting, translation, and compression do you find yourself having to make? Experiment with Aegisub's formatting options: which are the most useful for the type of clip you are working on?

Further Reading

On the historical, cultural, and theoretical dimensions of subtitling as an expanding translation practice, see Marie-Noëlle Guillot's (2018) chapter 'Subtitling on the cusp of its futures' in the *Routledge handbook of audiovisual translation*, as well as the updated core book *Subtitling: concepts and practices* by Jorge Díaz Cintas and Aline Remael (2021). Díaz Cintas's (2015) entry on 'Technological strides in subtitling' in the *Routledge encyclopedia of translation technology* gives a useful overview of the development of subtitling technologies. The BBC's online guidelines (BBC Academy, 2021a & b) contain a wealth of useful practical tips about how to edit and present subtitles, and make an interesting comparison with the guidelines issued by Netflix (Netflix, 2021a &b).

10 Software, Web, and Game Localisation

Key Questions

- What is localisation and how does it differ from translation?
- What types of localisation are there?
- What is the difference between software and game localisation?
- What file formats are used in localisation?
- Can we use a CAT tool for a localisation project?
- What are the main considerations when localising websites?
- Is subtitling for a game the same as subtitling other media?

Introduction

The growth in computing for work and home use in the 1990s not only brought about the first CAT tools (see Chapter 2), but also led to many other new information technology tools. These tools – software applications in particular – needed to be translated and adapted to be sold beyond the **locale** of origin, which is where the term **localisation** first appeared. We talk of locales rather than countries, not meaning a small area (as you might expect), but rather a region with a distinct language, as localisation caters to language communities rather than nationalities. Localisation involves linguistic, cultural, and technical adaptation of technology for an end-user group (Folaron, 2020). Jiménez-Crespo (2019: 299) defines it more comprehensively as the 'complex technological, textual, communicative and cognitive translational processes that introduce modifications to source interactive digital texts with the goal of rendering them usable in linguistic and sociocultural contexts other than those of production'. It can be applied to websites and portals as well as software and games. In this chapter, we introduce **software localisation**, **Web localisation**, and **game localisation**, processes that share similarities but differ in their production cycles, textual features, and genres (Jiménez-Crespo, 2013).

There have been largely pointless arguments as to whether localisation forms part of translation or vice versa, but we can safely say that localisation

DOI: 10.4324/9781003160793-10

brings some extra tasks along with those carried out as part of translation, such as testing, engineering, and updating accompanying documentation and support materials. Localisation is often a task with no clear endpoint, as software, games, and websites are continually developed and updated as part of an agile workflow (see Chapter 8), and localisation has to fit in with this fast development cycle and with larger development, marketing, and sales plans. This necessarily means that localisation is often carried out on an unfinished or untested product. In order to prepare a product for worldwide distribution, companies may speak of **GILT: Globalisation, Internationalisation, Localisation**, and **Translation**. We'll explain these related terms in the following section.

The GILT Edge

The term **globalisation** can have multiple meanings, but in the context of GILT, globalisation means consideration of the needs and consequences of making a product globally available. According to the now-defunct Localization Industry Standards Association (LISA), this means integration of localisation throughout a business, and adjusting plans and designs to support a global market (Esselink, 2000). The key reason to implement a globalisation strategy is to increase sales and to enter markets where, for reasons of choice or law, customers want to be addressed and to use products in their own language. An important first step in product design is internationalisation.

Internationalisation is the act of making a product (and related documentation) translatable and culturally adaptable from the very outset of its development. Translatable text should be in **strings** (see Box 10.1), ideally in a standalone file to prevent translators from breaking program code. **Character encoding** should be in a format that will work for other character sets and input methods (*Unicode* works for most character sets). Date, time, and currency formats should be editable. Text boxes presented to the user should not be in a fixed size so as to accommodate longer or shorter strings if necessary.

Localisation, as discussed, involves the project management, translation, and cultural adaptation of a product, followed by testing and publication. This can be done in-house by a company but due to projects' size and complexity is often outsourced to the sizeable localisation industry that has built up since the 1990s to provide localisation services at scale. As with other translation processes discussed in this book, localisation makes use of technology and automation where possible, often utilising CAT and similar tools built specifically for localisation and MT. There is also a tendency towards tight turnaround times for simultaneous shipment ('**simship**') of products in different locales.

Companies that provide localisation services are known as LSPs (as discussed previously) or **multi-language vendors** (**MLVs**). These companies usually outsource in turn to **Single Language Vendors** (SLVs) or freelance translators. The number of locales catered to for software, game, and website localisation is growing, with preference often tiered based on market size: the first-tier locales are often Japan and FIGS (France, Italy, Germany, and Spain), followed by BRICS (Brazil, Russia, India, China, and South Africa), then '**long-tail**' locales for which the return on investment is expected to be slower. Since the 1990s, most software development has been in the USA, but particularly for games, Japan and China have been the source of a growing amount of development.

Box 10.1: Software Strings

In computer-aided translation, we translate in segments, which are usually sensible blocks of text, separated by language-specific cues (see Chapter 2). However, in software development (and thus localisation), text may be machine readable without being meaningful to a human reader. We thus work on **strings**: sequences of characters of variable length, the end of which is marked with a *termination character*.

Software Localisation

The first step in a localisation project is analysis, to assess whether all content can and should be localised. This means checking for internationalisation, estimating the effort for localisation, and choosing the best tools to use. When the project has been approved, the next step involves preparation of a **localisation kit** for translation. The localisation project is managed by a project manager, whose job is to ensure effective communications and timely delivery of a project (as in Chapter 8). A software product or video game might comprise a number of different files and applications, along with related 'help' documentation made available online or in print. The software itself is often made up of a number of folders containing executable files (such as .EXE for Windows environments) with accompanying resource files or localisation files (such as .PO or Portable Object files for Linux environments) in multiple languages that can be reintegrated by developers after the text strings have been translated. Executable files are compiled from source files that, along with the resource or localisation files, can usually be read within a text editor. Nonetheless, they are likely to have file format-specific tags and complex hierarchies that should be maintained (see Figure 10.1, for example). Ideally, these will be delivered as part of the localisation kit with detailed instructions and reference materials.

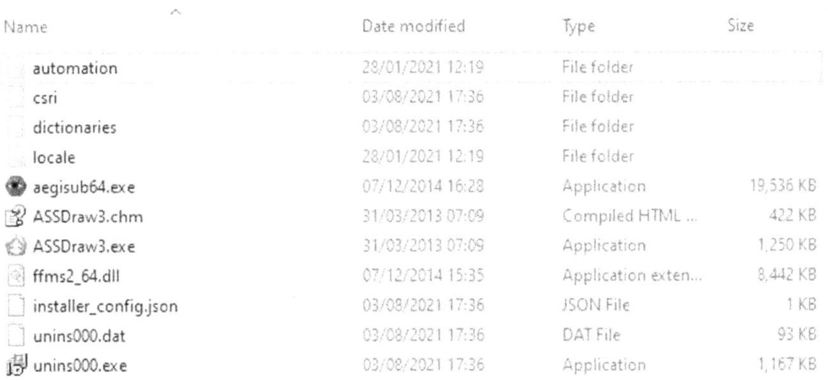

Name
Date modified
Type
Size
automation 28/01/2021 12:19 File folder
csri 03/08/2021 17:36 File folder
dictionaries 03/08/2021 17:36 File folder
locale 28/01/2021 12:19 File folder
aegisub64.exe 07/12/2014 16:28 Application 19,536 KB
ASSDraw3.chm 31/03/2013 07:09 Compiled HTML ... 422 KB
ASSDraw3.exe 31/03/2013 07:09 Application 1,250 KB
ffms2_64.dll 07/12/2014 15:35 Application exten... 8,442 KB
installer_config.json 03/08/2021 17:36 JSON File 1 KB
unins000.dat 03/08/2021 17:36 DAT File 93 KB
unins000.exe 03/08/2021 17:36 Application 1,167 KB

Figure 10.1 File manager view of the files and folders for Aegisub.

Title bar
Menu bar
Icons
Editing pane
Match pane
Tabs
Status bar
Project Edit Go To View Tools Options Help
Tian Ji goes horse racing
Over two thousand years ago, there lived a person called Tian Ji who liked horse racing
Dictionary
Machine Translation
Multiple Translations
Notes
Comments
Segment Properties

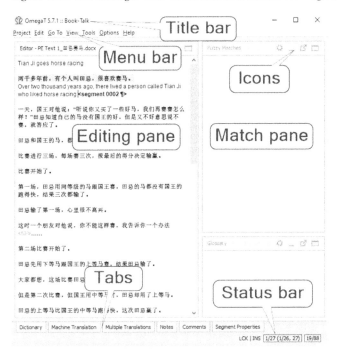

Figure 10.2 UI elements labelled in Omega-T 5.7.1.

The **user interface** (**UI**) of a software application will often contain dialog boxes, menus, and strings to be translated (see Figures 10.2 and 10.3). Dialog boxes are used for options and settings, menus are usually drop-down command options, and strings might contain error messages, tips, or status messages (Esselink 2000). There tends to be a strong focus on terminology in localisation projects and it is important that terms are consistent within a UI. There may be a need to translate different versions of strings (singular and plural, for example) to be used with **variable** characters (such as % or $), which can be replaced by different words when presented to the end user. Menu commands may have **shortcut** or **hotkey** options. A shortcut is a key combination (usually with ALT or CTRL when using Windows) set within the operating system, program, or by the users themselves, that will produce a convenient shortcut for a common task. These are usually denoted using an ampersand (&) character in strings within a resource file. Text to be translated is contained within quotation marks, so it is important to avoid using quotation marks or other symbols (such as $ or &) that have another purpose within this environment.

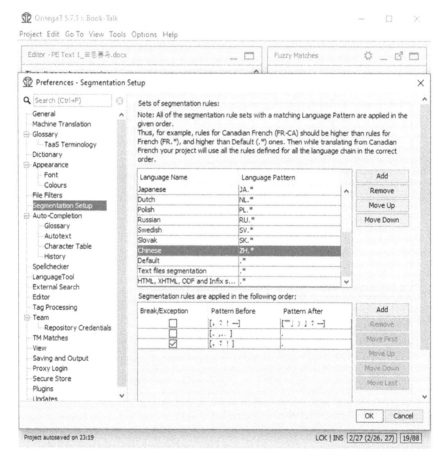

Figure 10.3 Segmentation Setup dialog box in Omega-T 5.7.1.

Following translation comes an engineering and testing phase to check for bugs and layout or linguistic problems. After a final quality assurance (QA) check has found all bugs to be removed, a final project review is carried out to assess processes and quality in order to improve for the following iteration.

Software Localisation Tools

One of the key features of CAT tools, as described in Chapter 2, is the import of many file formats so that the text to be translated within files can be presented to the user within a familiar interface. The tool can then export a target version that looks and functions just like the original. However, *executable* file types for software are beyond the remit of a regular CAT tool and need a specialist tool to rebuild a working version of the software in the target language. There are a number of software localisation tools on the market that lock away code and tags for multiple file formats, only making the translatable content visible to the translator. These tools, such as Alchemy Catalyst, RWS Passolo, Phrase Strings, and Lokalise essentially work as TM tools do, allowing translators to leverage previous work and ensuring that all segments or strings are translated, while also managing project management steps. The advantage of these tools is the capability of previewing UI updates and recompiling software so that the localised version behaves like the source version. This should ideally mean that localisation is easily added to an agile development cycle, wherein a prioritised list of updates and additions for software is attended to during a one- or two-week 'sprint', and even a continuous delivery cycle, in which updates may be released at any time. The aim of responsively developing working software according to customer needs means that updates will be published rapidly, necessitating the identification of new strings and pushing them to a localisation cycle that is just as quick, with localisation taking place almost alongside development.

Box 10.2: Okapi Tools

While software and Web localisation files may be provided in file formats that are easily opened by your chosen CAT tool, some more complex files may be difficult to work with. For example, a CAT tool such as memoQ has a filter for .PO files, often used for web localisation, but these may not work in practice. Particularly for those of you who are more technically confident, you might try tools from the Okapi Framework. Okapi tools are a set of free and open-source components and applications for localisation. The Okapi Rainbow tool, for example, is a toolbox to launch various localisation tasks and is useful for converting files from one format to another. There is also a very easy-to-use Okapi plugin for the open-source CAT tool Omega-T (see Omega-T in Figure 10.2), which can extend its file-handling capabilities. Many of these tools have graphical interfaces, although some require the use of the command line. Detailed instructions are beyond the remit of this book, but you can investigate further at https://okapiframework.org.

Working with a Software Localisation Tool – Lokalise

Setting up a project within a software localisation tool will follow similar steps to those described in Chapter 8. So, for example, if you are a project manager working for an MLV and have been tasked with translating some strings into Japanese for a simple smartphone app undergoing an update as part of an agile workflow, there may be an existing project to work with or you may have to set up a new project. Let's say that you have been asked to test Lokalise, a web-based software localisation tool that links with many other cloud-based tools and repositories. All of the tools listed above (and others) offer a free demo period, but Lokalise is a user-friendly option that does not require you to download software, as it is SaaS (see Chapter 8). Like many tools, Lokalise has a navigation pane on the left-hand side of the screen. If we click on the

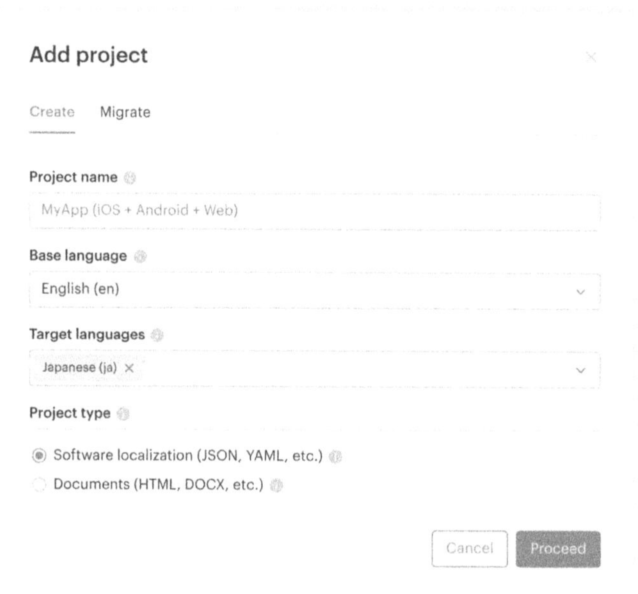

Add project

Create   Migrate

Project name

MyApp (iOS + Android + Web)

Base language

English (en)

Target languages

Japanese (ja) ×

Project type

● Software localization (JSON, YAML, etc.)
○ Documents (HTML, DOCX, etc.)

Cancel   Proceed

Figure 10.4 Lokalise Project Setup dialog.

Projects view and click New Project, the new project window as shown in Figure 10.4 will be similar to other CAT or localisation tools.

As with some other tools, we can link to online repositories via an API or

Upload localization files

Figure 10.5 Lokalise file upload dialog.

upload files. Localisation tools, however, tend to cater to a greater range of file formats than most CAT tools, as you can see in Figure 10.5.

Then, in the Editor view, you can begin to translate text in strings as displayed by Lokalise as shown in Figure 10.6, making use of matches from a TM (TMs are shared between 'team members' in Lokalise but can be activated per project). The tool will offer up to five TM proposals, up to 25 glossary entries, and MT outputs from publicly available engines by default. When translating, remember that words preceded with an ampersand (such as &File) will create a shortcut key for a menu or dialog item that uses the letter directly following the ampersand. You will need to decide whether that letter should be used and to ensure that no shortcut keys are repeated in any menu or dialog resources. Before completing the translation, you can preview

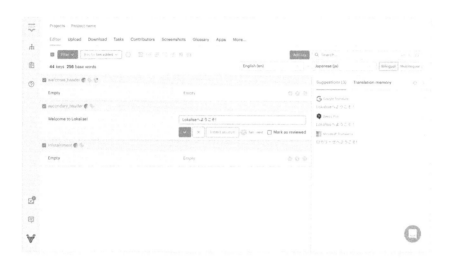

Figure 10.6 Lokalise Editor view.

how your translation will look within the Download menu. When complete, the file may be downloaded or exported via an API, ready to review and test.

Website Localisation

One of the materials that usually accompanies localised software and games is a multilingual website. This is also increasingly expected of international organisations. For large organisations, this will mean website localisation for far more locales than all but the most globalised software applications. According to Yunker (2021), an organisation that wants to reach more than 90% of global internet users will have to support over 40 languages on their website. At the time of writing, the world's most multilingual website (jw.org) supports well over 1,000 languages. Not all organisations can afford to (or have the interest to) support a **fully localised** website. Some offer **partial localisation,** whereby portions of the site are made available in multiple languages. Others add an MT button and accept the risk in having the text translated automatically, leaving images untouched. While high-quality translation into many languages will make your message understandable to a broader audience, web localisation involves many other considerations aside from language support.

Jiménez-Crespo (2013: 1) calls web localisation 'a communicative, technological, textual and cognitive process by which interactive digital texts are modified for use by the audiences around the world other than those originally targeted'. Many of the same principles as in software localisation apply, such as support for languages and character encodings, clear separation of code and content, and the use of templates to maintain consistency of style. However, web localisation requires a specific focus on technical, cultural, and marketing aspects to successfully transmit an organisation's message to users in a target locale.

Technical Considerations

Websites will be viewed on lots of different screens, through different browsers operating on multiple operating systems. Hopefully, developers will have chosen an architecture that is flexible enough to cater to these variations, but the choice of image and its size must work for users on large and small screens, on tablets and smartphones. A website should load quickly, even in a locale with slow internet speeds and sporadic access. This means optimising the number and quality of images – supporting many large images across multiple locales brings an associated resource cost in internet server time and bandwidth. Images should not have embedded text, as this can't be updated or translated.

While the default locale for a website should follow the location of the user's IP address, users will often have to manually change the target locale to the one that suits their needs. They do this using what Yunker (2010) calls a **global gateway**. Yunker (2010: 9) defines the global gateway as 'the visual and technical elements you employ to direct users to their localized websites and applications'. By clicking on a globally understandable icon, the user should be able to browse through a list of language names (perhaps in English and in the respective language and character set) to toggle between languages. It's best to avoid flags, as they do not map neatly to linguistic and cultural locales and, in some areas, can be contentious (Yunker, 2010).

According to Jiménez-Crespo (2013), the process of web localisation is similar to the example in Chapter 8. Localisation managers and engineers prepare a project, sending it to specialists and freelance translators to carry out, overseen by project managers, with specialist testing for quality and usability before publication. CAT tools may be used for web localisation, but there are also specialised tools (such as Smartling or Easyling) that can work either standalone or with a CAT tool, adding in functionality to

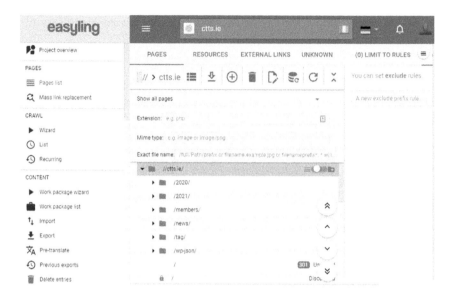

Figure 10.7 Easyling resources view.

preview the site before saving changes and finalising a project. In Figure 10.7, Easyling has automatically searched or *crawled* for pages within a website and allows the user to translate their selected webpage within the tool, export to a CAT tool, or outsource translation for a cost.

The files themselves may be HTML (HyperText Mark-Up Language) or HTML5, with CSS (Cascading Style Sheets) to adjust page style. Some sites use database formats and Javascript may be used for scripting. For translation from common **content management systems** such as WordPress or Drupal, strings are usually exported to a Portable Object Template or .POT file for translation, with one .PO file produced per target language. See Box 10.2 for a note about the use of .PO files.

Within web files, it's also important to update the LANG attribute to specify language and to translate ALT text for descriptions of images and **ARIA labels**. ARIA labels offer a text description for objects on-screen and are used by assistive tools such as screen readers so that blind and partially sighted users can navigate websites (see Chapter 12).

Cultural Considerations

Singh and Pereira (2005) propose several levels of website localisation, from a standardised (monolingual) website, to a localised website (with most content translated), to a culturally adapted website. A culturally adapted website incorporates comprehensive adaptation of content and functionality for the target locale. Reinecke and Bernstein (2011) find that users tend to work faster and with fewer errors within a culturally adapted interface. Significantly, they also report a superior user experience. For a culturally adapted website, the choice of colours, images, and icons will need to fit with your target locale and intended audience. What does the colour signify in the target locale? What are the global and local colour trends? Should images show people or animals and, if so, how should they look? What is the appropriate style of dress and body language for images with people? If images are chosen dynamically based on location (if there's an 'explore nearby' button, for example), how can you ensure that these are appropriate for a user? Pym (2011) notes that users rarely read a website in full, preferring to scan through information. If so, are there areas of the screen that are likely to receive more attention?

Hofstede's (2011) six dimensions of culture may be helpful when answering these questions – or as a basis for analysis of cultural adaptation for existing websites. Is the target culture one where individualism trumps membership of a social group? Is the power dynamic hierarchical or is the target locale more egalitarian? Is uncertainty and ambiguity acceptable or avoided in the target locale? Is there a major division between gender roles and expectations? Do most people in the target locale plan for the long term or think mainly in the short term? Is there a tendency towards indulgence or restraint? Ultimately, the website should 'speak' to its target audience, which is where marketing comes in.

Marketing Considerations

Choosing the right cultural fit means speaking in a language that users can understand and using images that fit with their expectations and preferences. However, we also need to think about the keywords that they might use to search for a site. Multilingual **search engine optimisation** (SEO) will ensure that your site has the most popular keywords to rank highly on search engines in many target locales. Related social media profiles should use hashtags that are popular in the target locale (Desjardins, 2017) for indexing posts or tweets, and not assume that emojis are understood everywhere in the same way.

Web localisation, as with software and game localisation, is increasingly an ongoing endeavour. Outdated content will give a bad impression and result in fewer return visits. Even worse, cultural or geopolitical insensitivity could lead to negative publicity and in the past has resulted in whole sites being blocked in restrictive target locales.

Game Localisation

At the time of writing, the most valuable type of entertainment worldwide is video games, with a market value of well over USD$100 billion. As a result, game localisation forms a large and growing portion of the global language services market. Game localisation combines software localisation, audiovisual translation (see Chapter 9), and the cultural considerations of web localisation (known in game localisation circles as **culturalisation**). There are many types of games that may be localised: high-budget games from large publishers (often called AAA – triple-A – games), mobile or casual games, or massively multi-player online games, for example.

As this sector grew, a localisation special interest group (https://igda.org/sigs/localization) was formed as part of the International Game Developers Association (IGDA), and this group published a set of best practices in 2011, updated in 2012 (https://igda.org/resources-archive/best-practices-for-game-localization), in an attempt to standardise the industry. These guidelines explain the aim of culturalisation as to make a game meaningful in the target locale, considering history, religion, ethnicity, and geopolitical sensitivities, as well as providing guidelines for internationalisation and localisation.

Mejías Climent (2021: 226) describes games as the 'most complex' audiovisual products and defines them as audiovisual texts generated by software that allows onscreen interaction following a set of rules. Conversely, in their comprehensive book about game localisation, O'Hagan and Mangiron (2013: 65) prefer to consider games as software programs that 'incorporate written text and graphics as well as audio, often with full motion pictures'. By any definition, the list of assets to be translated for a video game is long and the task complex.

Game Localisation Processes

Game localisation can happen concurrently with development or afterwards, either in-house or outsourced to a localisation agency. It involves a similar localisation engineering step to software localisation, where files or *assets* are prepared for translators with instructions, reference materials, code, and style guides. Before translation, translators are often expected to familiarise themselves with the game by playing and reading about it. The IGDA guidelines suggest a length of at least three days for this period of **familiarisation**, and up to a month for massively multiplayer role-playing games. Translators are then expected to work with developers on a target-language style guide and glossary of common terms. The term '**translatable assets**' is used for the various elements of a game to be localised. This includes in-game text, art, video, and audio assets within the game, and printed materials in case of a physical release. Some dedicated tools have been developed to manage the localisation process for this diverse set of assets, such as XLOC and Gridly, and game development engines such as Unity and Unreal Engine incorporate some localisation-specific features and guidelines (Rivas Ginel, 2022). In-game text may be in the UI in menus, system or help messages, and tutorials, as well as descriptive texts and written dialogues. In the past, these have usually been translated using spreadsheets, but there is increasing use of CAT tools in the game industry, particularly memoQ, and even some use of MT. Consistency of terminology for the game or platform is important, but narrative and dialogue text needs to be creative, engaging, and not repetitive. Art assets such as maps or signs embedded within the game need to be translated, although this is often managed by developers who will just include the text string in files sent to translators. Where cost is an issue, these assets may not be translated at all.

Video and audio assets are translated using subtitles and/or dubbing, although the workflow is unlike standard audiovisual translation. Subtitles are translated with other translatable assets as above. Some of the key requirements for translated subtitles as described in Chapter 9 are often ignored in gaming subtitles, in favour of non-typical fonts, three-line titles, and 96-character lines. The IGDA guidelines simply suggest the use of brightly-coloured text with a dark outline. For audio, dubbing scripts are prepared and studios and voice actors hired. For a **voiceover** section, the dubbed audio may not need to be synchronised with video, but for much of the game, these will need to be either time-constrained, synchronous with other audio, or **lip-synchronous**. In addition, there may be 'stitches': short audio clips that can be triggered at appropriate points within the game, possibly with variables that can be slotted together (O'Hagan & Mangiron, 2013). Players will go through a series of **game situations** within a game, with different levels of interactivity and different implications for dubbing synchrony: the player may receive a task in audio or written instruction, they may be in interactive game action, there may be a restricted interaction for dialogue, or a cinematic clip with no interaction possible at all. A fully localised and customised AAA game may be dubbed into eight or nine languages, with over 100 actors per language, which represents a huge cost and effort. At the time of writing, games localisation companies are looking at using artificial voices, in order to save costs for some secondary characters.

The final stage is linguistic QA, which again is a little different to the QA stages described in Chapters 2 and 11. First of all, testers need to be gamers with strong target-language skills. They are charged with finding bugs and might also query some translation decisions, then with testing that bugs have been fixed without causing new issues. Once a game has been published, the process will usually repeat with regular updates, patches, ports to other platforms, and possible sequels, with the sometimes with the added complication of user input, as some games allow modification and co-creation by gamers under the limits of a EULA (End User Licensing Agreement).

Culturalisation

For a game to become successful, it needs to fit effectively within the target culture. At a macro level, as demonstrated by O'Hagan and Mangiron (2013), this may mean adjusting or adapting the game to fit with the expectations of gamers in the target locale, perhaps to do with the look and feel, character expressions, or game mechanics (making the game easier or more difficult). At the micro level, changes might be in the use of linguistic variation for characterisation or a domesticating translation strategy.

A major focus for culturalisation is carefully checking elements of the game that may be offensive or contrary to common religious preferences within the target culture, checking the provenance and meaning of sounds, songs, and effects within a game. The appropriate use of gender or gender-neutral language is often considered important. There are also regulatory requirements depending on the target locale, forbidding the use of certain symbols, graphic violence, or spatters of blood. The content of some games might present ethical concerns to a translator who objects to offensive content, but there may also be concerns about addictive content and monetisation strategies, especially within casual games for smartphones and tablets. Many such games are initially free to play, foregoing a charge for installation in favour of the use of microtransactions within the game or *lootboxes*, consumable virtual items to customise avatars or to aid game progress.

Conclusion

Although localisation only came about in the 1990s, it is a huge and growing industry, facilitating access to software, websites, and video games for a global audience. Localisation is characterised by complex workflows with many files and assets to translate, a combination of restrictive (e.g. UI and system messages) and creative (website text, game narrative) translation, a consideration for aesthetics, and an acute sensitivity to the target culture. As with other areas of translation discussed within this book, localisation is undergoing change, with the focus on production velocity necessitating an ever-faster schedule and the use of automation where possible, not just in the use of MT, but also for automating workflow steps and even the use of synthetic voices for some game characters. The industry is a major source of employment in specific locations worldwide, such as San Francisco, Dublin, Berlin, and Tokyo, and the increased use of MT in localisation workflows has been associated with new roles involving critical use of technology and of legacy data (O'Brien & Rossetti, 2020).

Follow-Up Tasks and Reflection

1. GILT is a standard process sequence for software localisation. What do you think would be the effect of removing one of these steps?
2. Choose two localised websites from two internationally known organisations. How do these sites compare? What images do they use? Would you consider each version to be fully localised and culturally adapted based on your understanding of this chapter? If you compare countries at www.hofstede-insights.com/country-comparison, do the results fit with what you find in your comparison?
3. Find video walkthroughs of a section of a game online for two different locales, ideally in two languages that you know. Has everything been localised? What has been left out? Why might this be?

4. Localised material has to be not just culturally, but also politically acceptable. Websites have been blocked for whole regions due to content that is considered inappropriate, offensive, or ill-judged. To what extent do you think it's acceptable for an organisation to accede to censorship in order to access a locale? What problems might this cause outside of the target locale?

Further Reading

This chapter provides a brief introduction to localisation, but there is plenty of further reading that you might find useful and informative. Esselink's (2000) *A practical guide to localisation* is a little dated but still useful, and Dunne & Dunne's (2011) *Translation and localization project management: The art of the possible* goes into detail on localisation project management. Jiménez-Crespo also has a book on localisation to come in this series. His (2013) *Translation and web localization* and Yunker's website at www.bytelevel.com are excellent resources for web localisation. Key readings for video game localisation are O'Hagan & Mangiron (2013) *Game localization: Translating for the global digital entertainment industry*, Bernal-Merino (2014) *Translation and localisation in video games*, and Mejías-Climent (2021) *Enhancing video game localization through dubbing*.

11 Translation Quality Assurance

Key Questions

- What is translation quality?
- Why is it important to consider quality when we use translation tools and technologies?
- What sorts of impact can tools and technologies have on the quality of translations?
- What are the main tools and technologies which aim to measure or enhance translation quality?
- What are the main benefits and risks for translation quality when using tools and technologies?
- What do key terms like translation quality assurance, assessment, and control mean?
- Who uses translation quality assurance features, and what does this mean for translators and others involved in translation processes?
- How do translation tools and technologies support industry-wide quality standards such as those produced by the International Organization for Standardization (ISO)?

Introduction

Translation quality is a longstanding challenge for the profession and for researchers and teachers of translation, as well as for students keen to improve the quality of their work. The different tools and technologies we outline in this volume have brought new challenges in relation to translation quality, but also new opportunities. Translation tools and technologies can be harnessed in translation projects in really varied combinations. Translation memory (TM), machine translation (MT), terminology management and dedicated **Quality Assurance (QA)** or **Quality Control (QC)** tools and features are used and applied before, during, and after the translation

DOI: 10.4324/9781003160793-11

process, often without translators' knowledge or consent. The tools are regularly used in ways not anticipated by their designers: large organisations commission bespoke add-ins or workarounds for their own needs, and individual users may misapply the tools, adopt them in idiosyncratic ways and combinations or tweak settings to suit their own preferences. The increasingly complex array of tools and features available, and this variability in how they are applied, has effects on translation quality which can be difficult to predict, spot, and manage. This chapter places the focus on the user of the main types of tools and highlights some important questions to consider in relation to translation quality when we work with them.

Even just stating clearly what we mean by translation quality is a challenge. When five specialists, each of whom had decades of experience working in the industry, research and training, attempted this in a series of linked articles, they eventually agreed to disagree 'strongly' with one another about which definition was better (Koby et al., 2014). Translation quality is part of a wider debate about what quality itself means across a vast range of fields, linked to the work on agreed standards for many industries led by bodies like the European Committee for Standardization (CEN) and the International Organization for Standardization (ISO). It's hard to agree on what acceptable or high-quality translation might be, because needs and preferences vary hugely. For MT specialist Kirti Vashee (2021), 'comparing different translations of the same source material is often an exercise in frustration or subjective preference at best. Every sentence can have multiple correct, accurate translations', and even experts disagree with one another's judgements.

Yet, as any student of translation knows from first-hand experience, the quality of different translations is assessed, compared, and scored every day. It may be a challenge, or even an impossibility, to agree on a single definition, but in practice, translation quality is defined, evaluated, and built in to translation processes. For instance, at the European Union's Directorate General for Translation, quality is 'never absolute but depends on both context and situation. [It] concerns products and services, as well as the processes involved' (Drugan et al., 2018: 42). The leading German scholar of translation quality, Juliane House, stresses this important dual aspect: assessing quality means 'both retrospectively assessing the worth of a translation and prospectively ensuring the quality in the production of a translation' (2015: 2). This matters in two ways for the tools and technologies now integral to translation production: first, the tools can be used to assess the 'worth' of the translation *product* in certain ways, and second, more commonly, they are used to try to ensure quality in translation *processes* as well as any future product these processes will result in.

All the tools described in this volume can be used to measure and improve translation quality in different ways. Some are mainly used before translation begins, some during the translation, revision and editing workflow, and some post-delivery of translated materials. Others still can be used at one remove from individual translation projects, to manage processes and approaches so that important aspects of translation quality can be guaranteed or checked.

Since the 1990s, as translation tools and technologies have been integrated more widely in translation processes, researchers and users have observed various effects on the quality of the translations produced. Tools can enhance quality in a range of useful ways, but they also have a potentially detrimental impact, often without users noticing. Research has demonstrated that translators tend not to realise when problems arise, especially when they are first learning to use the tools (Christensen & Schjoldager, 2011), though awareness of this tendency, careful use and well-designed review processes can help mitigate the risks (Gamal, 2020: 9–10).

Benefits for Translation Quality

What are the main benefits of using translation tools and technologies for translation quality? Above all, they enable translation of useful quality that could not otherwise be provided at all, due to constraints on translator availability, cost, or time. As we learned in Chapter 6, since around 2016, free online NMT systems have been offering hugely improved translation quality for a far higher number of language pairs, providing access to information in some contexts where translation is literally lifesaving, such as multilingual crisis communication during natural disasters, particularly where funding is limited or there are not enough trained professional translators (Federici et al., 2019). Users combine translation technologies with automatic speech recognition (ASR) and other tools or devices such as phones in novel ways, notably among deaf users of sign languages, for example (Shterionov, 2021). One evident benefit for translation quality is that technology makes possible the sharing of information which could simply not otherwise be provided in as many languages, though this of course involves risks as well as benefits.

The headline benefit in adopting TM and terminology management tools is their potential to enhance consistency across different translators, and from one project to the next. Large volumes of source language (SL) content can be translated to otherwise impossible deadlines by teams of translators and others in supporting roles sharing terminology and TMs. As we learned in Chapters 2, 3, and 7, high-quality previously translated content can be leveraged and reused, thus improving consistency across time and ensuring high-quality material is exploited efficiently. The vendors of MultiTerm and Trados, for example, stress that centralised online resource-sharing, with TMs and termbases updated in real time, results in 'more accurate and consistent translation whenever different translators work on related materials', and allows work to be shared 'among different translators for a faster turnaround, where before this might have created quality control challenges' (RWS, 2021). Figure 11.1 gives an illustration of typical checks in the Phrase TMS Editor, which has introduced the option of conducting partial checks on particular features rather than having to run full QA checks with lots of potential false negatives.

Figure 11.1 List of QA checks in Phrase, with partial Terminology QA check selected.

Some QC steps are intended for use before translation begins, to prevent some human error. For example, project managers and terminologists can *lock* segments, figures and tags (that is, prevent editing by other users) to ensure they are not deleted or mishandled during translation processes. Key project terminology can be researched and approved by dedicated terminology leads then imposed on all translators, to enhance consistency across a given project and also across future translation projects. Inconsistent terminology or failing to use approved terms, including trademarks and company style rules, has been shown to be one of translation clients' main frustrations regarding translation quality (Warburton, 2021) and has been a significant driver of the adoption of the tools in many commercial sectors.

While the tools have features to anticipate and prevent some human error in the first place, their automated QC features during and after translation are the most widely understood and used in the industry. Basic TM quality checks are outlined in Chapter 2 and typically include checking on the fly and post-translation for empty target segments, unopened segments (implying translators have missed these, a common problem in projects with hundreds of files), significant differences in SL and TL segment length, partial translation, incompatible/inconsistent translations of the same SL content, unedited fuzzy matches/MT, failure to respect approved terminology/TM content, issues with numbers/dates, tags, spaces, and so on. All TM, localisation and subtitling tools provide a range of such automated QC/QA features and processes, typically performed on multiple files at once then generating reports which highlight possible errors for users to review (see Figure 11.2 for an illustration).

Figure 11.2 Illustration of batch task options including Translation Quality Assessment in Trados Studio 2022.

Terminology management and TM tools can be linked to project management tools to run batch tests for extremely large text quantities, often split across thousands of files and many different file types. Translation project content often involves significant repetition across large numbers of files with only a few words in each, making it impractical and costly for human checks on consistency; the tools support this much more effectively than human project managers or translation leads can. Localisation tools also check for bugs, layout and linguistic issues (see Chapter 10), and are increasingly integrated into standard TM tools, so quality checks can also be conducted on a broader range of content types such as gaming strings. Subtitling tools can be integrated within larger projects to ensure video content is translated consistently with other source text material, and to ensure text length rules are not broken (see Chapter 9). Spelling and grammar checks are integrated in almost all translation tools, often using standard Microsoft dictionaries and offering options to prioritise matches from client terminology databases.

In addition to these checks during translation projects, QA and QC features are also often applied at one further remove from the translation process, and this can frequently happen without translators' awareness. Project management tools and TM QA and report features are used during project reviews to map and improve quality in relation to translation processes. Translation providers and clients typically do this sort of review to extend perceived benefits beyond the individual translation project, sometimes as part of 'continuous improvement' quality management approaches. Where mistakes are identified, processes can be reviewed to prevent future occurrences, with improved quality usually the stated aim. However, increasingly detailed and specific data on individual translator performance is available, particularly by linking project management tools with translation production/checking tools and features (see Chapter 8). There are clear risks as well as benefits in the increasing integration of more and more complex translation tools and technologies, whether for translators, clients, or translation quality overall.

Risks for Translation Quality

The potential for negative impact on the quality of translations has been one of the principal concerns voiced in relation to the use of translation tools and technologies from their earliest days, sometimes due to a failure to distinguish between CAT tools and (early) MT. Canadian researcher Lynne Bowker showed nearly two decades ago that translators accept matches from database content without noticing or correcting errors (2005: 18). Related to this is a significant risk in the adoption of translation tools and technologies for translation: misplaced confidence in the tools' capacity to enhance quality. Companies selling tools have regularly claimed or implied that the tools can do far more than is the case even today. For instance, RWS state that in their 2022 version of Trados Studio, 'an enhanced [fully automated] Translation Quality Assessment provides an easier way to objectively evaluate the quality of a translation', yet as we have seen, most translation quality specialists and researchers would question whether fully 'objective' evaluation of translation quality, or even a shared definition of the term, is possible.

Known problems of human-computer interaction and human error when using translation tools and technologies are risks for translation quality as they are in other spheres of computer use, sometimes exacerbated by the ways in which tools require human translators to work. Translation tools are typically more efficient and accurate at certain tasks, such as handling figures, tags, and numbers, but this means that human editors and translators may not pay as much attention to these features and miss serious errors where they do arise. For example, where a statistic is incorrect or nonsensical in a source text, translators often spot and query this, but when all figures have been automatically replaced in target segments prior to translation, such issues are more likely to slip through the net. A frequent challenge is human quality checks missing errors because the tools' automated QA checks flag so many false negatives (e.g. flagging multiple tag 'errors' when there is no error), and indeed false positives (where errors are accepted as accurate translations, perhaps because database content is flawed). The temptation is to click quickly through and override these, thus missing a few real, even serious, errors. Users of CAT tools have flagged concerns about the growing amount of time needed to learn and implement such new features (particularly as additional features are added to each new update to the tools), the extra steps introduced to their workflow, and having to move between additional interfaces or shut projects to perform QA processes, disrupting the flow of translation (Goldsmith, 2018). The cluttered screen common when using translation tools and information overload (see Chapters 2 and 12) also make it more challenging for translators to spot errors.

As with any database content, poor-quality material can be recycled and have a long-term impact on overall translation quality (the 'Garbage In, Garbage Out' principle). If low-quality human or machine translations are approved and added to a TM, they can continue to be imposed on frustrated translators during future projects. Large organisations generally appoint TM leads who must check any queried segment with senior linguists for the relevant language pair before deciding whether to delete or edit existing content, a cycle which often takes weeks or months. This also relies on translators flagging the problems they spot rather than just accepting them because they are approved in the client TM. Translators may also click through to accept previously approved matches without noticing false friends, fuzzy matches and where MT output is integrated in suggestions, known negative features such as gender bias (Savoldi et al., 2021), more readily than they would produce such low-quality content independently, particularly when working to tight deadlines as is common in the translation industry.

All languages are not equally well supported by translation tools and this can lead to inconsistent levels of quality across multilingual translation projects. These inconsistencies are very difficult to spot or address, as no project manager or QA specialist can hope to be competent in the tens of languages involved in large-scale projects. A risk for translation quality is that the gulf between language pairs with rich resources and those with very few continues to grow, with little or no QC and far less useful MT output for most of the world's non-endangered languages (Ranathunga et al., 2021).

The segment-based approach to translation imposed by most tools has been criticised for its impact on overall style at the level of the whole text. Where large text volumes are split among several or many translators, individuals' different translation styles can combine with this segmented approach to produce low-quality results even if careful editing is part of the workflow. Translators are disempowered by imposed TM and terminology database content when they are given limited information as to its provenance, sometimes not even whether suggestions come from MT or approved translations. Some risks for translation quality are linked to limited training, working conditions, 'social quality' (see Chapter 12) and individual translators' experience of using the tools, and all of these are hard to measure. Especially for less experienced translators, there is a risk of focusing on learning how to navigate using the translation tool rather than on the quality of the translation. The complicated interaction of different tools, perhaps at different stages in a project life cycle, has not been thoroughly researched so a lot of the impacts are unknown and hard to predict. However, as newer tools and approaches, such as ASR, have emerged and been integrated into workflows by translators, studies have indicated negative impact on translation quality as one of the clear risks (Ciobanu, 2016).

Specialist Tools for Translation Quality Assurance

Mainly at the enterprise level, some dedicated QC and QA tools are in use, notably Yamagata's QA Distiller and ApSIC Xbench. These carry out automated, but highly customisable, quality checks on large volumes of translated content across hundreds of file types and without the user needing licences or access to proprietary tools. This means an agency project manager can perform automated QA checks without having access to all the different tools individual translators may be using. Users can identify errors and correct automatically across all files in a project using batch replacement mode, and there are features designed to limit the problem of large numbers of false positives (automated checks identifying 'errors' which are not in fact errors), if the user is willing to invest time identifying common error patterns.

Yamagata has made QA Distiller available as a free download (with a recommended donation to Translators Without Borders in return, and support available only to paying users), and it works for over 90 languages. An illustration of QA Distiller's interface to manage Omissions, Inconsistencies, Formatting, and Terminology is presented in Figure 11.3. This gives a sense of the types of errors the tools can identify, and the customisable options available to the user.

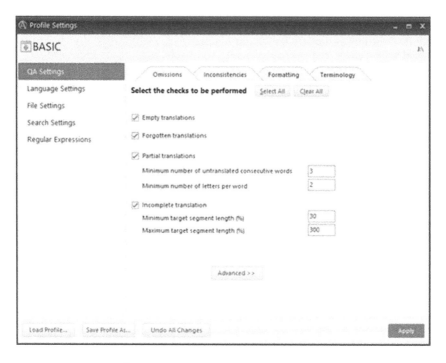

Figure 11.3 QA Distiller 10 automated translation and terminology checks.

Large companies and translation service providers often also produce their own tools or macros in-house to perform similar automated quality checks.

Dedicated QA tools are not commonly taught in university translation programmes, as they require large volumes of translated data to demonstrate their features properly, are cumbersome to set up for training outside real world contexts and are mainly aimed not at the individual user but at the enterprise level (dedicated project managers or quality managers in agencies or large translation clients). Their functions mirror features found in TM and terminology tools, such as multilingual spell checking, and common translation error checking, but they allow users to batch process QA checks on multiple file formats without owning a specific CAT tool, for example. They may be used to assess translators' work and rank its quality without their knowledge. They are affected by the same risks for translation quality as the TM features outlined above (false negatives, false positives, false confidence in their output, human judgement being weakened), and like other translation tools, their manufacturers often make strong but vague claims about making QA and terminology checks 'easy' – see for example Xbench's marketing material: 'Easy Quality Assurance and Terminology. ApSIC Xbench provides simple and powerful Quality

Assurance and Terminology Management in a single package. Just load files in any of the dozens of CAT formats supported and get your translation quality to the next level' (www.xbench.net).

Some key terms including 'translation quality assurance', 'quality assessment', 'quality control', 'quality evaluation' and 'quality management' have been used in this discussion without thus far defining them. In large part, this is because the tools manufacturers themselves either omit to define the terms they adopt, use various terms interchangeably, or offer their own definitions which don't match those typically used by academics or those working in the translation profession. The dominant TM software Trados includes references to Quality Control, Quality Assessment and Quality Assurance with the explanation that 'While we refer to the actual checking of translations as "Quality Control" and the setting up of processes to ensure quality as "Quality Assurance", [we] simply [use] the term "Quality Assurance" in Trados Studio' (www.web-translations.com/blog/quality-control-features-in-trados). This means that many translators may not realise there is a difference. A useful overview of a range of terms and approaches to translation quality is included in the free online resources provided by the Multidimensional Quality Metrics (MQM) framework (see https://themqm.org/mqm-terminology). Designed for application to either human or machine translation (as outlined in Chapter 6), MQM can also be used as part of a quality management system but is a way of approaching the evaluation of quality rather than a translation tool. In practice, many translation providers adopt approaches such as these rather than using specific automated QA tools, recognising that human judgement combined with metrics is the most effective way to measure and enhance translation quality at present.

A final aspect to consider, then, when learning about translation tools and quality is how translation QA features, tools and approaches are used in the industry and what this means for translators and others involved in translation projects. Many of the technologies used to measure and enhance translation quality are deployed by managers working in large organisations or for translation providers. Their motivation includes guaranteeing or improving translation quality, but they may also be driven by considerations such as enhanced sales, differentiating their services from those of rivals, measuring individual translator productivity, increasing translation delivery speeds or consistency across different projects, achieving better returns for investment, or designing processes which can be applied efficiently across different translation projects, language pairs and 'resources' (human translators). Users of these tools and features include dedicated quality managers at international organisations. Tools providers are likely to have these management-level users in mind when designing quality management features, given the size and importance of the contracts they oversee. Developers also keep in mind, and even work directly for the agencies and translation providers, who are increasingly signed up to industry-wide quality standards such as those produced by the ISO, particularly ISO 17100:2015, which stipulates requirements for the 'core processes, resources, and other aspects necessary for the delivery of a quality translation service that meets applicable specifications' (ISO, 2015). Note the emphasis not on the quality of the translation *product*, or the translator, but on the quality of the business *processes* and the 'service', i.e. the company, agency, or organisation.

This seems particularly important for the likely reader of this volume, who is unlikely to have significant power at these levels, and as we move on to the final chapter, on human factors in relation to translation technologies. Translation quality management tools and approaches have shifted significant decision-making power from individual human translators, proof readers and editors to the more distant levels of the project and even cross-project management of processes to which translators must then adapt and conform. What does this increasing lack of agency mean for translation quality? The complex balance between translators' skills and professional judgement, built up over decades of experience, with the top-down imposition of processes intended to measure or improve general quality levels is linked to issues of professional autonomy, trust, and motivation, as we will see in Chapter 12. It is not clear how these developments and the continuing automation of quality assessment processes will affect translation quality in future. Approaches such as User-Centred Translation (Suojanen et al., 2014), large-scale user feedback or ratings, and online translation communities suggest some possible different ways of adopting technology to improve translation quality, although these can also pose some new challenges and risks for quality too. Kirti Vashee has concluded that 'maybe we need more focus on improving the man-machine [sic] interaction and [to] find more elegant and natural collaborative models' (Vashee, 2021). Läubli and Green (2020: 380) stress a problematic imbalance in such human-machine interaction, however: 'Research as well as commercial state-of-the-art systems still hinder true mixed-initiative translation: humans can learn how to handle novel machinery, but the machinery itself has trouble learning from human input'. It is also important to acknowledge the wider picture of AI being led by a tiny unrepresentative section of the world's inhabitants, dominated by overwhelmingly male developers based in WEIRD (Western, Educated, Industrialised, Rich, Democratic) countries. When we learn to use translation tools and adopt the design and processes they impose, as for any technology, it is urgent and necessary to do so critically and reflectively. There is much for language and translation specialists to do to challenge, as well as being challenged by, current technological approaches to translation quality.

Follow-Up Tasks and Reflection

1. Look at the Multidimensional Quality Metrics (MQM) *Gentle Introduction*, *MQM Error Typology* and *MQM Scorecards* (https:// themqm.org/). Why do you think the industry needed these approaches?

Would they be useful in relation to the assessment of your own translations?

2. How would you define the concept of 'translation quality'? In a small group, take a few minutes to write your own one-sentence definition then compare with everyone else's definitions. What sort of themes or key words appear in most of your definitions?

3. Which aspects of translation quality are translation tools and technologies not able to evaluate without human input? Are any of these likely to be achievable for computers alone in the next decade, in your view?

4. How are QA checks implemented in the CAT tools you have used so far? Run QA checks on the translation projects you have created after reading earlier chapters of the book. How useful are they? Are there any errors (false positives, false negatives)?

5. What does the approach taken in design and implementation of translation tools and technologies tell us about how the industry thinks about translation quality?

Further Reading

There are lots of studies, theories, and discussions of translation quality and translation quality assessment in both academic and industry publications. The recommendations here are ones where significant attention is paid to tools and technologies, rather than just theoretical or general discussions. With apologies for the immodest self-recommendation, the author of this chapter Joanna Drugan gives a critical overview of the concept of translation quality in relation to tools in Chapters 2 and 3 of *Quality in professional translation: assessment and improvement* (2013). Stephen Doherty's (2016) journal article discusses 'The impact of translation technologies on the process and product of translation'. The chapters included in Joss Moorkens et al.'s edited collection from 2018, *Translation quality assessment: From principles to practice*, cover a range of technologies and contexts with perspectives from professional users, developers, and academic researchers. Minako O'Hagan's (2020: 17) introductory chapter to the *Routledge handbook of translation and technology* focuses on the 'disruptive entanglement of human and machine', and asks 'what it is to be human and a translator in the technologizing age': important background context for anyone reflecting on how technologies affect translation quality.

12 Human Factors in Translation Tools and Technologies

Key Questions

- What are human factors and how might they affect how you work with translation tools?
- What physical constraints might prevent you from working efficiently?
- How might cognitive ergonomics be a helpful way to think about your interactions with a translation tool?
- How might the intentions of developers change how you work within a tool?
- What organisational factors might motivate translators?
- What tools can I use if I have a visual impairment and how can I help visually impaired translation colleagues?

Introducing Human Factors

In the preceding chapters, we wrote about the capabilities and features of CAT tools in the context of translation or localisation projects. Here and there, we also mentioned the ways that translators might interact with translation tools and technologies as part of their work. In this more theoretical chapter, we focus on those interactions using the concept of **human factors**, also known as **ergonomics**. According to the International Ergonomics Association (IEA, 2022), the discipline of human factors looks to understand 'interactions among humans and other elements of a system' to improve both human well-being and the efficiency of overall performance. To do this, we might investigate 'physical, cognitive, sociotechnical, organizational, environmental and other relevant factors' to see how humans interact with each other, their tools, and their environment (IEA, 2022).

In the years since O'Brien (2012) notably framed translation as an example of human-computer interaction, we have seen **workplace research** published in Translation Studies that reports and measures these interactions, often offering recommendations and advice based on their findings. Most

DOI: 10.4324/9781003160793-12

translators work on a freelance basis (Pielmeier & O'Mara, 2020), which makes them difficult to access for workplace studies. As a result, studies of freelance translators are usually based on surveys or interviews, whereas in-house teams in companies or institutions have been the subject of direct studies using methods such as screen recording and ergonomic assessments (Ehrensberger-Dow & Hunziker Heeb, 2016), key-logging and eye-tracking (Teixeira & O'Brien, 2017), and ethnography (Milošević & Risku, 2020). We won't summarise these studies here (although you can investigate further, beginning with the Further Reading section at the end of the chapter), but will instead try to introduce the main themes in the sections that follow, with the aim of helping you to use translation tools and technologies effectively.

Physical and Cognitive Ergonomics and Translation Technology

The ideal for translation, as with any immersive task, is to achieve a state of 'flow', being energised and fully engaged in the activity of the moment. O'Brien et al. (2017) associate this with an acceptable cognitive load, but warn that **cognitive overload** or **cognitive friction** – when something goes wrong or causes irritation – can disturb this flow state. Good practice in ergonomics should enable the user of a tool to achieve a state of flow, without causing distress or disturbance. In this section, we consider how physical and cognitive ergonomics might affect a translator and their ability to work efficiently and effectively. Physical ergonomics looks at well-being and efficiency regarding a user's situation and surroundings, whereas cognitive ergonomics looks at the alignment of a product with the user's cognitive abilities.

As translation is a form of human-computer interaction, it follows that translators spend a lot of time sitting at a desk in front of a computer screen (not unlike students and academics). Aside from their on-screen activities, they are affected by the quality of their work environment – seating, heat, light, and noise levels – and their physical positioning at the desk. Many translators now prefer to have a two-screen setup so that they can keep their CAT editing interface open on one while accessing different resources on another, but many freelance translators in particular do not have a dedicated workstation and use a laptop only, potentially causing posture problems and neck pain. Whether using one or two screens, long hours spent staring at screens may lead to vision problems. Poor desk and mouse/keyboard layouts can cause tendonitis or repetitive strain injury (RSI) and carpal tunnel syndrome. Experienced translators tend to primarily use the keyboard only, making use of keyboard shortcuts for frequently-used operations. Some tech-savvy translators use **macros** (programmed sequences of activities or commands) and **regular expressions** (text strings that run specific searches) to provide personalised shortcuts, minimising keyboard use. A growing proportion of translators use **automatic speech recognition** (**ASR**) for translation and post-editing, either to avoid RSI or during periods of recovery, but also to aid productivity. Many CAT tools work well with ASR, allowing users to verbalise keyboard commands as well as entering text, and memoQ even has a dedicated iOS app for translation dictation.

A difficulty related to both the use of CAT tools and the addition of ASR is a high learning curve (see also Chapter 2). From the early days of TM tools, users found the complexity of the UI (user interface) off-putting, as documented in Lagoudaki's study in 2009. She felt that 'systems usability and end-users' demands seem to have been of only subordinate interest' in translation tool development (Lagoudaki, 2009: 17). García (2008: 55) called TM 'an obtrusive tool that translators need to learn and adjust to before they can achieve the gains in productivity and consistency it promises'. Good ergonomic design should empower the user by foregrounding usability and avoiding distractions, thus making it intuitive to learn a new tool rather than slow and painful, but there have been complaints in translator studies of users having to get used to a new tool rather than having a tool that fits with their way of working.

Thankfully, translation tool developers, on the whole, are very responsive to user complaints, and contemporary tools tend to be more stable and user-friendly than those of the early 2000s. Despite this, surveys will still find users who are unhappy with the stability and basic functionality of their current tool and who complain that their tool lacks customisability, has an overly complex UI, and does not offer enough flexibility in segmentation. We might also add that what translators and users say they want from a tool in surveys and correspondence may not actually be useful when added or might be difficult to implement in a usable way. Large desktop or workstation-based CAT tools are unwieldy pieces of software incorporating years of design decisions that will be difficult to change or reverse. The addition of new functionality will often have an unanticipated knock-on effect, such as the decision to allow the merging of segments in Trados Studio 2017, causing unpredictable effects on the target text file (Filkin, 2016). The removal of little-used features can still bring an avalanche of complaints. There have been suggestions that some UI customisability is available in many CAT tools, but that users are not aware of the possibility to make changes that could help them to use the tool more efficiently. A key point here would be that, if some element of a CAT tool seems difficult or awkward, it's probably worth investigating how it might be adjusted rather than just accepting the default option.

At the time of writing, there are two main types of CAT tools (as introduced in Chapter 2): workstation-based, feature-rich tools with busy interfaces, a range of powerful features, and PM and QA functionality, and cloud-based SaaS tools, often with comparatively minimal UIs, little customisability, and fewer features. Some users will prefer the decluttered SaaS UIs, and are happy to accept fewer features, especially considering they had no intention of finding out exactly how to use them or which menu they were buried in anyway. Other 'power' users will prefer to have everything revealed to them, accepting that the initially high cognitive load when working within a busy interface as a necessary step in learning. When you are choosing or evaluating a CAT tool, it is worth thinking about which category of user you mainly fall into. As noted in Chapter 2, developers have introduced colours, icons, and menu systems to help guide the user around busy, feature-rich interfaces. Kappus and Ehrensberger-Dow noted in 2020 that Trados Studio 2017, one such feature-rich tool, had over 2,000 functions and commands, of which only a small number could be included in icons or menus on-screen at any one time. Their conclusion was that it might be more effective to introduce a simple interface to students first, then to build towards bigger, feature-rich tools.

Two other areas in which contemporary tools diverge, i.e. sub-segment matching and MT presentation, are discussed in Chapter 7. Again, it's down to user preference whether they would like to see sub-segment or MT matches in a drop-down menu, separate to the segment match suggestions elsewhere on-screen, or automatically propagated as the UI updates the user's translation proposal. What we see in both options is that users are less likely to be faced with a blank target segment and no proposals, as more resources are incorporated into translation tools. This presents the cognitive difficulty of reading, evaluating, and managing a number of resources in order to produce a target text to a defined quality level that fits the translation brief and conforms to stylistic guidelines. If the user is presented with too many proposals to sift through, the task can take longer than translating from scratch and become self-defeating. Getting this cognitive balance right is a significant challenge for CAT UI designers.

Some recommendations for working with translation tools and technologies are to make sure that your workspace is comfortable and allows you to sit straight and to adjust your posture regularly; take regular breaks – both for your eyes by looking at something at distance every so often and for your body by taking a short walk; explore customisability options within your translation interface to make it best suit your needs; make good use of keyboard shortcuts and try other input modes, such as ASR; try to avoid on-screen and off-screen interruptions that distract from tasks. Ubiquitous technology has tended to make us more distracted, bringing down the average length of time spent on tasks. It might be helpful to remove some distractions, such as smartphones or even internet access, to improve and extend periods of focussed attention (see also the checklist in Box 12.1).

Box 12.1: Physical Ergonomic Checklist

- Can your chair be adjusted so that you sit upright, with your feet flat on the ground and lower back supported?
- Are your elbows bent at 90 degrees and wrists straight when using the mouse and keyboard?

- Is your monitor directly in front of you, just below eye level?
- Is there enough light in your workspace?
- Do you take regular breaks to stand up or adjust your posture?
- Do you take regular eye breaks to look away from the monitor and refocus every 20 to 30 minutes?

Organisational Ergonomics

As part of human factors, there are also organisational aspects of translation work that might help or hinder a translator in achieving a state of 'flow'. These can be investigated by asking the question: Who does what and why? This is outside of the direct interaction of the user and their translation tool but will of course affect the user's well-being and efficiency. If we look at the dynamics of development of the translation tool itself, there is a school of thought that believes that technology is neutral, a tool to be used for good or ill. On the other hand, many ethicists and philosophers believe that technology engenders a specific worldview (Winner, 1983) or at least reflects the values of the designer (Moorkens, 2022). One way to see this influence in technology is in what a tool or software product allows or *affords* you to do, generally referred to as **affordances**. When Gibson (2014) originally introduced the concept in 1979, it was related to what the environment offered a person or animal, but a subsequent redefinition by Norman (1988) regarding product design relates to the *perceived actions* afforded by an object. So, in a translation tool, what are the affordances and what are the limitations? Well, as an example, CAT tools generally force users to follow a set segment-by-segment translation process. When we look at recordings of how users translate within a CAT tool, most follow this intuitive process but sometimes break from it to check for coherence or to go back over some previous segments.

One aspect of work organisation that is changing at the time of writing, particularly in areas of the translation market that focus most on scale, velocity, and productivity rather than quality, is increased automation and digitally mediated work. While variable pricing and automatic **'lights-out' project management** might not be expected to affect the ability of a translator to work immersively, the context is a lack of control over work and the isolation of not having a human point of contact in the workplace. This is particularly notable in translation **platform** work, which 89% of respondents to Pielmeier and O'Mara's (2020) survey say that they have experienced.

Many language service providers ask their translators (or *linguists*, as they are usually termed in the industry) to work via dedicated platforms in order to control workflows and to maximise data security. However, there are also companies whose work is entirely mediated via platforms, restricting translator autonomy within rigidly-defined workflow steps. Fırat (2021) notes some key attributes common to translation platforms, such as their enablement of peer-to-peer transactions, cutting out a middle person and offering translation buyers access to a large crowd of freelance workers, and replacing trust relationships and quality scores with rating systems. This is probably the most restrictive area of the contemporary translation marketplace, where sociotechnical concerns most affect the ability of translators to produce their best work. The translation editing interfaces on these platforms are nonetheless likely to resemble those discussed in Chapter 2 and elsewhere in this book, although without the rich suite of features available in larger workstation tools.

Software increasingly collects data from users, which can aid with development decisions and help with personalisation, but can also be used to monitor time spent or can be merged with other data to make inferences about the user. The extent to which users can access or control the data collected within their CAT tools such as TMs, activity data including keystrokes and mouse clicks, and **metadata** (data about data, e.g. date, time, or translator of a segment) will vary depending on organisational choices (see Chapter 8). The autonomy allowed or restrictions imposed on a translator can make a big difference to their feelings of job satisfaction and motivation in their work. This is a point made by Abdallah (2014) who proposed that **social quality** – the decisions made that support or disempower the translator – should be considered indivisible from **process quality** and **product quality**. Process quality often refers to whether the translation process follows the workflow steps as defined by standards such as the ISO standards for translation or post-editing, with the assumption that a high-quality process is more likely to produce a high-quality translation product.

Chapter 11 introduced various measures of translation product quality, but an organisational decision that affects human factors is the level of quality required for a translation project. In order to translate content as quickly and effectively as possible, many large organisations now have a tiered approach to product quality whereby translations are produced according to two or three defined quality levels. At the lowest level, low-risk, short shelf-life content is machine translated; at the medium level, low-risk and medium-term content is post-edited (light post-editing or full post-editing according to the fitness for purpose, as described in Chapter 6), and at the top level, full translation quality is produced using CAT tools and various resources such as those described throughout this book.

Bednárová-Gibová (2021: 403) reports that the aspects of work organisation that are most effective in keeping the agency translators she surveyed happy at work are their 'working environment, the text type they translate, time pressure and the ability to maintain concentration'. Working alone, as many translators tend to do, was not associated with unhappiness as long as the work environment was considered to be positive and without distraction. Conversely and rather predictably, this suggests that a physical and digital working environment that functions poorly will be a cause of unhappiness.

Accessibility in Translation Tools and Technologies

While translation tool developers have in recent years become far more responsive to user requirements than previously, the ability of translators with accessibility needs to work with existing tools is hampered by the functionality of many such tools. In particular, visually impaired translators who rely on **assistive technologies** have found that they don't interact well with many CAT tools. Assistive technologies for blind users are often **screen readers**, which either transform text on-screen into synthesised speech, often at high speeds, or use *braille displays*, converting on-screen text to braille characters. As a result of this limited interaction, blind translators are at a disadvantage when trying to carry out a translation within a CAT tool in order to deliver a quality translation that maintains the formatting of the original document(s). This is an ongoing problem that Rodríguez Vázquez and Mileto (2016: 120) call a 'so far unexplored branch of translational ergonomics'.

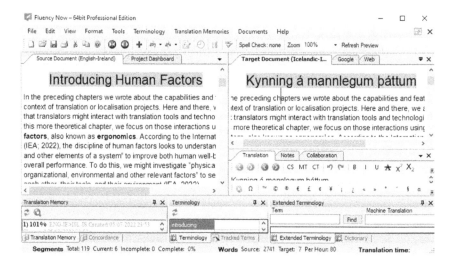

Figure 12.1 Fluency Now 4.21 editing interface.

Ideally, CAT tools would include accessible descriptions without reference to colours or formats, a comprehensive list of shortcuts, and a start-up guide for visually impaired users. Aside from text on-screen, screen readers also convert labelled icons and shortcuts to audio. In a web-based tool, this means using **ARIA labels** (attributes intended specifically for accessibility), as specified in W3C Web Content Accessibility Guidelines (www .w3.org/WAI/standards-guidelines). At the time of writing, some tools are not accessible even on their welcome page, others do not offer labels and assistance within the editing interface, and accessible user guides are seldom produced. Fluency Now, produced by Western Standard, appears to be the most accessible of current CAT tools (see Figure 12.1). Once users learn one or two unlabelled commands, those within the editing interface and fuzzy match percentages are all compatible with assistive technologies, with tags for formatting elements that can be automatically read and shortcuts for toggling between source and target text and terminology windows. There appear to be some accessibility difficulties with the integrated alignment tool. See Figure 12.2 for the Fluency Now Speech to Command menu.

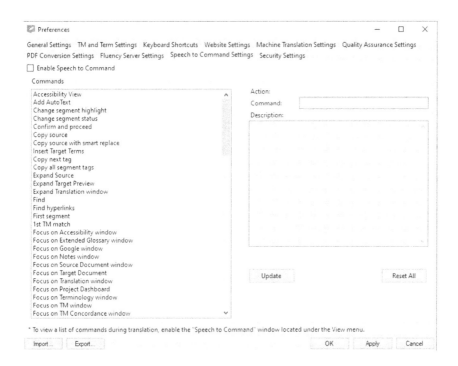

Figure 12.2 Fluency Now 4.21 Speech to Command menu.

For users who are visually impaired, we suggest trying a number of tools, if possible with a sighted translator, to assess their usability for your needs. You might also try the free demo version of Fluency Now due to its reputation as the most accessible of workstation-based CAT tools, taking advantage of the free web training session if available. We also recommend networking with other blind and visually impaired translators via groups such as TheRoundTable mailing list (http://lists.screenreview.org/listinfo.cgi /theroundtable-screenreview.org). to share advice on the use of translation tools with assistive technologies. For tool developers, we understand that it's difficult to retrospectively make your software accessible, but appeal to you to include accessible labels, to work with visually impaired translators to create a start-up guide, and to make your standard tools easily accessible to all users. For translation trainers, we suggest that due to the limited accessibility of CAT tools, you allow for extra and dedicated support to visually impaired translation students where possible (following the call from Figiel, 2018).

Conclusion

We still have much to learn about human factors in translation, and the dynamic technological landscape means that our interactions are changing all the time. However, an awareness of ergonomics should mean that we allow ourselves to be interrupted less frequently and to arrange the part of our working lives that we can control – our physical environment and our interaction with tools and technologies – in order to work more happily and efficiently. It's important also to be aware of the organisational aspects of our tasks that can affect our productivity and well-being. After all, translation, as noted by Risku (2002: 529), 'is done not only by the brain, but also by complex systems, systems which include people, their specific social and physical environments and all their cultural artefacts.' Finally, universal access to translation tools would be ideal but is not currently a reality. There are tools that cater better to visually impaired users that we might try, and for those who do not require assistive technology, an awareness of the limitations of contemporary tools should help to aid (and advocate for) others with accessibility needs.

Follow-Up Tasks and Reflection

1. Think about the different tools that you have explored through this book from an ergonomic point of view. Which did you find most intuitive to learn, and why? Which was the least intuitive? Approximately what proportion of available features would you estimate you now know how to use? Are there any that remain unclear to you?
2. In general, which features of translation tools do you find most helpful in making your work more efficient? Do they also help to make it more enjoyable, or the opposite?
3. Take a close look at the UI (User Interface) for the tool with which you are most familiar. What are its most, and least, helpful features? Are there any features from other tools that you would like to see added to it, and if so, why?
4. Finally, draw up a list of the *minimum number* of features that you consider essential for efficient translation in a CAT tool. How does that list compare with what you actually find in your most familiar tool?

Further Reading

This chapter introduces the concepts of human factors and ergonomics, but you may read about these in more detail in the following articles. Maureen Ehrensberger-Dow has published a great deal in this area, with some key work being Ehrensberger-Dow & Hunziker Heeb (2016) on *Investigating the ergonomics of a technologized translation workplace* and Kappus & Ehrensberger-Dow (2020) on 'The ergonomics of translation tools: Understanding when less is actually more', which compares a fully-featured and a SaaS CAT tool. Sharon O'Brien's work with Ehrensberger-Dow et al. (2017) investigates 'Irritating CAT tool features that matter to translators', and Teixeira & O'Brien (2017) report on 'Investigating the cognitive ergonomic aspects of translation tools in a workplace setting' with the use of biometrics.

Afterword

Key Questions

- What new developments are likely in the near to mid-term future?
- How will they change the translation industry?
- How far and in what ways can MT be expected to improve?
- Who is now doing MT research?
- What new developments in CAT tools may be around the corner?
- How are these technologies becoming increasingly interconnected?
- What might future translation tools look like?
- How will such developments affect the work and career prospects of translators?

In recent years translation tools and technologies have advanced at a remarkable pace, and there is every indication that this will continue for the foreseeable future. TM has become an almost ubiquitous tool for professional translators of all types, and is even starting to be used in literary and other types of 'creative' translation (Youdale & Rothwell, 2022). CAT tools have acquired new features designed to extract more leverage from legacy translation data and prompt the user with different types of useful proposals, including from MT. This has already made the modern translation environment 'an *extended cognitive system* involving a human translator, a TM tool, an MT engine, and sometimes other human translators or editors' (Balashov, 2020: 351, emphasis original). Moving into the **cloud** has also made many tools more collaborative, allowing linguists to share data in real time as well as facilitating project management (Chapter 8), potentially across multiple language pairs and time zones. Large LSPs are increasingly using **platforms** to put translation buyers in direct contact with freelance suppliers, assessing the job's languages and domain, and routing it to an appropriate linguist automatically, without the intervention of a project manager; platforms can also require linguists to compete directly for jobs on price. These trends towards cloud-based project automation and the fusion of the linguistic and financial aspects of professional translation look set to continue and exert increasing influence on the market.

Parallel and complementary developments in MT have been even more far-reaching than those in conventional CAT, prompting visions of the future in which the system's output would be consistently good enough not to need human intervention at all. In 2016 the influential technology think-tank TAUS published a *Translation Technology Landscape Report* in which it envisioned a point of 'singularity' in the translation industry, when NMT would be available in around 20,000 language pairs, for unrestricted domains, ubiquitously embedded in devices, and trained on corpora of user-selectable data:

> What we predict is that the world will get accustomed to what we call Fully Automatic Useful Translation (FAUT) and will more and more accept this as the norm for standard translation.
>
> (Massardo et al., 2016: 11)

TAUS hypothesised the advent of this singularity in 2030, but in some respects it has already arrived. MT has come of age and become truly useful, at least in some 'major' language pairs, to the point where, for many use cases (limited-life, -risk, and -value information, informative documents not for publication) it can be used with no, or only light, post-editing. As with CAT tools, MT's remit is starting to expand beyond technical domains into more 'creative' areas, with research currently being undertaken into its effectiveness and acceptability in literary translation (Toral & Way, 2018; Hadley et al., 2021). Meanwhile, TAUS has repositioned itself as an online marketplace 'for language data monetization and acquisition' (TAUS, n.d.), in which data sellers (LSPs, translators, data producers) can offer their domain-specific TMs for sale to data buyers, including MT providers and enterprises, for purposes of training specialised MT systems.

While these developments have in many contexts made the individual translator's task easier and more efficient, they have also changed it in ways that are making many professionals concerned about their future roles and livelihood. There is a fear that MT is not only driving down rates but will deskill translation in a growing number of domains by reducing it to post-editing, if it does not soon supplant the human translator altogether. In contrast to this pessimistic outlook is CSA Research's vision of the technology-enhanced *augmented* translator (Lommel, 2018a), empowered by increasingly user-friendly and connected tools to be more creative as well as more efficient. This vision, harking back to the initial motivation for TM (see Chapter 1), is close to reality for those who have built an interoperating suite of supporting tools for their work, particularly so for the increasing number of translators who make effective use of AI-supported technologies such as ASR to augment their translation practice (see Chapter 12).

There has been pushback from translator associations, voices in academia and industry, and translators themselves in response to the use of translation tools and technologies to introduce reductive modes of work. Organisations that impose restrictive post-editing workflows for inadequate remuneration, particularly in the AVT space, have reported a 'talent crunch', as skilled translators simply choose not to accept poorly paid work that is not varied, motivating, and satisfying (Stasimioti, 2022; see also Chapter 9). Many other organisations have developed a tiered quality system depending on product line or text type, whereby certain low-risk and low-value content is machine translated, possibly with the aid of automatic quality estimation, middle value but low-risk content is post-edited, and higher value content is translated by computer-aided specialist linguists (see for example Kelly, 2020). This is even true of the higher or 'premium' end of the translation market, where Jemielity (2018), among others, says that demand and prices remain strong for translation of high-risk or high-value content. Gartner Research (Elliot et al., 2022) predicts continued and pronounced tiering in what they call the '**localisation** hyper-automation' era, when humans will focus on strategic and critical requirements, leaving simpler work to NMT with risk automatically flagged. The 'human-in-the-loop' model of NMT training and development (TAUS n.d.; Vashee, 2021) also promises to open up new career opportunities for linguists to use their high-level language and cultural skills in creating and maintaining translation training data, and evaluating and improving machine-generated output. Suggestions from O'Brien and Rossetti (2020: 114) include 'management of linguistic resources' (e.g. **data curation** and evaluation), 'training, development, and testing of MT engines; translation and editing; quality assurance for products in specialised markets and target cultures; or copywriting and **transcreation**', alongside longstanding roles such as vendor or project management. Massey (2021: 76) feels that there are huge opportunities for translators to 'make fuller use of their capacities and to adopt more visible, agentic roles' within organisations. What seems certain is that these innovations will change the translation industry in fundamental ways, some of which we aim to outline below.

Huge resources are being put into MT research at the time of writing, with industry and academic efforts moving in slightly different directions. The effectiveness of NMT as a tool for end users, as an example of cutting-edge AI, and as a way to maximise the interconnectedness (and thus value) of their international network, has led big technology companies to expand their MT research teams, to the extent that major research efforts now originate mostly from these companies rather than academic researchers. Well-resourced technology industry teams have a budgetary advantage to afford the cost of competitive salaries and of energy and powerful computing equipment, plus they often have access to large amounts of training data. An example of contrasting approaches from industry and academia is MT for **low-resource languages**. Industry teams are mostly behind research in massively multilingual NMT, as reported in Chapter 6. These *multilingual* systems boost the output quality of MT for low-resource languages such as Faroese and Hausa. Conversely, academic research tends to focus on maximising the quality of *bilingual* systems for low-resource languages by finding or creating extra training data or exploring alternative MT models (see Haddow et al., 2022). The combined effect of this research will be the availability of high-quality resources and useful MT in a greater number of the very numerous 'long-tail' languages that have so far been left behind in the translation technology revolution, with immense implications for the economic and social wellbeing, and linguistic and cultural equality, of the countries and regions involved (Bapna et al., 2022; NLLB team et al., 2022). For instance, MT promises to allow the voices and ideas of people in less published or less widely known languages to come to the attention of readers, activists, scholars, allies and others around the world, while ideas and texts in already dominant languages might increase their reach into even more languages.

Ongoing efforts to make MT more efficient have decreased the amount of time, cost, and electricity (and thus CO_2 emissions) required to train MT systems (see Heafield et al., 2021 and Jooste et al., 2022), but concurrent efforts to improve output quality, particularly for multilingual systems, mean that **language models** for translation or text generation are growing larger and require longer training, outpacing the innovations in training efficiency. Dodge et al. (2022) called for publication of CO_2 emissions related to MT research to make this counterintuitive situation more transparent to readers. The continued use of huge amounts of power for computing, especially at a time when many national networks are approaching their limits, cannot possibly be sustainable.

There is continuing interest in improved **evaluation metrics** and in document-level MT production and evaluation, with the publication of the first document-level metrics (see BlonDe from Jiang et al., 2022), which should in time lead to contextually aware MT, with greater consistency across sentence boundaries. This fits with the predictions (and prescription) of MT research by Lommel (2021), who feels that so-called 'responsive MT' should automatically adapt to the subject domain based on user feedback and automatically match with requirements for applicability and usability.

Improvements in MT quality in general have become more difficult to attain as NMT technology has matured. However, there is scope for better incorporation of MT into workflows, exemplified by the ideas in Responsive MT, research on MT in dubbing (Mejías-Climent & de los Reyes Lozano, 2021) and the increased use of MT (and synthetic voices) in game localisation. We are seeing increased automation outside of MT, such as workflow steps to remove excess effort and maximise efficiency, often based on feedback from translation activity data gleaned within translation platforms (Fırat, 2021). The impact of large language models for both (source) text generation and for translation is unclear at the time of writing. Future developments in NMT point towards incremental quality improvements, a greater range of languages supported, and improved integration of MT into workflows, tools, and technologies. However, there is also the certainty that another technology will in time supplant NMT, extending the limits of MT beyond what is currently possible.

For obvious reasons, the discussion around MT often focuses on financial gains achieved through the use of MT systems in commercial and for-profit settings, and the consequences this is having on professional translators and translation trainees. However, recent years have also seen an increase in the use of MT and other translation technology solutions in not-for-profit contexts. These trends are the subjects of growing research activities in translation including, for example, the use of MT in non-governmental organisations (Rico Pérez, 2019), as part of the provision of public legal or health services (Vieira et al., 2021), and crisis translation scenarios (Federici & O'Brien, 2019). The role of MT in language learning is also an area of growing interest among scholars in Translation Studies and language learning (Carré et al., 2022).

The ubiquity of MT in today's digital society (Vieira et al., 2022) and its growing importance in a number of settings has resulted in calls for developing MT literacy (Bowker & Ciro, 2019), not only in current and future professional translators but in non-professional users as well. As Dorothy Kenny puts it, 'all users should have some basic understanding of how the technology works, so they can use it intelligently and avoid common pitfalls' (2022a: vi). The growing realisation that MT and other text automatically generated by neural systems reflects and exacerbates societal bias should serve to highlight the need for a critical and ethical approach to MT usage. As Kenny (ibid.) writes, 'users should have some basic knowledge of the ethical issues that arise when we use machine translation', since MT, 'like all communication technologies, [...] can be used for nefarious causes or positive humanitarian purposes'. Critically exploring both the former and the latter will be of utmost importance in the training of future translators.

As should be clear by now, the authors of this book, while remaining alert to the potential risks and threats inherent in increasing computerisation of the translation process, take a pragmatic and broadly positive view of the development of translation technologies and are reasonably optimistic about their future. We see them as likely to open up new opportunities for linguists, by both increasing the range and quality of resources available to the translator, and by creating additional expert roles, especially around data curation, linguistic/cultural advocacy and consultancy, and quality control. Within the computerised translation environment of the future, the distinction between human and machine-sourced translation proposals, between TM and MT, may disappear completely, while the translation engine becomes able to interact more flexibly and effectively with a user-configurable range of other online data sources (e.g. termbases, dictionaries, and corpora). What we consider important, and hope to facilitate with this book, is an interest in keeping abreast of the capabilities of new translation tools and technologies. As noted by Esselink (2022), technologies have tended to be introduced by LSPs and translation employers rather than by translators themselves. We consider that familiarity with developing technologies and an understanding of their benefits (as well as the new challenges and risks they will continue to present) should be empowering for translators, allowing them to advise others knowledgeably about the appropriateness of their use. This optimistic vision of a constructive future collaboration between human linguists and machines seems an appropriate note on which to close this book, for the moment at least.

Bibliography

Abdallah, K. (2014). Social quality. Key to collective problem solving in translation production networks. *Proceedings of the 6th Riga Symposium on Pragmatic Aspects of Translation*, 5–18.

Ahmad, K., & Rogers, M. (2001). Corpus linguistics and terminology extraction. In S. E. Wright & G. Budin (Eds.), *Handbook of terminology management* (Vol.2, pp. 725–760). John Benjamins.

Ahrenberg, L. (2015). Alignment. In S.-W. Chan (Ed.), *Routledge encyclopedia of translation technology* (pp. 395–408). Routledge.

Akhulkova, Y., Hicket S. and Hynes, R. (2022). *Language technology atlas: The definitive map to language technology*. Nimdzi. https://www.nimdzi.com/language-technology-atlas/

Alcina, A. (Ed.). (2011). *Teaching and learning terminology: New strategies and methods*. John Benjamins.

Allwood, J. (2009). Multimodal corpora. In A. Lüdeling & M. Kytö (Eds.), *Corpus linguistics. An international handbook* (Vol. 1, pp. 207–225). Mouton de Gruyter. DOI: 10.1515/booksetHSK29/html

ALPAC. (1966). *Language and machines: Computers in translation and linguistics. A report by the Automatic Language Processing Advisory Committee, Division of Behavioral Sciences, National Academy of Sciences, National Research Council (1416)*. National Academy of Sciences. http://www.nap.edu/openbook.php?isbn=ARC000005

Anthony, L. (2013). A critical look at software tools in corpus linguistics. *Linguistic Research*, *30*(2), 141–161. DOI: 10.17250/khisli.30.2.201308.001

Arthern, P. J. (1979). Machine translation and computerized terminology systems: A translator's viewpoint. In *Translating and the Computer: Proceedings of a Seminar, London, 14th November, 1978* (pp. 77–108).

Atril. (n.d.). *Déjà Vu X3 videos—AutoWrite*. Atril Solutions. https://atrilsolutions.zendesk.com/hc/en-us/articles/205542431-D%C3%A9j%C3%A0-Vu-X3-videos

Austermühl, F. (2001). *Electronic tools for translators*. St. Jerome.

Austermühl, F. (2012). Using concept mapping and the web as corpus to develop terminological competence among translators and interpreters. *Translation Spaces*, *1*(1), 54–80. DOI: 10.1075/ts.1.09aus

Avila, C. (2018). *How to use upLIFT fragment recall and fuzzy repair in SDL Trados Studio*. Trados. https://www.trados.com/blog/how-to-use-uplift-fragment-recall-and-fuzzy-repair-in-sdl-trados-studio.html

Bahdanau, D., Cho, K., & Bengio, Y. (2016). Neural machine translation by jointly learning to align and translate. ArXiv. http://arxiv.org/abs/1409.0473

Baker, M., & Saldanha, G. (Eds.). (2009). *Routledge encyclopedia of translation studies* (2nd ed). Routledge.

Balashov, Y. (2020). The translator's extended mind. *Minds and Machines, 30*(3), 349–383. DOI: 10.1007/s11023-020-09536-5

Bapna, A., Caswell, I., Kreutzer, J. et al. (2022). Building machine translation systems for the next thousand languages. ArXiv. https://arxiv.org/abs/2205.03983.

Bar-Hillel, Y. (1960). The present status of automatic translation of languages. In F. L. Alt (Ed.), *Advances in computers* (Vol. 1, pp. 91–163). Elsevier. DOI: 10.1016/S0065-2458(08)60607-5

BBC Academy. (2021a). *How do I create subtitles?* https://www.bbc.com/academy -guides/bbc.com/academy-guides/how-do-i-create-subtitles/

BBC Academy. (2021b). *BBC subtitle guidelines.* https://bbc.github.io/subtitle -guidelines/

Bednárová-Gibová, K. (2021). Organizational ergonomics of translation as a powerful predictor of translators' happiness at work? *Perspectives, 29*(3), 391– 406. DOI: 10.1080/0907676X.2020.1753788

Ben Milad, K. M. (2021). *Comparative evaluation of translation memory (TM) and machine translation (MT) systems in translation between Arabic and English* [PhD thesis, Swansea University]. https://cronfa.swan.ac.uk/Record/ cronfa57439

Bernal-Merino, M. Á. (2014). *Translation and localisation in video games: Making entertainment software global.* Routledge. DOI: 10.4324/9781315752334

Birdsong, D. (2014). *Second language acquisition and the critical period hypothesis.* Routledge.

Bononno, R. (2000). Terminology for translators—An implementation of ISO 12620. *Meta: Translators' Journal, 45,* 646–669. DOI: 10.7202/002101AR

Boulton, A. (2015). Applying data-driven learning to the web. In A. Leńko-Szymańska & A. Boulton (Eds.), *Multiple affordances of language corpora for data-driven learning* (pp. 267–296). John Benjamins. DOI: 10.1075/scl.69.13bou

Bowker, L. (2002). *Computer-aided translation technology: A practical introduction.* University of Ottawa Press.

Bowker, L. (2003). Terminology tools for translators. In H. Somers (Ed.), *Computers and translation: A translator's guide* (pp. 49–65). John Benjamins.

Bowker, L. (2005). Productivity vs quality? A pilot study on the impact of translation memory systems. *Localisation Focus, 4,* 13–20.

Bowker, L. (2015). Terminology and translation. In H. J. Kockaert & F. Steurs (Eds.), *Handbook of terminology* (Vol. 1, pp. 304–323). John Benjamins. DOI: 10.1075/hot.1.ter5

Bowker, L. (2019). Terminology. In M. Baker & G. Saldanha (Eds), *Routledge encyclopedia of translation studies* (3rd edition, pp. 579–583). Routledge.

Bowker, L., & Ciro, J. B. (2019). *Machine translation and global research: Towards improved machine translation literacy in the scholarly community.* Emerald Publishing Limited. DOI: 10.1108/9781787567214

Bowker, L., & Pearson, J. (2002). *Working with specialized language: A practical guide to using corpora.* Routledge. DOI: 10.4324/9780203469255

Brown, P., Cocke, J., Della Pietra, S. et al. (1988). A statistical approach to French/ English translation. In *Proceedings of the Second Conference on Theoretical and*

Methodological Issues in Machine Translation of Natural Languages. TMIMTNL 1988, Pittsburgh, USA. https://aclanthology.org/1988.tmi-1.19

Cabanellas, G. (2014). *The legal environment of translation*. Routledge. DOI: 10.4324/9781315763989

Cabré, Mª. T. (1999). *Terminology: Theory, methods, applications*. John Benjamins.

Cabré, Mª. T. (2003). Theories of terminology: Their description, prescription and explanation. *Terminology, 9*(2), 163–200.

Candel-Mora, M. Á. (2017). Criteria for the integration of term banks in the professional translation environment. *Sendebar. Revista de Traducción e Interpretación, 28*, 243–260.

Carré, A., Kenny, D., Rossi, C. et al. (2022). Machine translation for language learners. In D. Kenny (Ed.), *Machine translation for everyone* (pp. 187–207). Language Science Press. DOI: 10.5281/zenodo.6760024

Castilho, S., Moorkens, J., Gaspari, F., et al. (2018). Evaluating MT for massive open online courses. *Machine Translation, 32*, 255–278. DOI: 10.1007/s10590-018-9221-y

Cerrella Bauer, S. (2015). Concepts, tools and methods: Managing terminology projects. In H. J. Kockaert & F. Steurs (Eds.), *Handbook of terminology* (Vol. 1, pp. 324–340). John Benjamins. DOI: 10.1075/hot.1.man1

Chan, S.-W. (Ed.). (2015a). *Routledge encyclopedia of translation technology*. Routledge. DOI: 10.4324/9781315749129

Chan, S.-W. (2015b). The development of translation technology: 1967-2013. In S.-W. Chan (Ed.), *Routledge encyclopedia of translation technology* (pp. 1–46). Routledge.

Christensen, T. P., & Schjoldager, A. (2011). The impact of translation-memory (TM) technology on cognitive processes: Student-translators' retrospective comments in an online questionnaire. In B. Sharp, M. Zock, M. Carl, et al. (Eds.), *Proceedings of the 8th International NLPCS Workshop: Special theme: Human-Machine Interaction in Translation* (pp. 119–130). Samfundslitteratur.

Ciobanu, D. (2016). Automatic speech recognition in the professional translation process. *Translation Spaces, 5*, 124–144. DOI: 10.1075/ts.5.1.07cio

Corpas Pastor, G., & Durán-Muñoz, I. (Eds.). (2018). *Trends in e-tools and resources for translators and interpreters*. Brill/Rodopi. DOI: 10.1163/9789004351790

Costa, H., Corpas Pastor, G., & Durán-Muñoz, I. (2018). Assessing terminology management systems for interpreters. In G. Corpas Pastor & I. Durán-Muñoz (Eds.), *Trends in e-tools and resources for translators and interpreters* (pp. 57–84). Brill/Rodopi.

De Bessé, B. (1997). Terminological definitions. In S. E. Wright & G. Budin (Eds.), & J. C. Sager (Trans.), *Handbook of terminology* (Vol. 1, pp. 63–74). John Benjamins.

De Moraes, N. (2007). Déjà Vu X Professional: A review of version 7.5, Part II. *ATA Chronicle, 36*(9), 33–38.

Deane-Cox, S., & Spiessens, A. (Eds.). (2022). *Routledge handbook of translation and memory*. Routledge.

Declercq, C. (2015). Editing in translation technology. In S.-W. Chan (Ed.), *Routledge encyclopedia of translation technology* (pp. 480–493). Routledge. DOI: 10.4324/9781315749129.ch30

Desjardins, R. (2017). *Translation and social media*. Palgrave Macmillan.

Di Nunzio, G. M., & Vezzani, F. (2021). On the reusability of terminological data. In *Proceedings of the 10th National Conference of AIUCD: Digital Humanities for Society: E-Quality, Participation Rights and Values in the Digital Age*, 183–186.

Díaz, N., & Zetzsche, J. (2022). *The translator's tool box* (Version 15). https://www.academiaclp.com/course/the-translators-tool-box

Díaz Cintas, J. (2015). Technological strides in subtitling. In S.-W. Chan (Ed.), *Routledge encyclopedia of translation technology* (pp. 632–643). Routledge.

Díaz Cintas, J., & Massidda, S. (2020). Technological advances in audiovisual translation. In M. O'Hagan (Ed.), *Routledge handbook of translation and technology* (pp. 255–270). Routledge.

Díaz Cintas, J., & Remael, A. (2021). *Subtitling: Concepts and practices* (2nd edition). Routledge.

Doddington, G. (2002). Automatic evaluation of machine translation quality using n-gram co-occurrence statistics. *Proceedings of the Second International Conference on Human Language Technology Research*, 138–145.

Dodge, J., Prewitt, T., Tachet des Combes, R. et al. (2022). Measuring the carbon intensity of AI in cloud instances. In *2022 ACM Conference on Fairness, Accountability, and Transparency*, 1877–1894. DOI: 10.1145/3531146.3533234

Doherty, S. (2016). The impact of translation technologies on the process and product of translation. *International Journal of Communication, 10*, 947–969.

Dowling, M., Lynn, T., Poncelas, A. et al. (2018). SMT versus NMT: Preliminary comparisons for Irish. In *Proceedings of the AMTA 2018 Workshop on Technologies for MT of Low Resource Languages* (LoResMT 2018), 12–20. https://aclanthology.org/W18-2202

Drouin, P. (2006). Termhood experiments: Quantifying the relevance of candidate terms. In H. Picht (Ed.), *Modern approaches to terminological theories and applications* (pp. 375–391). Peter Lang.

Drugan, J. (2013). *Quality in professional translation: Assessment and improvement*. Bloomsbury.

Drugan, J., Strandvik, I., & Vuorinen, E. (2018). Translation quality, quality management and agency: Principles and practice in the European Union institutions. In J. Moorkens, S. Castilho, F. Gaspari et al. (Eds.), *Translation quality assessment: From principles to practice* (pp. 39–68). Springer. DOI: 10.1007/978-3-319-91241-7_3

Dunne, K. J., & Dunne, E. S. (2011). *Translation and localization project management: The art of the possible*. John Benjamins.

Durban, C. (2022). Translation, time, technology—Who's counting? In M. Kubánek, O. Klabal, & O. Molnár (Eds.), *Teaching Translation vs. Training Translators: Proceedings of the Translation and Interpreting Forum Olomouc* (pp. 11–19). Palacký University.

Ehrensberger-Dow, M., & Hunziker Heeb, A. (2016). Investigating the ergonomics of a technologized translation workplace. In R. Muñoz Martín (Ed.), *Reembedding translation process research* (pp. 69–88). John Benjamins. DOI: 10.1075/btl.128.04ehr

Elithorn, A., & Banerji, R. (1984). Artificial and human intelligence. Edited review papers presented at the *International NATO Symposium on Artificial and Human Intelligence, Lyon, France, October 1981*. North-Holland.

Elliot, B., Rigon, G., Lee, A., et al. (2022). *Market guide for AI-enabled translation services* (No. G00741813; pp. 1–22). Gartner Research. https://www.gartner .com/doc/reprints?id=1-2AAOC19B&ct=220613&st=sb&submissionGuid= 2bdffc80-1ade-4633-8374-3e99335dae93

Enríquez Raido, V. (2014). *Translation and web searching*. Routledge.

EMT Board. (2022). *European master's in translation competence framework 2022.* European Commission.

Esselink, B. (2000). *A practical guide to localization*. John Benjamins.

Esselink, B. (2022). Thirty years and counting: A global industry growing up. *Journal of Internationalization and Localization, 9*(1), 87–95.

Evans, D. (n.d.). *Corpus building and investigation for the humanities: An on-line information pack about corpus investigation techniques for the humanities.* University of Birmingham. https://www.birmingham.ac.uk/Documents/college -artslaw/corpus/Intro/Unit1.pdf

Exel, M., Buschbeck, B., Brandt, L., et al. (2020). Terminology-constrained neural machine translation at SAP. In *Proceedings of the 22nd Annual Conference of the European Association for Machine Translation*, 271–280. https://aclanthology .org/2020.eamt-1.29

Federici, F. M., Gerber, B., O'Brien, S., et al. (2019). *The international humanitarian sector and language translation in crisis situations: Assessment of current practices and future needs.* INTERACT The International Network on Crisis Translation. https://doras.dcu.ie/23708/

Federici, F. M., & O'Brien, S. (Eds.). (2019). *Translation in cascading crises.* Routledge. DOI: 10.4324/9780429341052

Fernández, T., Flórez de la Colina, M. A., & Peters, P. (2011). Terminology and terminography for architecture and building construction. In A. Alcina (Ed.), *Teaching and learning terminology: New strategies and methods* (pp. 11–35). John Benjamins.

Figiel, W. (2018). Studying translation from the perspective of blind students in Poland. In P. Bouillon, S. Rodríguez, & I. Strasly (Eds.), *Proceedings of the 2nd Swiss Conference on Barrier-free Communication: Accessibility in Educational Settings* (pp. 36–39).

Filkin, P. (2016). Bridging the divide… merging segments. *Multifarious Blog.* https://multifarious.filkin.com/2016/11/21/bridging-the-divide-merging -segments/

Firth, J. R. (1957). *Papers in linguistics, 1934–1951.* Oxford University Press.

Fırat, G. (2021). Uberization of translation: Impacts on working conditions. *The Journal of Internationalization and Localization, 8*(1), 48–75. DOI: 10.1075/jial .20006.fir

Flanagan, K. (2015). Subsegment recall in translation memory—Perceptions, expectations and reality. *Journal of Specialised Translation, 23.* https://jostrans .org/issue23/art_flanagan.pdf

Folaron, D. (2020). Technology, technical translation and localization. In M. O'Hagan (Ed.), *Routledge handbook of translation and technology* (pp. 203-219). Routledge.

Forcada, M. L. (2010). Machine translation today. In Y. Gambier & L. van Doorslaer (Eds.), *Handbook of translation studies* (Vol. 1, pp. 215–223). John Benjamins. https://doi.org/10.1075/hts.1.mac1

Gale, W. A., & Church, K. W. (1993). A program for aligning sentences in bilingual corpora. *Computational Linguistics*, *19*(1), 75–102.

Gamal, S. (2020). The memory of knowledge: An analytical study on translators' perceptions and assessment of CAT tools with regard to text genre. *International Journal of Linguistics and Translation Studies*, *1*, 1–18. DOI: 10.36892/ijlts. v1i2.47

Garcia, I. (2008). Translating and revising for localisation: What do we know? What do we need to know? *Perspectives*, *16*(1–2), 49–60. DOI: 10.1080/09076760802517630

Garcia, I. (2014). Computer-aided translation. In S.-W. Chan (Ed.), *Routledge encyclopedia of translation technology* (pp. 68–87). Routledge.

Gaspari, F., & Hutchins, J. (2007). Online and free! Ten years of online machine translation: Origins, developments, current use and future prospects. In *Proceedings of Machine Translation Summit XI: Papers. MT Summit 2007, Copenhagen, Denmark*. https://aclanthology.org/2007.mtsummit-papers.27

Gibson, J. J. (2014). *The ecological approach to visual perception*. Psychology Press. https://doi.org/10.4324/9781315740218

Goldsmith, E. (2018). SDL Trados Studio 2019: Avoiding featuritis. *Signs & Symptoms of Translation*. https://signsandsymptomsoftranslation.com/2018/07 /26/studio-2019/

Gornostay, T. (2010). Terminology management in real use. In *Proceedings of the 5th International Conference Applied Linguistics in Science and Education*, 25–26.

Gough, J. (2019). Developing translation-oriented research competence: What can we learn from professional translators? *The Interpreter and Translator Trainer*, *13*(3), 342–359. DOI: 10.1080/1750399X.2019.1656404

Graham, Y., Baldwin, T., Dowling, M., et al. (2016). Is all that glitters in machine translation quality estimation really gold? In Y. Matsumoto & R. Prasad (Eds.), *Proceedings of COLING 2016, the 26th International Conference on Computational Linguistics: Technical Papers* (pp. 3124–3134). The COLING 2016 Organizing Committee. https://aclanthology.org/C16-1294

Granda, R., & Warburton, K. (2001). Terminology management as data management. In *Proceedings of the 2001 Conference of the IBM Centre for Advanced Studies on Collaborative Research* (CASCON 01). https://dl.acm.org/ doi/10.5555/782096.782100

Guerberof-Arenas, A., & Toral, A. (2020). The impact of post-editing and machine translation on creativity and reading experience. *Translation Spaces*, *9*(2), 255–282. https://doi.org/10.1075/ts.20035.gue

Guillot, M.-N. (2018). Subtitling on the cusp of its futures. In L. Pérez-González (Ed.), *Routledge handbook of audiovisual translation* (pp. 31–47). Routledge.

Hadley, J. L., Taivalkoski-Shilov, K., Teixeira, C., & Toral, A. (Eds.). (2022). *Using technologies for creative-text translation*. Taylor & Francis.

Haddow, B., Bawden, R., Miceli Barone, A. V. et al. (2022). Survey of low-resource machine translation. *Computational Linguistics*, *48*(3), 673–732. DOI: 10.1162/ coli_a_00446

Hassan Awadalla, H., Aue, A., Chen, C., et al. (2018). *Achieving human parity on automatic Chinese to English news translation*. https://www.microsoft.com/en-us /research/publication/achieving-human-parity-on-automatic-chinese-to-english -news-translation/

Heafield, K., Zhu, Q., & Grundkiewicz, R. (2021). Findings of the WMT 2021 shared task on efficient translation. In *Proceedings of the Sixth Conference on Machine Translation*, 639–651. https://aclanthology.org/2021.wmt-1.68

Hearne, M., & Way, A. (2011). Statistical machine translation: A guide for linguists and translators. *Language and Linguistics Compass* 5(5), 205–226. DOI: 10.1111/j.1749-818X.2011.00274.x.

Heylen, K., & De Hertog, D. (2015). Automatic term extraction. In H. J. Kockaert & F. Steurs (Eds.), *Handbook of terminology* (Vol. 1, pp. 203–221). John Benjamins.

Hofstede, G. (2011). Dimensionalizing cultures: The Hofstede model in context. *Online Readings in Psychology and Culture*, 2(1). DOI: 10.9707/2307-0919.1014

House, J. (2015). *Translation quality assessment: Past and present*. Routledge. DOI: 10.4324/9781315752839

Hutchins, W. J. (1986). *Machine translation: Past, present, future*. Ellis Horwood.

Hutchins, W. J. (1995). Machine translation: A brief history. In E. F. K. Koerner & R. E. Asher (Eds.), *Concise history of the language sciences: From the Sumerians to the cognitivists* (pp. 431–445). Pergamon.

International Ergonomics Association. (n.d.). *What is ergonomics?* https://iea.cc/what-is-ergonomics/

International Organization for Standardization. (2015). *ISO 17100:2015*. https://www.iso.org/standard/59149.html

International Organization for Standardization. (2017). *ISO 18587:2017*. https://www.iso.org/cms/render/live/en/sites/isoorg/contents/data/standard/06/29/62970.html

Isabelle, P. (1993). Bi-textual aids for translators. In *Proceedings of the 8th Annual Conference of the UW Centre for the New OED and Text Research*, 1–15.

Jemielity, D. (2018). Translation in intercultural business and economic environments. In S.-A. Harding and O. Carbonell Cortés (Eds.), *Routledge handbook of translation and culture* (pp. 533–557). Routledge.

Jiang, Y., Liu, T., Ma, S., et al. (2022). BlonDe: An automatic evaluation metric for document-level machine translation. In M. Carpuat, M.-C. De Marneffe, & I. V. Meza Ruiz (Eds.), *Proceedings of the 2022 Conference of the North American Chapter of the Association for Computational Linguistics: Human Language Technologies* (pp. 1550–1565). Association for Computational Linguistics. DOI: 10.18653/v1/2022.naacl-main.111

Jiménez-Crespo, M. A. (2013). *Translation and web localization*. Routledge.

Jiménez-Crespo, M. A. (2019). Localization. In M. Baker & G. Saldanha (Eds.), *Routledge encyclopedia of translation studies* (pp. 299–304). Routledge. DOI: 10.4324/9781315678627-64

Johnson, M., Schuster, M., Le, Q. V., et al. (2017). Google's multilingual neural machine translation system: Enabling zero-shot translation. *Transactions of the Association for Computational Linguistics*, 5, 339–351. DOI: 10.1162/tacl_a_00065

Jooste, W., Haque, R., & Way, A. (2022). Knowledge distillation: A method for making neural machine translation more efficient. *Information*, 13, 88. DOI: 10.3390/info13020088

Kageura, K., & Marshman, E. (2020). Terminology extraction and management. In M. O'Hagan (Ed.), *Routledge handbook of translation and technology* (pp. 61–77). Routledge.

Kalchbrenner, N., & Blunsom, P. (2013). Recurrent continuous translation models. *Proceedings of the 2013 Conference on Empirical Methods in Natural Language Processing*, 1700–1709. https://aclanthology.org/D13-1176

Kappus, M., & Ehrensberger-Dow, M. (2020). The ergonomics of translation tools: Understanding when less is actually more. *The Interpreter and Translator Trainer*, 14(4), 386–404. DOI: 10.1080/1750399X.2020.1839998

Kay, M. (1997) [1980]. The proper place of men and machines in language translation. *Machine Translation*, 12(1/2), 3–23.

Keller, N. T. (2010). Integrating multiword terms in terminology management systems: A case study. *Proceedings of T21N Translation in Transition*. Translation in Transition 2010. http://www.t21n.com/articles.php

Kelly, N. (2020). *The translation tech trifecta*. Born to Be Global. https://borntobeglobal.com/2020/11/18/the-translation-tech-trifecta/

Kenny, D. (2018). Machine translation. In J. P. Rawling & P. Wilson (Eds.), *The Routledge handbook of translation and philosophy* (pp. 428–445). Routledge.

Kenny, D. (Ed.). (2022a). *Machine translation for everyone: Empowering users in the age of artificial intelligence*. Language Science Press. https://langsci-press.org/catalog/book/342

Kenny, D. (2022b). Introduction. In D. Kenny (Ed.), *Machine translation for everyone* (pp. v–viii). Language Science Press. https://langsci-press.org/catalog/book/342

Knight, D. and Adolphs, S. (2020). Multimodal corpora. In M. Paquot & S. T. Gries (Eds), *A practical handbook of corpus linguistics* (pp. 351–369). Springer.

Koby, G. S., Fields, P., Hague, D. R., et al. (2014). Defining translation quality. *Tradumàtica: Tecnologies de la traducció*, 12, 413–420. DOI: 10.5565/rev/tradumatica.76

Kocmi, T., Federmann, C., Grundkiewicz, R., et al. (2021). To ship or not to ship: An extensive evaluation of automatic metrics for machine translation. In *Proceedings of the Sixth Conference on Machine Translation* (pp. 478–494). https://aclanthology.org/2021.wmt-1.57

Koehn, P. (2009). *Statistical machine translation*. Cambridge University Press. DOI: 10.1017/CBO9780511815829

Koehn, P. (2020). *Neural machine translation*. Cambridge University Press.

Koehn, P., Hoang, H., Birch, A., et al. (2007). Moses: Open source toolkit for statistical machine translation. In *Proceedings of the 45th Annual Meeting of the Association for Computational Linguistics Companion Volume Proceedings of the Demo and Poster Sessions* (pp. 177–180). https://aclanthology.org/P07-2045

Koerner, E. F. K., & Asher, R. E. (Eds.). (1995). *Concise history of the language sciences: From the Sumerians to the cognitivists*. Pergamon.

Koller, W. (1995). The concept of equivalence and the object of translation studies. *Target*, 7(2), 191–222.

Krings, H. P., & Koby, G. S. (2001). *Repairing texts: Empirical investigations of machine translation post-editing processes*. The Kent State University Press.

Lagoudaki, P. M. (2009). *Expanding the possibilities of translation memory systems: From the translator's wishlist to the developer's design* [PhD thesis, Imperial College London]. http://hdl.handle.net/10044/1/7879

Läubli, S., Castilho, S., Neubig, G., et al. (2020). A set of recommendations for assessing human–machine parity in language translation. *Journal of Artificial Intelligence Research*, 67, 653–672. DOI: 10.1613/jair.1.11371

Läubli, S., & Green, S. (2020). Translation technology research and human–computer interaction (HCI). In M. O'Hagan (Ed.), *Routledge handbook of translation and technology* (pp. 370–383). Routledge.

Laviosa, S., & Liu, K. (2021). The pervasiveness of corpora in translation studies. 翻譯季刊 *(Translation Quarterly)*, *101*, 5–20.

Lee, K., Fırat, O., Agarwal, A., et al. (2018). Hallucinations in neural machine translation. In *ICLR 2019 International Conference on Learning Representations*. https://openreview.net/forum?id=SkxJ-309FQ

Leńko-Szymańska, A., & Boulton, A. (Eds.). (2015). *Multiple affordances of language corpora for data-driven learning*. John Benjamins.

Licht, D., Gao, C., Lam, J., et al. (2022). *Consistent human evaluation of machine translation across language pairs*. arXiv. https://arXiv.2205.08533

Lilt. (n.d.). *What is interactive, adaptive MT?* https://support.lilt.com/kb/what-is-interactive-adaptive-mt

Lommel, A. (2018a). Augmented translation: A new approach to combining human and machine capabilities. In *Proceedings of the 13th Conference of the Association for Machine Translation in the Americas (Volume 2: User Track)*, 5–12. https://aclanthology.org/W18-1905

Lommel, A. (2018b). Metrics for translation quality assessment: A case for standardising error typologies. In J. Moorkens, S. Castilho, S. Doherty, et al. (Eds.), *Translation quality assessment. From principles to practice* (pp. 109–127). Springer. DOI: 10.1007/978-3-319-91241-7_6

Lommel, A. (2021). *Responsive machine translation: The next frontier for MT*. CSA Research. https://csa-research.com/Blogs-Events/Blog/responsive-MT-Test

Marshman, E., Gariépy, J. L., & Harms, C. (2012). Helping language professionals relate to terms: Terminological relations and termbases. *Journal of Specialised Translation*, *18*, 30–56. https://www.jostrans.org/issue18/art_marshman.pdf

Massardo, I., van der Meer, J., & Khalilov, M. (2016). *TAUS translation technology landscape report*. Translation Automation User Society.

Massey, G. (2021). Exploring and expanding the plus of translators' power: Translatorial agency and the communicative constitution of organizations (CCO). *Cultus*, *14*, 62–82. https://www.cultusjournal.com/files/Archives/Cultus_202114.pdf

Matecat. (n.d.). *Guess tag position*. https://guides.matecat.com/guess-tag-position

McEnery, T., Xiao, R., & Tono, Y. (2006). *Corpus-based language studies: An advanced resource book*. Routledge.

Mejías-Climent, L. (2021). *Enhancing video game localization through dubbing*. Springer.

Mejías-Climent, L., & Lozano, J. de los R. (2021). Traducción automática y posedición en el aula de doblaje: Resultados de una experiencia docente. *Hikma*, *20*(2), 203–227. DOI: 10.21071/hikma.v20i2.13383

Melby, A. K. (1982). Multi-level translation aids in a distributed system. In *Proceedings of the 9th Conference on Computational Linguistics* (Vol. 1, 215–220). DOI: 10.3115/991813.991847

Melby, A. K. (2012). Terminology in the age of multilingual corpora. *Journal of Specialised Translation*, *18*. https://www.jostrans.org/issue18/art_melby.php

Melby, A. K. (2015). TBX: A terminology exchange format for the translation and localization industry. In H. J. Kockaert & F. Steurs (Eds.), *Handbook of terminology* (Vol. 1, pp. 393–424). John Benjamins. DOI: 10.1075/hot.1.tbx1

Melby, A. K., & Wright, S.-E. (2015). Translation memory. In S.-W. Chan (Ed.), *Routledge encyclopedia of translation technology* (pp. 662–677). Routledge.

Melby, A. K., Lommel, A., & Vésquez, L. M. (2015). Bitext. In S.-W. Chan (Ed.), *Routledge encyclopedia of translation technology* (pp. 409–424). Routledge.

memoQ. (n.d.a). *Muses.* https://docs.memoq.com/ggl-tst/Things/things-muses.html

memoQ. (n.d.b). *Partial matches (Longest Substring Concordance).* https://docs.memoq.com/ggl-tst/Things/things-partial-matches-longest-substr.html?Highlight=LSC

Microsoft. (2022). *Microsoft terms of use.* Microsoft Legal. https://www.microsoft.com/en-us/legal/terms-of-use

Milošević, J., & Risku, H. (2020). Situated cognition and the ethnographic study of translation processes: Translation scholars as outsiders, consultants and passionate participants. *Linguistica Antverpiensia, New Series – Themes in Translation Studies, 19.* DOI: 10.52034/lanstts.v19i0.545

Minsky, M., & Papert, S. (1969). *Perceptrons: An introduction to computational geometry.* MIT Press.

Mitchell-Schuitevoerder, R. (2020). *A project-based approach to translation technology.* Routledge. DOI: 10.4324/9780367138851

Mitkov, R. (2022). Translation memory systems. In S. Deane-Cox & A. Spiessens (Eds.), *Routledge handbook of translation and memory* (pp. 364–380). Routledge.

Moorkens, J. (2022). Ethics and machine translation. In D. Kenny (Ed.), *Machine translation for everyone* (pp. 121–140). Language Science Press. https://langsci-press.org/catalog/book/342

Moorkens, J., Castilho, S., Gaspari, F., & Doherty, S. (2018). *Translation quality assessment from principles to practice.* Springer. DOI: 10.1007/978-3-319-91241-7

Muegge, U. (2007). Disciplining words: What you always wanted to know about terminology management. *TC World Magazine, 2*(3), 17–19.

Nagao, M. (1984). In A. Elithorn & R. Banerji (Eds.), *A framework of a mechanical translation between Japanese and English by analogy principle* (pp. 97–103). NATO. https://cir.nii.ac.jp/crid/1571698598998536832

Nesselhauf, N. (2015). *Corpus linguistics: A practical introduction.* http://www.as.uni-heidelberg.de/personen/Nesselhauf/files/Corpus%20Linguistics%20Practical%20Introduction.pdf

Netflix. (2021a). *Timed text style guide: General requirements.* https://partnerhelp.netflixstudios.com/hc/en-us/articles/215758617-Timed-Text-Style-Guide-General-Requirements

Netflix. (2021b). *English timed text style guide.* https://partnerhelp.netflixstudios.com/hc/en-us/articles/217350977-English-Timed-Text-Style-Guide

Nissim, M., van Noord, R., & van der Goot, R. (2020). Fair is better than sensational: Man is to doctor as woman is to doctor. *Computational Linguistics, 46*(2), 487–497. DOI: 10.1162/coli_a_00379

Nkwenti-Azeh, B. (2001). Term banks. In M. Baker (Ed.), *Routledge encyclopedia of translation studies* (pp. 249–251). Routledge.

NLLB team, Costa-Jussà, M. R., Cross, J., et al. (2022). *No language left behind: Scaling human-centered machine translation.* arXiv. https://arxiv.org/abs/2207.04672

Norman, D. A. (1988). *The psychology of everyday things.* Basic Books. http://www.gbv.de/dms/bowker/toc/9780465067091.pdf

O'Brien, S. (2012). Translation as human–computer interaction. *Translation Spaces*, *1*. DOI: 10.1075/ts.1.05obr

O'Brien, S., & Rossetti, A. (2020). Neural machine translation and the evolution of the localisation sector: Implications for training. *The Journal of Internationalization and Localization*, 7(1–2), 95–121. DOI: 10.1075/jial.20005.obr

O'Brien, S., Ehrensberger-Dow, M., Connolly, M., et al. (2017). Irritating CAT tool features that matter to translators. *HERMES – Journal of Language and Communication in Business*, 56, 145–162. DOI: 10.7146/hjlcb.v0i56.97229

O'Hagan, M. (Ed.). (2020). *Routledge handbook of translation and technology*. Routledge. DOI: 10.4324/9781315311258

O'Hagan, M., & Mangiron, C. (2013). *Game localization: Translating for the global digital entertainment industry*. John Benjamins.

O'Keeffe, A., & McCarthy, M. J. (Eds.). (2022). *Routledge handbook of corpus linguistics* (2nd edition). Routledge.

Olohan, M. (2016). *Scientific and technical translation*. Routledge.

Panou, D. (2013). Equivalence in translation theories: A critical evaluation. *Theory and Practice in Language Studies*, *3*(1), 1–6. DOI: 10.4304/tpls.3.1.1-6

Papineni, K., Roukos, S., Ward, T., et al. (2002). Bleu: A method for automatic evaluation of machine translation. In P. Isabelle, E. Charniak, & D. Lin (Eds.), *Proceedings of the 40th Annual Meeting of the Association for Computational Linguistics* (pp. 311–318). Association for Computational Linguistics. DOI: 10.3115/1073083.1073135

Parasuraman, R., Sheridan, T. B., & Wickens, C. D. (2000). A model for types and levels of human interaction with automation. *IEEE Transactions on Systems, Man, and Cybernetics – Part A: Systems and Humans*, *30*(3), 286–297. DOI: 10 .1109/3468.844354

Pareja-Lora, A., Blume, M., Lust, B. C., et al. (Eds.). (2019). *Development of linguistic linked open data resources for collaborative data-intensive research in the language sciences*. MIT Press.

Penn-Pierson, J. (n.d.). *Introduction to Lilt Translate*. Lilt Knowledge Base. https://support.lilt.com/hc/en-us/articles/1500005205482-Introduction-to-Lilt -Translate

Pérez-González, L. (Ed.). (2018). *Routledge handbook of audiovisual translation*. Routledge. DOI: 10.4324/9781315717166

Pérez-Ortiz, J. A., Forcada, M. L., Sánchez-Martínez, F. (2022). How neural machine translation works. In D. Kenny (Ed.), *Machine translation for everyone* (pp. 141–164). Language Science Press. https://langsci-press.org/catalog/book/342

Phrase. (n.d.a). *CAT pane (TMS)*. https://support.phrase.com/hc/en-us/articles /5709683926812

Phrase. (n.d.b). *MT quality estimation (TMS)*. https://support.phrase.com/hc/en-us/ articles/5709672289180

Picht, H. (2006). *Modern approaches to terminological theories and applications*. Peter Lang.

Pielmeier, H., & O'Mara, P. (2020). *The state of the linguist supply chain*. CSA Research. https://cdn2.hubspot.net/hubfs/4041721/Newsletter/The%20State %20of%20the%20Linguist%20Supply%20Chain%202020.pdf

Popiolek, M. (2015). Terminology management within a translation quality assurance process. In H. J. Kockaert & F. Steurs (Eds.), *Handbook of terminology* (Vol. 1, pp. 341–359). John Benjamins.

Pym, A. (2011). *Website localizations.* Oxford University Press. DOI: 10.1093/oxf ordhb/9780199239306.013.0028

Quah, C. K. (2006). *Translation and technology.* Palgrave Macmillan.

QYResearch. (2021). *Captioning and subtitling solutions market size, global trends 2027.* https://reports.valuates.com/market-reports/QYRE-Auto-916/global -captioning-and-subtitling-solution

Ranathunga, S., Lee, E.-S. A., Skenduli, M. P., et al. (2021). *Neural machine translation for low-resource languages: A survey.* arXiv. https://arXiv.2106.15115

Rathjens, D. (1985). The seven components of clarity in technical writing. *IEEE Transactions on Professional Communication, PC-28*(4), 42–46. DOI: 10.1109/ TPC.1985.6448848

Rei, R., Stewart, C., Farinha, A. C., et al. (2020). COMET: A neural framework for MT evaluation. In *Proceedings of the 2020 Conference on Empirical Methods in Natural Language Processing* (EMNLP), 2685–2702. DOI: 10.18653/v1/2020 .emnlp-main.213

Reinecke, K., & Bernstein, A. (2011). Improving performance, perceived usability, and aesthetics with culturally adaptive user interfaces. *ACM Transactions on Computer-Human Interaction, 18*(2), 8:1–8:29. DOI: 10.1145/1970378.1970382

Reiss, K. (1981). Type, kind and individuality of text: Decision making in translation. *Poetics Today, 2*(4), 121–131. DOI: 10.2307/1772491

Ricks, R. (2020). *Aegisub tutorials—YouTube.* https://www.youtube.com/playlist ?list=PLqazFFzUAPc7BgGTaDAvvsGEoLolq09YP

Rico Pérez, C. (2019). Mapping translation technology and the multilingual needs of NGOs along the aid chain. In F. M. Federici & S. O'Brien (Eds.), *Translation in cascading crises* (pp. 112–131). Routledge.

Risku, H. (2002). Situatedness in translation studies. *Cognitive Systems Research, 3*(3), 523–533. DOI: 10.1016/S1389-0417(02)00055-4

Rivas Ginel, M. I. (2022). Video game localisation tools: A user survey. In *De la hipótesis a la tesis: Traductología y lingüística aplicada* (pp. 295–324). Comares.

Rodriguez Vazquez, S., & Mileto, F. (2016). On the lookout for accessible translation aids: Current scenario and new horizons for blind translation students and professionals. *Journal of Translator Education and Translation Studies (TETS), 1*(2), 115.

RWS. (n.d). *UpLIFT.* https://docs.rws.com/813470/422215/trados-studio-2021-sr2 /uplift

RWS. (2021). *Where to now for translation project management?* https://www .rws.com/localization/products/resources/where-now-for-translation-project -management/

Sager, J. C. (1990). *A practical course in terminology processing.* John Benjamins.

Savoldi, B., Gaido, M., Bentivogli, L., et al. (2021). Gender bias in machine translation. *Transactions of the Association for Computational Linguistics, 9,* 845–874. DOI: 10.1162/tacl_a_00401

Schäler, R. (2009). Localization. In M. Baker (Ed.), *Routledge encyclopedia of translation studies* (pp. 157–161). Routledge.

Schipack, A. (n.d.). *TMS translation management systems.* Nimdzi. https://www .nimdzi.com/tools/#tms

Schmitz, K. D. (2009). *Applied principles of terminology work.* Terminology Summer School, Cologne. http://www.termnet.org/downloads/english/events/ tss2009/TSS2009_KDS_TerminologyWork.pdf

Sennrich, R., Haddow, B., & Birch, A. (2016). Neural machine translation of rare words with subword units. In *Proceedings of the 54th Annual Meeting of the Association for Computational Linguistics* (Volume 1: Long Papers), 1715–1725. DOI: 10.18653/v1/P16-1162

Shterionov, D. (Ed.). (2021). *Proceedings of the 1st International Workshop on Automatic Translation for Signed and Spoken Languages* (AT4SSL). Association for Machine Translation in the Americas. https://aclanthology.org/2021 .mtsummit-at4ssl.0

Shuttleworth, M. (2015). Translation management systems. In S.-W. Chan (Ed.), *Routledge encyclopedia of translation technology* (pp. 678–691). Routledge.

Singh, N., & Pereira, A. (2005). *The culturally customized web site: Customizing web sites for the global marketplace*. Routledge.

Snell, B. M. (Ed.). (1979). *Translating and the Computer: Proceedings of a Seminar, London, 14th November, 1978*. North-Holland.

Snover, M., Dorr, B., Schwartz, R., et al. (2006). A study of translation edit rate with targeted human annotation. In *Proceedings of the 7th Conference of the Association for Machine Translation in the Americas: Technical Papers*, 223–231. https://aclanthology.org/2006.amta-papers.25

Somers, H. L. (1992). Current research in machine translation. *Machine Translation*, 7(4), 231–246. DOI: 10.1007/BF00398467

Somers, H. L. (2003). *Computers and translation: A translator's guide*. John Benjamins.

Star. (2018). *What is a dual fuzzy?* STAR Translation Services. https://www.star-ts .com/transit/dual-fuzzy/

Stasimioti, M. (2022). What to do about the talent crunch in media localization. *Slator*. https://slator.com/what-to-do-about-the-talent-crunch-in-media -localization/

Steurs, F., De Wachter, K., & De Malsche, E. (2015). Terminology tools. In H. J. Kockaert & F. Steurs (Eds.), *Handbook of terminology* (Vol. 1, pp. 222–249). John Benjamins.

Storm, E. (n.d.). *What is interactive, adaptive MT?* Lilt. https://support.lilt.com/hc/ en-us/articles/360058203753-What-is-Interactive-Adaptive-MT

Strubell, E., Ganesh, A., & McCallum, A. (2019). Energy and policy considerations for deep learning in NLP. In *Proceedings of the 57th Annual Meeting of the Association for Computational Linguistics*, 3645–3650. DOI: 10.18653/v1/ P19-1355

Suojanen, T., Koskinen, K., & Tuominen, T. (2014). *User-centered translation*. Routledge. DOI: 10.4324/9781315753508

Systran. (n.d.). *Neural translation powered by translation memories and fuzzy matching*. https://www.systransoft.com/translation-products/integrations/neural -translation-powered-by-translation-memories-and-fuzzy-matching/

TAUS. (n.d.). *Data marketplace*. https://datamarketplace.taus.net/

Teixeira, C., & O'Brien, S. (2017). Investigating the cognitive ergonomic aspects of translation tools in a workplace setting. *Translation Spaces*, 6, 79–103. DOI: 10.1075/ts.6.1.05tei

Temmerman, R. (2000). *Towards new ways of terminology description: The sociocognitive approach*. John Benjamins.

Ten Hacken, Pius. (2015). Terms and specialized vocabulary. In H. J. Kockaert & F. Steurs (Eds.), *Handbook of terminology* (Vol. 1, pp. 3–13). John Benjamins.

Toral, A. (2019). Post-editese: An exacerbated translationese. *Proceedings of Machine Translation Summit XVII: Research Track*, 273–281. https://aclanthology.org/W19-6627

Toral, A. (2020). Reassessing claims of human parity and super-human performance in machine translation at WMT 2019. In *Proceedings of the 22nd Annual Conference of the European Association for Machine Translation*, 185–194. https://aclanthology.org/2020.eamt-1.20

Toral, A., & Way, A. (2018). What level of quality can neural machine translation attain on literary text? In J. Moorkens, S. Castilho, F. Gaspari, et al. (Eds.), *Translation quality assessment: From principles to practice* (pp. 263–287). Springer. DOI: 10.1007/978-3-319-91241-7_12

Trados. (2022). *eBook: Going places with Trados.* SDL. https://www.trados.com/download/going-places-with-trados/

Tran, C., Bhosale, S., Cross, J., et al. (2021). Facebook AI's WMT21 news translation task submission. *Proceedings of the Sixth Conference on Machine Translation*, 205–215. https://aclanthology.org/2021.wmt-1.19

Troussel, J.-C., & Debussche, J. (2014). *Translation and intellectual property rights: Final report.* Az Európai Unió Kiadóhivatala. https://data.europa.eu/doi/10.2782/72107

Van der Meer, J. (2021). *A journey into the future of the translation industry.* Translation Automation User Society. https://www.taus.net/resources/blog/a-journey-into-the-future-of-the-translation-industry

Vanmassenhove, E. O. J. (2019). *On the integration of linguistic features into statistical and neural machine translation* [PhD thesis, Dublin City University, School of Computing]. https://doras.dcu.ie/23714/

Varantola, K. (1992). Words, terms, translators. In *EURALEX 92 Proceedings: Papers Submitted to the 5th EURALEX International Congress on Lexicography in Tampere, Finland*, 121–128. Tampereen yliopisto. https://www.euralex.org/elx_proceedings/Euralex1992_1/019_Krista%20Varantola%20-Words,%20terms%20and%20translators.pdf

Vashee, K. (2021a). *The challenge of defining translation quality.* GALA Global. https://www.gala-global.org/knowledge-center/professional-development/articles/challenge-defining-translation-quality

Vashee, K. (2021b). *The human-in-the-loop.* ModernMT Blog. https://blog.modernmt.com/human-in-the-loop

Venuti, L. (Ed.). (2021). *The translation studies reader* (4th ed.). Routledge.

Vieira, L. N., O'Hagan, M., & O'Sullivan, C. (2021). Understanding the societal impacts of machine translation: A critical review of the literature on medical and legal use cases. *Information, Communication & Society*, 24(11), 1515–1532. DOI: 10.1080/1369118X.2020.1776370

Vieira, L. N., O'Sullivan, C., Zhang, X., et al. (2022). Machine translation in society: Insights from UK users. *Language Resources and Evaluation*. DOI: 10.1007/s10579-022-09589-1

Warburton, K. (2008). Managing enterprise terminology. *LISA Forum Europe: The Business Impact of Operating Without Standards.* http://www.infoterm.info/pdf/activities/INL/INL129-130.pdf.

Warburton, K. (2010). Extracting, preparing, and evaluating terminology for large translation jobs. In *Proceedings of the Seventh Language Resources and Evaluation Conference.* Language Resources and Evaluation Conference

(LREC), Valletta, Malta. https://www.researchgate.net/publication/274712625
_Extracting_preparing_and_evaluating_terminology_for_large_translation
_jobs

Warburton, K. (2011). *Language standards as a cornerstone for business strategies—Implications for the design of academic curricula.* International Cooperation on Education about Standardization. https://slideplayer.com/slide /708373/

Warburton, K. (2014). *Developing a business case for managing terminology.* Termologic. http://termologic.com/wp-content/uploads/2014/06/roi-article -warburton.pdf

Warburton, K. (2015). Managing terminology in commercial environments. In H. J. Kockaert & F. Steurs (Eds.), *Handbook of terminology* (Vol. 1, pp. 360–392).

Warburton, K. (2021). *The corporate terminologist.* John Benjamins.

Warburton, K., & Wright, S. E. (2019). A data category repository for language resources. In A. Pareja-Lora, M. Blume, B. C. Lust, et al. (Eds.), *Development of linguistic linked open data resources for collaborative data-intensive research in the language sciences* (pp. 69–97). MIT Press.

Way, A. (2010). Panning for EBMT gold, or 'remembering not to forget'. *Machine Translation, 24*(3), 177–208. DOI: 10.1007/s10590-010-9085-2

Way, A. (2018). Quality expectations of machine translation. In J. Moorkens, S. Castilho, F. Gaspari, et al. (Eds.), *Translation Quality Assessment: From Principles to Practice* (pp. 159–178). Springer. DOI: 10.1007/978-3-319-91241-7_8

Weaver, W. (1975 [1949]). Translation. In W. N. Locke & A. D. Booth (Eds.), *Machine translation of languages: Fourteen essays* (pp. 15–23). Greenwood Press.

Wikipedia. (2021). Smartcat. In *Wikipedia.* https://en.wikipedia.org/wiki/Smartcat

Wikipedia. (2022). Edit distance. In *Wikipedia.* https://en.wikipedia.org/w/index .php?title=Edit_distance&oldid=1099296255

Winner, L. (1983). Technologies as forms of life. In R. S. Cohen & M. W. Wartofsky (Eds.), *Epistemology, methodology, and the social sciences* (pp. 249–263). Springer. DOI: 10.1007/978-94-017-1458-7_10

Wordfast. (n.d.). *Wordfast Anywhere project manager tool manual.* http://www .wordfast.net/wiki/Wordfast_Anywhere_Project_Manager_tool_Manual

Wright, S. E. (2015). Language codes and language tags. In M. O'Hagan (Ed.), *Routledge encyclopedia of translation technology* (pp. 536–549). Routledge.

Wright, S. E., & Budin, G. (1997). *Handbook of terminology management. Volume 1: Basic aspects of terminology management.* John Benjamins.

Wright, S. E., & Budin, G. (Eds.). (2001). *Handbook of terminology management. Volume 2: Application-oriented terminology management.* John Benjamins.

Xiao, R. (2010). Corpus creation. In N. Indurkhya & F. J. Damerau (Eds.), *Handbook of natural language processing* (2nd ed., pp. 147–165). Chapman & Hall.

Xiao, R., & McEnery, T. (2010). What corpora can offer in language teaching and learning. In E. Hinkel (Ed.), *Handbook of research in second language teaching and learning* (Vol. 2, pp. 364–380). Routledge.

Youdale, R., & Rothwell, A. (2022). Computer-assisted translation (CAT) tools, translation memory, and literary translation. In S. Deane-Cox & A. Spiessens (Eds.), *Routledge handbook of translation and memory.* Routledge.

Yunker, J. (2010). *The art of the global gateway: Strategies for successful multilingual navigation* (2nd ed). Byte Level Books.

Yunker, J. (2021). *The 2021 web globalization report card*. Byte Level Research. https://bytelevel.com/reportcard2021/

Zaretskaya, A., Corpas Pastor, G., & Seghiri, M. (2015). Integration of machine translation in CAT tools: State of the art, evaluation and user attitudes. *SKASE Journal of Translation and Interpretation, 8*, 76–88.

Zetzsche, J. (2016). *The 267th tool box journal: An electronic journal for translation professionals*. https://internationalwriters.com/toolkit/

Zetzsche, J. (2020). *The translator's tool box: A computer primer for translators* (Version 14). https://www.internationalwriters.com/toolbox/

Zetzsche, J. (2022). *The 336th tool box journal: An electronic journal for translation professionals*. https://internationalwriters.com/toolkit/

Zito, A. (Director). (n.d.). *Localization tools: Discovering new TMS together (UX reviews)*. https://www.youtube.com/playlist?list=PLSpSKUS7GX2W7j-UaR99AnYBHi2mH2uVY

Index

abbreviation 9, 10, 43, **61**, 65, 71,
    84, 131
accessibility 152–154, 208–210
accessible description 208
acronym 60, **61**, 65
Across 26, 43, 48
active terminology lookup 58, 59,
    69–71
adaptation 174, 184
adequacy 100, 107
Adobe: InDesign 12, 17; PDF 12, 17,
    41–42, 81–84
Advanced Sub-Station Alpha (.ASS)
    160, 171
Aegisub 158–163, 171–172, *177*; Style
    Editor *160*, 170; Style Manager 161;
    subtitle edit box 159; Translation
    Assistant 161–163; user interface (UI)
    159–160; visual typesetting 160–161
aesthetics 188
affordance 206
agile development cycle 179
agile workflow 130, 148, 175, 180
Alchemy Catalyst 179
aligned data interchange formats 49–53
alignment 9, 19, 34, 40–49, 51, 53–54,
    100, 104, 114–115, 166, 169, 209
ALPAC Report 4
ALT text 184
amanuensis *see* assistant
ambiguity 3, 12, 24, 99, 164, 185
ampersand (&) character 178, 181
analysis 3–9, 23, 30, 66, 78, 84, 99,
    108, 125, 138, 176, 185
AntConc 80, 83–90, 93–95
antonym 62
Apertium RBMT 112
application programming interface (API)
    144, 181; key 19, 122–124, 143

Arabic 39–40, 158
ARIA label 184, 208
artificial intelligence (AI) 3, 97, 101,
    105, 112, 123, 124, 164, 169,
    172, 200, 214, 215; explainable AI
    (xAI) 102
artificial neuron 6, 102–103; weights
    101–104
artificial voice 187–188, 216
assistant 11, 21
assistive technology 184, 208–210
audience 183–185, 188
audio 186, 208; 'stitch' 187; stream
    154; track 156, 169; waveform 156,
    159, 170
audiovisual translation (AVT) 152,
    173, 185, 187, 215
authorship 111
automatic quality estimation 215
automatic speech recognition (ASR)
    102, 153, 154, 163, 164, 169, 170,
    192, 197, 203–205, 214
autotext 18
autotype 18

Baidu 77, 94
bandwidth 183
base 88, 94
base form *see* canonical form
batch processing 197–198
BBC 153–154, 173
Berne Convention 111
bias 109, 111, 196, 217
bigram 100, 118
binary code 14, 15, 18, 42, 179,
    182, 186
bitext 19, 22, 23, 30, 33–36, 40, 44,
    50, 53–54
black box 36, 102, 105, 109, 112

BLEU (Bilingual Evaluation
Understudy) 108–109
blind and partially sighted user 184, 208
BlonDe 216
Boolean operators 82
braille display 208
brain 102
brand 35, 55, 193
BRICS (Brazil, Russia, India, China,
South Africa) 176
bug 178–179, 187, 194
business management system (BMS)
131–132, 150
byte pair encoding (BPE) 105

CafeTran Espresso 12, 26, 47
calibration set 107
candidate 18, 36, 43, 47, 82, 100, 126
canonical form 63, 70
carpal tunnel syndrome 203
CAT tool 4–7, 11–32, 74, 113–129,
130–151, 163–164, 174–175, 179,
181, 183, 186, 195–199, 202,
204–214; architecture 25–30, 131;
certification 31, 144; cloud-based
6, 12, 20, 22, 26–28, 30, 126, 131,
163, 171, 183; editor 15–17, 27, 28,
38, 41, 49, 52, 150, 163, 181, 207,
209; environment 13–16, 15–21, 20,
25, 27–28, 59, 72, 110, 125–126,
128, 131–132, 142, 149–150, 199;
history of 6–7, 11–14, 25, 32; hybrid
architecture 27–28; licence 9, 26,
28–29; mobile app 27; platform 7,
28, 31, 111, 143, 150, 206–207,
213, 216; server-based 22, 26, 28;
'team' edition 26, 131; training 31;
workfile 16, 29, 49, 142; workflow
2, 21–25, 34, 97–98, 111–112, 197;
workstation-based 22, 26, 28–29,
143, 163, 164, 203, 204, 207, 209
celluloid film 157
censorship 189
character: encoding 160, 175, 182;
input method 175; set 175, 183
characters per line (CPL) 165–167, 171
characters per second (CPS) 155,
165–167, 171
chunk 41, 104, 105
citation form *see* canonical form
clause-splitting 128
client 6–7, 15, 22, 25, 29, 31, 36,
40–41, 60, 130, 133, 135, 138–139,
143, 145–146, 148, 150, 161, 163,
194, 196
client (PC) 26
closed captions 153
cloud 6, 26–27, 112, 133, 143, 149,
163, 172, 180, 204, 213; repository
2, 5, 66, 97, 180–181
CO_2 emissions 112, 216
codebreaking 3
cognitive: abilities 203; balance 205;
distraction 155; effort 2, 9, 12, 20,
28, 31, 107, 120, 122, 129, 204,
205; friction 203; overload 20, 28,
37, 196, 203; system 213
coherence 24, 164, 206
cohesion 24
collaboration 22, 26, 29, 149–150,
200, 213
collocate 88, 91–95; table 80, 88–90,
94, 96
collocation 56, 63, 70, 76, 91, 93–95
collocational span 95
collocator *see* collocate
COMET 109
command line 180
communications 131–132, 147, 176
complexity 2, 25–28, 101, 130, 204
computer 3–4, 6, 11, 19, 26, 81, 97,
101, 102; Apple Macintosh 12; IBM
PC 12
computing time 106
concept 3, 56–57, 60, 62, 64, 99;
interlingual 99; map 74, 89; network
58, 62, 64
concordance search 18, 41, 66, 71, 92,
117, 120
concordancer 66, 74, 77, 80, 83, 89,
90, 93, 94, 95; parallel 76, 92
confidentiality 29–30, 39, 124,
137–138, 140
connectivity 26–27, 164
consistency 7, 12, 18, 22, 35, 42, 55,
57, 59–60, 66–67, 72, 101, 104–105,
107–108, 114, 116–117, 178, 182,
186, 192–194, 199, 204, 216
constraint 101, 154–156, 163, 165,
169, 187, 192
content management system (CMS) 184
context 3, 7, 12, 17, 34–37, 40, 60, 62,
65–67, 75, 77, 92, 94, 104, 127–128,
164, 174, 191–192, 206
continuing professional development
(CPD) 8, 31

continuous delivery cycle 179
convergence of TM and MT 104, 121, 125, 128, 172
copywriting 215
corpus (pl. corpora) 37, 67–68, 74, 77, 75–95, 96, 99, 108, 214, 217; analysis 77, 80, 83, 89, 95; annotated *see* tagged; applications for translators 80–93; bilingual 67, 76, 79, 93; building 78, 104; comparable 9, 69, 79; compilation 81, 82; control 79; crawled 53; definition 78; developmental 79; diachronic 79; dynamic 79; general language 79; interlanguage *see* learner; learner 79; linguistics 78, 80, 93, 95; monitor *see* dynamic; monolingual 67, 79, 93, 100; monomodal 79; multilingual 76, 79; multimodal 79; native 79; online 81; open 101; orthographic *see* plain; package 80; parallel 5, 9, 40, 53, 76, 79–80, 100–101, 103–104, 106, 111; plain 79; quality 78; query 77; raw *see* plain; reference 79; sample *see* static; sampling 78; specialised 79; spoken 79; static 79; sub-corpus 95; sublanguage 79; synchronic 79; tagged 68, 79; target 79; tools 80; translation 69; types 79–80; written 79
country code 22
crisis translation 217
critical period 1
Cross-Lingual Semantic Textual Similarity (XSTS) 107
cross-platform 12, 157, 158, 163
crowdsourcing 105, 107, 108, 207
cryptography 3
culturalisation 185, 187–188
culture 2, 3, 11, 57; adaptation 34; six dimensions of (Hofstede) 185; source 1, 76; target 76–77, 185, 187–188, 215
currency format 175
customisation 12–13, 93, 146, 166, 187–188, 204–205

data 5, 6, 11, 22, 30, 35, 49, 67, 71–72, 78, 100, 119, 143–146, 195, 198, 214; back-translated 106; bilingual 9; buyer 214; conversion 50; curation 215, 217; empirical 78; evaluation 215; exchange 13, 22, 28, 34; legacy 22,

188; manager 130; market 31; monetisation 214; ownership 28, 30, 111; parallel 101; personal 112; scraping 106, 111; security 29–30, 143, 206; seller 214; sharing 25, 27, 29, 132–133, 213; sparsity 106; speech 78; translation 12, 98–101
database 13, 22, 30, 33, 55, 111, 115–119, 123, 138, 146, 149, 184, 194–196
data-driven decision-making (DDDM) 93
data-driven language learning 96
data-driven learning (DDL) 77, 90, 93, 96
date format 18, 175
decision-making power 200
deep learning 128
DeepL 112, *122*, 126; alternative translations *126*; Glossary 126
definiendum 64
definiens 64
definition 16, 56–57, 60, 64–65, 67, 70; circular 64; terminology-oriented 65
Déjà Vu 14, 17, 18, *20*, 26, 29, 38, 47, 116, 117, 118, 121; Assemble 38, 119; AutoWrite 121; DeepMiner 121; Lexicon 66, 117–121; TEAMserver 149
deskilling 214
desktop publishing (DTP) 130
developer 10, 20, 28, 30, 72, 107, 108, 114, 163, 176, 183, 186, 200, 204, 205, 208, 209
diagram 58, 65, 79
dialog 177, *178*, 181
dialogue 154, 169, 186
dictionary 3, 43, 75, 79, 94, 98–99, 118, 121, 194, 217; bilingual 3; paraphrase 128
dictionary form *see* canonical form
direct assessment 107
direct RBMT 98
discount 39, 139, 140
disempowerment 149
Disney+ 153
documentation 13, 60, 128, 175–176
domain 1, 4, 7, 9, 22, 25, 34–35, 40, 55–62, 64–65, 67–69, 76–78, 81–82, 89, 99, 106, 114, 116, 119, 122, 124, 138–139, 145–148, 213–214, 216; subdomain **61**, 146–148; unrestricted 214

Downsub 172
Drupal 184
dubbing 187, 189, 216; synchrony 187
dynamic TM analysis (DTA) 121

Easyling 184, *184*
edit distance 36–38, 40, 107
efficiency 2, 7, 30, 33, 35, 43, 60, 66,
  72, 94, 99, 112, 120, 195, 202, 203,
  206, 214, 216
email 26, 28–29, 138, 140–141,
  143–145, 149; address 18, 138, 141;
  notifications 148
emoji 185
EMT competences 7–8
encyclopaedic information 62–65
end user 6, 27, 109, 178, 187, 215
energy consumption 101, 106, 112,
  143, 216
equality 154, 216
equivalence 9, 34, 40, 42–43, 50, 53,
  56, 64, 68, 70, 94, 100, 114–115,
  118, 120, 169
ergonomics 17, 202–203, 206, 208,
  210–211; cognitive 32, 203–206,
  211; organisational 206–208;
  physical 203–206
Esperanto 99
ethnography 203
EULA (End User Licensing Agreement)
  187
Europarl corpus 90–91
European Commission 7, 13, 99;
  Directorate General for Translation
  (DGT) 191
European Committee for
  Standardization (CEN) 191
European institutions 101
European Master's in Translation
  (EMT) Network 7
European Union 99, 123
Eurotra 99
eye-tracking 203

false negative 193, 196, 198
false positive 196–198
fansubbing 158, 161, 172
feedback loop 127
field *59–65*, 67
FIGS (French, Italian, German,
  Spanish) 176
file: conversion 179; executable 176,
  179; export 12–15, 19, 25, 41, 47,
  48, 49, 119, 181; format 12–13, 42,

53, 130, 179, 181; hierarchy 176;
  import 12–15, 22, 41, 51, 67, 179;
  localisation 176; management 22;
  pivot format 50; resource 176, 178
filename 35, 50, 157
filtering 14–15, 23, 41–42, 67, 77, 82,
  146, 179
flow state 203, 206
fluency 100, 105, 107
Fluency Now 12, *208*, *209*
font 15, 18, 20, 155, 159–160, 166,
  170, 187
footnote reference 18, 123
fragment 66, 115–116, 118–121, 130
frame 156, 159, 166
freeware 12, 42, 44–45, 83
frequency 66, 80–86, 90, 95, 116, 119
Fully Automatic Useful Translation
  (FAUT) 214
fuzzy index (Star Transit) 17, 24, 35,
  41, 49, 114, 116–117, 120, 130
fuzzy logic 37
fuzzy match repair 38, 119, 121, 123,
  128, 129
fuzzy match threshold 37, 40, 148

game 176, 185–187, 188; AAA
  (triple-A) 186–187; addictive content
  188; art asset 187; avatar 188;
  characterisation 187; co-creation
  187; developer 186; development
  engine 186; familiarisation 186; look
  and feel 187; lootbox 188; massively
  multiplayer online 186; mechanics
  187; mobile 186; monetisation 188;
  offensive content 188; outdated
  content 188; porting 187; sequel 187;
  situation 187; tester 187; translatable
  asset 186
'Garbage In, Garbage Out' 196
gender **61**, 105, 113, 185, 188; gender
  bias 196; grammatical 105, 118
General Data Protection Regulation
  (GDPR) 112
Georgetown-IBM experiment 3, 4, 98
gesture patterning 79
global gateway 183
globalisation 175, 182
globalisation, internationalisation,
  localisation, and translation (GILT)
  175–176
glossary 12, 16, 21–23, 56–59, 67,
  81, 121, 126, 131, 134, 142–143,
  181, 186

Google 6, 77, 80, 82, 93, 94; Docs
  24; Sheets 112; Translate 101, 112,
  122–123, 126
grammar checking 2, 19, 194
grammatical relations 91
graphic 15, 65, 186
graphical processing unit (GPU) 112
graphical user interface (GUI) 44,
  159, 180
Gridly 186

Handbrake 157, *158*
Happyscribe 163
hashtag 185
headword 63–64
hearing impaired audience 153–154
holonym 62, 64
homepage 81
HTER (Human-Targeted Translation
  Edit Rate) 109
HTML 13, 15, 17, 42, 184
HTML5 171, 184
human error 193, 195
human factors 200, 202–211
human judgement 108, 109, 198
human readable 101
human-computer interaction (HCI) 2,
  195, 200, 203
human-in-the-loop 215
hyperlink 59, 123
hyperonym 62, 64
hyponym 62; co-hyponym 62

IATE 72
IBM Translation Manager 12
inclusion 152
industry 7, 9, 30, 109, 131, 171, 186,
  188, 189, 191, 193, 196, 199, 206,
  215; consolidation 7, 8
inflection 16, 40
informant 78
information sharing 192
information technology (IT) 174
inline format 18, 43
inline tag 18, 49
intellectual property (IP) 31
inter-annotator agreement (IAA) 107
interlingua RBMT 98, 99
interlingual representation 99
intermediate representation 99
international organisation 182, 199
International Organization for
  Standardization (ISO) 191
internationalisation 175, 176, 186

internet 12, 26–27, 77, 82, 93, 111,
  182–183, 205
interoperability 72
interpreter 56, 75, 92, 95, 96
invoice 25, 130, 133
ISO 639–631 22
ISO 17100:2015 (en) 24, 200
ISO 18587 2017 110
ISO 3166–3161 22
isolation 206

Java 12
Javascript 184
job satisfaction 111, 207
judgement metrics 108

KANT 99
Kapwing 163
keyboard 16, 203; hotkey 178; shortcut
  70, 178, 203, 205
key-logging 203
keystroke 125, 207
keyword 77, 80, 82, 86, 91–95, 185
Keyword in Context *see* KWIC
  concordance
KWIC concordance 80, 85–87, 90,
  92, 96

L1 speaker 76, 78
label 58, 60, 208–210; *see also* ARIA
  label
lack of agency 200
LANG attribute 184
language: artificial 99; barriers 3, 6;
  code 22; controlled 101; gender-
  neutral 188; general 58; of habitual
  use 76; independence 21, 39;
  interface 158; L1 interference 76,
  93, 111; learning 1–2, 78, 92, 93,
  95, 154, 217; long-tail 216; low-
  resource 215, 216; morphologically
  rich 105; natural 78; non-alphabetic
  156; non-endangered 112; pivot
  3, 169; sign 79; sublanguage 4;
  supported 106, 112; universals 3,
  99; variety 78
language model 100–102, 112, 216
language pair 6, 22, 31, 43, 101,
  106, 111, 122–124, 126, 131, 134,
  136–140, 145–146, 165, 192, 196,
  199, 213, 214
language service provider (LSP) 7, 23,
  25–31, 35, 130–133, 136, 138–140,
  143–145, 147, 150, 153, 161, 163,

175, 195, 198–199, 206, 213–214, 218

laptop 27, 30, 203

layer 102; hidden 103; input *103*; output 102, *103*

layout 20, 51, 170, 178, 194

learning curve 30, 204

LetsMT.eu 113

Levenshtein distance *see* edit distance

leverage 4–5, 7, 11, 33–35, 40, 42, 66, 114–128, 130, 137–138, 143, 145, 150, 179, 192, 213

lexicography 58, 79

lexicon 4, 43, 99, 117

lexis 1, 3, 16

LF Aligner 42–47

licence 9, 13, 26, 197

Lilt Translate 126–128; baseline MT 127; Interactive and Adaptive MT 126, *127*

lingua franca 99

Linguee 92, 94

linguist 2, 9, 25, 27, 35, 49, 52, 78, 131–133, 136–150, 196, 206, 213, 215, 217–218; relevancy 146, 149; remuneration 141, 143, 215

linguistic/cultural advocacy 217

linguistic/cultural consultancy 217

Lionbridge Translation Workspace 27, 144, 149

lip-reader 154

local area network (LAN) 26

locale 22, 174, 182, 183, 184; code 51; first-tier 176; long-tail 176; target 18, 185–186, 188

localisable 18, 43

localisation 9, 28, 174–188; cultural adaptation 175; and development cycle 175; engineering 175, 178, 183, 186; game 174, 185–188, 189, 216; hyper-automation 215; industry 175; kit 176; manager 183; media 171; production cycle 174; project 178; simultaneous shipment ('simship') 175; software 13, 153, 174, 176–182, 185; testing 175, 178; tool 194; turnaround times 175; website 174, 179, 182–185; workflow 188

Localization Industry Standards Association (LISA) 72, 175

Logos 99

Lokalise 13, 179–181, *182*

machine learning 102, 128

machine translation (MT) 6, 9, 51, 74, 76, 97–113, 115, 122, 144–145, 148–149, 153, 163, 175, 182, 186, 188, 190–191, 195, 197, 199, 205, 207, 214–215, 217; adaptive 127; for assimilation 97; automatic evaluation metric (AEM) 108–110; CAT integration 19, 122–129; contextually aware 216; corpus-based 99; customisation 126; data driven 99–111; for dissemination 97; document-level 216; engine 53, 124, 125, 145, 164, 181, 213, 215; ethical issues 217; evaluation metric 104, 107, 199, 216; example based (EBMT) 5, 99–100; free online (FOMT) 2, 5, 101, 122, 124, 192; history 3–6, 98–101, 113; human evaluation 106–108, 112; hybrid 101; interactive 126; interactive, adaptive 110; literacy 217; neural *see* neural machine translation (NMT); phrase-based SMT (PBSMT) 100, 121; pre- and postprocessing 6, 98, 101; quality 98, 106–110, 112, 216; quality estimation (MTQE) 109; raw output 110, 111; research 215; 'responsive MT' 216; rule-based (RBMT) 3–5, 10, 98–99, 101, 105–106, 109, 118, 186, 194; *see also* direct RBMT, interlingua RBMT, transfer RBMT; sociotechnical issues 111–112; statistical (SMT) 6, 100–101, 103, 113; *see also* phrase-based SMT, word-based SMT; subsymbolic 101–102; symbolic 101; syntax-based SMT 100; tuning 100, 108; unidirectional 99; word-based SMT (WBSMT) 100

macro 13, 14, 198, 203

mapping 99–100, 104, 183, 195

market 28, 110–111, 131, 143, 153, 175–176, 185, 206–207, 214–215

marketing 34–35, 111, 175, 183, 185, 198

match 6, 12, 16, 23, 33–34, 36–41, 53, 70, 109, 116–117, 123, 137, 142, 146, 181, 194–196; 100% *see* exact match; 101% *see* context match; 102% *see* perfect match; band 38, 122, 125; context 35, 39; exact 23, 37, 39, 71, 122–123; fuzzy 19,

37–39, 51, 71, 116, 121–123, 125, 194, 196, 209; Lexicon 66; pane 121; penalty 36–37, 42; percentage 23, 50, 52, 70; perfect 37, 39; repetition 37; segment 126, 205; semantic 128; string 40, 70, 115, 116, 128; sub-segment 100, 115–116, 120–123, 128–129, 205; Target Fuzzy (Star Transit) *117*; terminology 23, *57*, 58, 69, 70
Matecat 18, 27, 31, 47, 123, 126, 150, 163; Guess Tags *123, 124*; outsourcing quote *150*
Matesub 163–172; editing interface 170; formatting 170; project setup 165–169; user interface (UI) 171
memoQ 17, 31, 35, 44, 48, 49, *50*, 52, 121, 179, 186, 204; LiveDocs 35, 44; Longest Substring Concordance (LSC) 120; Muse 121; Project Manager edition 27; Server 149
menu 16, 20, 24, 177, 181, 186, 204–205, 209
meronym 62
message 177, 186, 188
metadata 40–41, 49–51, 112, 148, 207
MÉTÉO 4
Microsoft 6, 101, 105, 194; Bing Translator 77, 94, 112, 123–124; Excel 17, 39, 44, 56, 67, 71, 72, 148; PowerPoint 12, 14, 41; Sharepoint 144; Terms of use 124; Word 6, 12, 13, 17, 18, 24, 52; Word bilingual table 29, 49, 51, *52*, 53
mind-mapping 74
minimum frequency value 68
misalignment 43–46, 48
mistranslation 101, 105, 111
mixed-initiative translation 200
ModernMT 123
modifier 91
monetisation 124, 188
monitoring 207
MonoConc 80
monolingual text generation 112, 216
morphology 39–40, 71
Moses 101
motivation 112, 199, 200, 207, 215
mouse 16, 159, 170, 203, 207
Multidimensional Quality Metrics (MQM) 107, 199–200
multilingual crisis communication 192
multilingualism 6, 99

MutNMT 112
MXLIFF 49, 53
MyMemory 123, 125, 142, 150, 164

named entity 43, 124
native speaker *see* L1 speaker
natural language processing (NLP) 40
navigation pane 180
necessary and sufficient conditions 64
negative publicity 185
net rate scheme 39, 146
Netflix 153–154, 166, *167*
networking 209
Neural machine translation (NMT) 6, 97–98, 101–113, 122, 128–129, 192, 214–217; attention mechanism 104; bias 105, 112; bilingual 106, 216; decoder 101–102, 104; domain-specific 105; encoder 49, 102–104; error 101, 105, 110, 112; fluent output 104–105, 112; hallucination 106; human parity 105, 108; interlingua 106; lexical diversity 105; massively multilingual 106, 216; multilingual 106; neural AEM (automatic evaluation metric) 109; overfitting 104; pre-processing 104; processes 104–105; quality 105–106, 128; recurrent encoder–decoder architecture 104; training 5, 31, 40, 53, 98, 103–104, 111–112, 124, 126–128, 197, 214–216; training data 100–109, 111, 112; transformer architecture 104, 112; untranslated word 106; 'zero-shot' 106
neural network 102–104; perceptron *103*
n-gram 80, 86–88, 90, 94, 100, 102, 108, 118, 119
Nimdzi 131
NIST 108
node *see* base
non-disclosure agreement (NDA) 29
non-Latin script 158
norm 76, 77, 214
Notepad++ 50, *51*

office software 11, 13, 18–19, 160
Okapi Tools 179; Rainbow 179
OmegaT 12, *16*, 26, 47, 58, *122*, *177*, 178; AutoCompleter 121
omission 101
online Help file 12

Online OCR 41
online streaming service 153
on-screen action 155
Ooona 163
Open Subtitle Editor 158
open-source 12, 26, 101, 123, 157, 158
OpenTM2 12
operating system 12, 178, 183; iOS
    204; Linux 12, 83, 176; Mac OS 12,
    13, 83; OS/2 12; Windows 12, 28,
    83, 176
optical character recognition (OCR) 41
outsourcing 175–176, 183, 186

paradigmatic relation 62; *see also*
    syntagmatic relation
paraphrase 109
parataxis 65
parsing 70, 99, 100
part of speech (PoS) 16, 60, **61**, 62, 65,
    67, 68, 164
Passolo 13, 179
payment 7, 109
peer-to-peer transaction 207
performance 105, 121, 125, 144, 202
Phrase Strings 179
phrase table 102
Phrase TMS 7, 24, 27, 31, *38*, 44, 49,
    51, *52*, 53, 120–125, 132, 143–150,
    163, 193; administrator 144–145,
    147; Autoselect 124; machine
    translation quality estimate (MTQE)
    124, *125*; Post-Editing Analysis 125
phraseology 2, 63, 66, 68, 70, 74, 88
placeable 18, 43, 124
plain text file 13–14, 51, 83, 156
plugin 72, 179
POEditor 149
polysemy 3
populate 35, 59, 61, 119, 123, 134,
    149
Portable Object (PO) file 176, 179, 184
Portable Object Template (POT) 184
PoS *see* part of speech
post-editing (PE) 6, 97–98, 108–111,
    115, 123–127, 146, 164, 203, 207,
    214–215; effort 109, 112; full 110,
    207; light 4, 110, 214; monolingual
    110; 'post-editese' 111; speed 110
posture 203, 205
predictive typing 6, 18, 110, 117, 121,
    123, 128
preposition 76–77, 88

pretranslation 23, 37, 71, 119–120,
    123, 125, 137, 148, 149
preview 17, *20*, 140, 156, 159,
    161–162, 179, 181, 183
pricing 144, 206, 213
product distribution 175
productivity 55, 66, 110, 143, 204,
    206, 210
professional autonomy 143
professional judgement 200
profit margin 139
program code 175
project 4, 6, 8, 9, 21–23, 25–28, 41,
    51, 55, 59–60, 114, 118–119, 126,
    130–131, 142, 144, 146–147, 150,
    161, 165, 175, 180–181, 183, 190,
    192–196, 199, 202; budget 139;
    cloud-based 27; communication 132;
    dashboard 142, 143, 149; deadline
    130, 132, 140, 143, 150, 192,
    196; delivery 131, 176; download
    143; due date 147; financials
    130–133, 137, 147, 214; global
    145; management 22–28, 30, 35,
    38–39, 41, 53, 130–150, 175–176,
    179–180, 183, 189, 193–195, 200,
    204, 206, 213, 215; multi-agent 133;
    multilingual 26, 132, 143; package
    29, 49, 143; preparation 125, 136;
    in progress 140, 141; return package
    29; review 195; revoke task 142,
    143, 149; settings 147, *148*; setup
    133–138, 140, 143, 147, 165; status
    132, 140; structure 136, 138, 147,
    149; task 25, 108, 135–143, 175,
    214; template 146; TM 137; user
    management 133, 140, 144–147;
    user permissions 144, 146–147, 149;
    workflow 23–25, 118, 131–135, 143,
    145–149, 164, 187, 191, 196, 207,
    216–217
proofreading 19, 138, 143, 200
propagation 19, 37, 110, 205
proposal 12, 16–17, 19–21, 23, 36, 38,
    51, 110, 117, 119–122, 124–128,
    132, 142, 148–149, 181, 205, 213
ProZ 28
purchase order (PO) 132, 140–141,
    143, 147

QA Distiller 197, *198*
quality assurance (QA) 9, 19–20, 23,
    130, 135–140, 143, 178, 190–201,

204, 215; automated 196; linguistic 187; specialist 196
quality control (QC) 190, 195, 197, 199, 217; automated 193
quoting 23, 39, 88, 130, 138, 150

ranking 16, 37, 71, 107–108, 124–125, 128, 185, 198
rate 130, 214
rating 207
readability 24, 154
reading difficulties 154
read-only 23, 36
read-write 23
real time 17, 26, 142–143, 192, 213
reference document 19, 29–30, 49, 108–109, 115, 120, 148–149, 186; *see also* bitext
register 60, **61**, 105
regular expression 203
regulatory requirements 188
repetitive strain injury (RSI) 203
report 38–39, 194, 195
representativeness 78, 81, 103
research 2–6, 11, 60, 68, 76, 78–79, 81, 99, 102, 106–108, 112, 123, 128, 131, 191–192, 200, 214, 216–217; academic 201, 215; industry 215; workplace 202
respeaking 154
return on investment 176, 199
review 24–25, 143, 192
reviewer 130
reviser 24–26, 29, 40, 49, 52–53, 130, 132, 138, 143
revision 23–25, 29, 76, 110, 143, 146
ribbon 13, 24, 133, 142, 143
Rich Text file 13
risk 18, 29–30, 35, 110–111, 182, 190, 195–197, 217–218
RWS Language Cloud 149

sales 175, 199
scale 107, 150, 206
screen 183, 185, 196, 203, 205; reader 184, 208; recording 203
scripting 167, 184
SDLXLIFF 49
search 86, 203; engine 77, 93, 95; hit 86, 93; internet 82; operator 77, 82, 95; phrase 77, 94–95; query 76, 94; result 82; truncated 71; wildcard 71; word 89

search engine optimisation (SEO) 185
search engine results page (SERP) 93
segment 3–9, 11, 14–19, 21, 23, 24, 26, 30, 33, 42–49, 51, 71, 103, 109, 117, 120–121, 124, 126–128, 136, 142, 148, 159, 176, 179, 195, 196, 204, 206, 207; active 13, 16, 17, 36–38, 46, 52, 116, 120–121, 124–125; boundary 15; locked 193; merge 46; parallel 106; revised 25; sign-off 25, 29; source 18, 19, 23, 33, 37, 48, 107, 114–115; speech 155, 156; status 23, 50; target 17, 19, 24, 104, 107–108, 193, 205; unmatched 115, 128; unopened 193; untranslated 17
segmentation 15, 42; rule 15, 42, 49
segment-by-segment translation 206
server 6, 26, 29, 131, 146, 183
similarity 16, 23, 36–37, 108–109, 116–117, 126, 128
simultaneous interpreting 154
singularity 214
Sketch Engine 74, 76, 80, 89–93, 95; dashboard *90*; Word Sketch *91*, 94; Word Sketch Difference *92*
Smartcat *21*, 27, 28, 44, 49, 51, 52, 58–59, 126
Smartling 183
smartphone 18, 41, 183, 188, 192, 205
social media 185
social quality 197
software 188; application 174, 182; compiling 176, 179; development 176; interface 120; resources 181; upgrade 28, 143, 163, 179
software as a service (SaaS) 6, 28, 131, 163, 180, 204, 211
sound effect 154
SPANAM 99
speech synthesis 208
speech-to-text software *see* automatic speech recognition (ASR)
spell-checker 2, 3, 19, 22, 36, 194, 198
spreadsheet 56–59, 120, 186; *see also* Microsoft Excel
Star Transit 19, 26, 34, 41, 47; 'Dual Fuzzy' lookup 116–117
status 25, **61**, 145, 149, 177
Stingray 47
stoplist 84, 88
string 15, 18, 23, 34–36, 39–40, 43, 70–71, 80, 95, 100, 107, 115–116,

118, 123, 128, 164, 175–181, 184, 187, 194, 203
string-based metric 109
style 76, 160, 183, 196; guide 186, 205
subordinate *see* hyponym
SubRip Text (.SRT) 156, *157*, 169, 171
subscription 89, 122, 123, 130, 144, 163
Subtitle Edit 158
subtitle editor 156; cloud-based 163–171; workstation-based 158–163, 172
Subtitle Workshop 158
subtitler 153–154, 156, 163–164, 171–172
subtitles 9, 111, 152–173, 187; active 159, 161, *171*; auto-generated 164, 168–170, 172; automated 153, 165; burnt in *see* hard coded; compression 160; condensed 154–155, 164; export 156, 171; file 157, 160, 161, 169; guidelines 155, 165–166, *167*; hard coded 153, 157, 171; in and out times 156, 159, 170; interlingual 154; intralingual 154; line break 155; line length 155, 171; list 156, 159, 162, 163, 170–172; live 154; meta-information 154; new line code 159; on-screen text 155; open 153, 157; reading speed 155–156, 160, 163–164, *168*; separation 155, 166; shot change 155; space on screen 155; speaker 160; spotting 154, 156, 159, 163–164, 166, 170, *171*, 172; time on screen 155, 166; timecode 156–157, 162; timeline 156, 159, 170; translated 152–155, *163*, 169, 187
superordinate *see* hyperonym
Swordfish 12, 47
synchronisation 156, 157, 170
synonym 56, 58, 62, 70, 109, 116, 126, 155, 164; cosmetic 71
syntagmatic relation 63; *see also* paradigmatic relation
syntax 1, 4, 39, 96, 98, 100, 110, 127, 155, 164
Systran 99, 122

tablet 12, 183, 188
tag 15, 18, 42, 50, 123–124, 148, 176, 179, 194–196, 209; inline 18–19, 42, 123; locked 193; placement 18, 124, 128
task-based evaluation 107, 108

TAUS (Translation Automation User Society) 110, 214
tautological definition *see* circular definition
TBX (TermBase eXchange) 71–72, 149
technical writing 116
technological unemployment 111
technology company 215
template 13, 67, 111, 140, 147, 182
temporal effort 107
term 23, 64, 85, 89; approved 193–194; boundary 64; candidate 68, 69; complex 69; cross-reference 56; duplicate records 67; embeddedness 66; example of usage 16, 56–57, 60, 64–65; field 60; less acceptable 66; multiword 58, 63, 71, 87, 114; non-hierarchical relations **62**, 64; paradigmatic relation 63, 65; preferred 66; recognition 65–66, 70; record 70, 149; signalling 65; syntagmatic relation 65; validation 68, 69; variant 56, 57, **61**; *vs.* word 58, 116, 119
term extraction 67–69, 74, 119; automatic 67–68; bilingual 68; hybrid 68; linguistic 68; manual 67, 68; monolingual 68; statistical 68
termbase 4, 12, 16–19, 21–23, 29, 57, 61, 63–72, 75–76, 81, 114–121, 126–128, 130, 132–134, 145–146, 148–149, 194, 196, 217; administrative information 61, 62; audiovisual content 56, 60; concept oriented 57, 59; corporate guidelines 60; creation 59–69; data category *see* termbase field type; data input 63, 67; entry 57, 61–62, 64, 116; entry level 58, **61**; export 72; graphic 56, 58, 59; hierarchical 57, 59, 67; import 72; index level **61**; *see also* language level; language level 58; maintenance 59; multilingual 56; notes field 63; online collaborative 72; prescriptive 66; source 57; structure 63, 72; term level 58, **61**; using for translation 69–71
termbase field type; free text 60, **61**; mandatory **61**, 62, 138, 145, 147, 148; multimedia 60; multiple **61**, 62; numeric 60, **61**; picklist 60, **61**

termhood 65–66

termination character 176

terminologist 26, 62, 64, 68, 132, 193

terminology 2, 7, 9, 19, 23, 55–73, 76, 84, 96, 101, 105, 110, 116, 124, 138, 178, 186, 193, 198–199, 209; automatic lookup *see* active terminology lookup; corporate 74; database *see* termbase; error 55; fuzzy lookup 70; lookup pane 69; research 60, 68

terminology extraction 43, 92

terminology management 6, 74, 153, 190, 192, 194, 199

terminology management system (TMS) 10, 71, 131

test set 104, 108

text: audiovisual 186; authentic 78; box 175; comparable 76; creative and literary 108; definition 1; digital 182; editor 2, 6, 13, 51, 176; embedded 183; formatting 159; function 76; idiomatic 77; in-game 186; machine readable 78, 176; not for publication 214; parallel 76–78, 81, 93; shelf-life 111, 207; source 5, 11–12, 15–19, 22–24, 29–30, 33–38, 41–47, 66, 69–70, 97, 127, 130, 136–138, 140, 149, 195, 209; tagged 49; target 12, 14, 15, 17, 18–20, 24–25, 29, 34–36, 41–44, 47, 70, 142–143, 155, 204–205, 209; time of publication 76; translatable 13, 14, 15; type 12, 34, 54, 76–78, 109, 207, 215

Tilde Translate 112

time format 175

time of publication 78

time pressure 207

time zone 130, 138, 145, 213

TMX (Transaltion Memory eXchange) 41, 44, 47–54, 148

TMXEditor 44

TMXMallaligner 43

token 83, 103, 104, 105; sentence ending 104

toolbar 13, 159, 161

tracked changes 24, 29, 38, 125

trademark 193

Trados 7, 31; AutoSuggest 121; Live Team 149; MultiTerm 59, 67, 192; Studio 17, 24, 26–27, 29, 35, 39, 47–50, 52, 69, 72, 92, 120–121, 123–124, 192, *194*, 195, 199, 204, 205; Team 2022 27; Teamworks 131; Translator's Workbench 13, *14*; upLIFT 120, 121; WinAlign 47

transcreation 215

transcription 79, 153–155, 164, 169; automated 170, 172

transfer RBMT 98, 99; analysis module 99; production module 99

translatable content 179

translation 146, 154, 175; activity data 216; agency *see* language service provider (LSP); automatic 2, 3, 9, 11, 19; *see also* machine translation; brief 205; budget 28, 110; buyer 110, 207, 213; compressed 172; constrained 171; copyright 111; creative and literary 213, 214; as derivative work 111; dictation 204; domesticating 187; error 7, 18–19, 23–24, 47, 101, 105–108, 110, 112–113, 117, 126–127, 172, 177, 185, 193–198, 200; ethics 2, 149, 188; extract 28, 30, 39; finalisation 19, 76, 183; gold standard 108; grid 118, 123; human 3, 97, 99, 100, 104, 106, 107–108, 110–111, 120, 122, 128; industry 214, 215; institutional 66; job 2, 6, 11, 17, 21, 23–25, 28, 30, 35, 39, 41, 52, 94, 110–111, 116, 118, 130, 133, 140–142, 144–145, 148–150, 155–156, 176, 214; legacy 5, 11, 33–35, 38, 40, 41, 44, 114, 126, 213; machine-aided 4; for non-governmental organisations 217; not-for-profit 217; preferred 94, 127; process 191, 200, 201; product 191, 200, 201; proposal 34, 35, 36, 37, 38, 40, 44, 76; review 24; revision 24; speed 110, 112, 114, 128, 136, 138, 139, 150, 166, 199, 208; student 2, 210, 217; supplier 138, 213; supply chain 150; tiered quality levels 176, 207, 215; trainer 8, 9, 210; *vs.* localisation 174

translation grid 23, 44, 45, 52

translation management system (TMS) 10, 27, 71, 131, 133, 140–145, 149–151, 163

translation memory (TM) 4–7, 9, 10, 12, 16–19, 21–24, 26, 29, 30–31, 33–41, 43–44, 47, 48– 51, 53–55, 66, 71, 76, 97, 110–111, 114–115, 117, 119, 120–121, 123, 125–126, 128–134, 137, 142–143, 145–146,

148–150, 164, 169, 179, 181, 190, 192–196, 198–199, 204, 213–214, 217; AI-enhanced 122; cleaning and maintenance 7; 'intelligent' 128; ownership 28, 30, 111
translation model 100, 101
translation process research 31
translation quality 191; 'good enough' 110; publishable 107, 109–111
Translation Studies 2, 202, 217; corpus-based (CBTS) 79–80
translation theory 34; equivalence 54; functionalism 54
translation unit (TU) 16, 19, 23, 25–26, 30, 33, 35–37, 39, 40–42, 48, 49, 50–53, 115–116, 120–121, 132, 137, 142, 149; confirmation 16–17, 19, 23, 41, 47–48, 89, 93, 95, 127–128, 132, 159, 171
translator 2–7, 9, 11–14, 16, 17–31, 34–41, 53, 55–60, 62, 64–72, 75, 77–78, 80, 91–97, 109–111, 116, 119, 120–121, 123–124, 126–133, 138–139, 141, 143, 149–150, 152–155, 171, 175, 179, 186–188, 191–193, 195–204, 206–208, 213–215, 217–218; associations 215; augmented 4, 21, 214; autonomy 7, 150, 200, 207; blind and visually impaired 209–210; early-career 2; freelance 6, 26–31, 35, 39, 60, 130, 138, 144, 150, 176, 183, 203, 207, 213; in-house 6; job satisfaction 111; as mediator 2; motivation 111; perception 110; performance 195; productivity 199; rating 200
Translators Without Borders 197
TranslatorsCafé 28
trigram 100
trust 200, 207
tutorial 186
tweet 185
typesetting 171

Unicode (UTF-8) 156, 175
unigram 100
university 4, 7, 9, 31, 80–81, 98, 99, 120, 198
Unreal Engine 186
URL 18, 77, 82, 84
usability 183, 204, 209, 216
user 144, 145, 169; complaint 204; documentation 13, 209; enterprise 6; experience (UX) 153, 154, 184; feedback 200, 216; preference 205
user interface (UI) 20–21, 159–160, 171, 177, 186, 204, 205
User-Centred Translation 200

variable 178, 187
Veed 163
vendor 27–28, 31, 138, 148, 192, 215; multi-language (MLV) 175, 180; single language (SLV) 176
video 154–161, 169, 187, 194; editing 152; navigation controls 159; stream 153; transcoding 157; viewer 159
visualisation 56
visually impaired user 208
voiceover 160, 187

W3C Web Content Accessibility Guidelines 208
Weaver Memorandum (1949) 3
Web as Corpus (WAC) 93–96
web designer 130
WebCorp 80
webpage 84, 184; Print view 81
website 8, 13, 35, 81, 83, 88, 95, 131, 132, 174–176, 183, 185, 188; colours 185; culturally adapted 184; fully localised 182; image 184, 185; multilingual 182; partially localised 182
WebVTT (Web Video Text Tracks) 171
WEIRD (Western, Educated, Industrialised, Rich, Democratic) 200
welcome page 209
wildcard 82, 88, 95
WinCaps 158
word 3, 145; base form 99; cloud 103; combination 76; compound 105; content 63; counting 3; embedding 103–105, 109; function 63, 84, 119; order 16, 40, 76, 109, 116; proximity 104; rate 24, 39, 111, 136–140, 146, 150; reordering 101; variation 105; *vs.* term 58, 116
Wordbee 27, 42, 144, 149, 163
Wordfast 44; Anywhere 27, 49, 123, 125, 132–143, 144, 146, 149, 150; AutoSuggest 121; Classic 12, 14, 27; Online Aligner 44; Pro 12, 26, 27, 48
Wordpad *157*
WordPress 144, 184

WordSmith 80
work environment 203, 207
WorldLingo 123, 125
WYSIWYG 18

Xbench 197, 198
XLIFF 49–51, 54
XLOC 186
XML 49–50, 71

XTM Cloud 27, 44, 49, 122, 144, 149,
  163; Advanced Text Aligner 43;
  Neural Fuzzy Adaptation 122

Yandex 112
YouAlign 42
YouTube 153, 158, 165, 171

zip archive 29